The Haunted Stage

THEATER: Theory/Text/Performance

Enoch Brater, Series Editor

Recent Titles:

Trevor Griffiths: Politics, Drama, History by Stanton B. Garner Jr.

Memory-Theater and Postmodern Drama by Jeanette R. Malkin

Performing America: Cultural Nationalism in American Theater
   edited by Jeffrey D. Mason and J. Ellen Gainor

Space in Performance: Making Meaning in the Theatre by Gay McAuley

Mirrors of Our Playing: Paradigms and Presences in Modern Drama
   by Thomas R. Whitaker

Brian Friel in Conversation edited by Paul Delaney

Sails of the Herring Fleet: Essays on Beckett by Herbert Blau

On Drama: Boundaries of Genre, Borders of Self by Michael Goldman

Contours of the Theatrical Avant-Garde: Performance and Textuality
   edited by James M. Harding

The Painted Word: Samuel Beckett's Dialogue with Art
   by Lois Oppenheim

Performing Democracy: International Perspectives on Urban
   Community-Based Performance
   edited by Susan C. Haedicke and Tobin Nellhaus

A Beckett Canon by Ruby Cohn

David Mamet in Conversation edited by Leslie Kane

The Haunted Stage: The Theatre as Memory Machine
   by Marvin Carlson

Staging Consciousness: Theater and the Materialization of Mind
   by William W. Demastes

Agitated States: Performance in the American Theater of Cruelty
   by Anthony Kubiak

Land/Scape/Theater edited by Elinor Fuchs and Una Chaudhuri

The
_H_aunted _S_tage

The Theatre as Memory Machine

Marvin Carlson

THE UNIVERSITY OF MICHIGAN PRESS
Ann Arbor

First paperback edition 2003

Copyright © by the University of Michigan 2001
All rights reserved
Published in the United States of America by
The University of Michigan Press
Manufactured in the United States of America
♾ Printed on acid-free paper

2006   2005   2004   2003   5   4   3   2

A CIP catalog record for this book is available from the British Library.

Library of Congress Cataloging-in-Publication Data

Carlson, Marvin A., 1935–
    The haunted stage : the theatre as memory machine / Marvin
Carlson.
        p.   cm. — (Theater—theory/text/performance)
    Includes bibliographical references and index.
    ISBN 0-472-11242-2 (alk. paper)
    1. Theater—Psychological aspects.   I. Title.   II. Series.
PN2071.P78   C37   2001
792'.01'9—dc21   2001003729

ISBN 0-472-08937-4 (pbk. : alk. paper)

To Daniel Mesguich

*whose ghost-filled productions have haunted
my memory as they have haunted this book*

For theatre is, in whatever revisionist, futurist, or self-dissolving form—or in the most proleptic desire to forget the theatre—a function of remembrance. Where memory is, theatre is.

—Herbert Blau, *The Audience*

Even in death actors' roles tend to stay with them. They gather in the memory of audiences, like ghosts, as each new interpretation of a role sustains or upsets expectations derived from the previous ones.

—Joseph Roach, *Cities of the Dead*

What, has this thing appear'd again tonight?

—Shakespeare, *Hamlet*

Contents

Acknowledgments   xi

one
The Haunted Stage: An Overview   1

two
The Haunted Text   16

three
The Haunted Body   52

four
The Haunted Production   96

five
The Haunted House   131

six
Ghostly Tapestries: Postmodern Recycling   165

Notes   175

References   187

Index   193

Acknowledgments

The basic concerns and interests that this book addresses were first developed in a series of reports and discussions that took place as a part of the ongoing Working Group in Performance Analysis of the International Federation of Theatre Research, and I am extremely grateful to the continuing members of that group, and especially to Sarah Bryant-Bertail, Erika Fischer-Lichte, Janelle Reinelt, Freddie Rokem, and Eli Rozek, for helping me to clarify my thoughts on this subject. A departed member of this group, Michael Quinn, was especially helpful at an early stage of the work in both conversations and writings. Although I hope that this study will contribute something to an awareness of the provocative relationship between the theatre, haunting, memory, and ghosts, I am certainly not the first to notice this relationship and must express my deepest gratitude for the fascinating and stimulating insights into this subject provided by the two theorists whose thinking has most haunted my own in this research, Herbert Blau and Joseph Roach. The epigraphs drawn from each that open this study suggest how closely some of their concerns resonate with my own.

The reader will quickly discover how important to my study are examples from the living theatre. I must also express my profound gratitude to the many theatre artists in many countries and traditions whose work I have been privileged to see and who have instructed and inspired me in this speculation upon certain aspects of that highly complex and challenging cultural phenomenon, the theatre.

The Haunted Stage: An Overview

*A*popular saying among students of Ibsen is that "all of his plays could be called *Ghosts*," and, indeed, the images of the dead continuing to work their power on the living, of the past reappearing unexpectedly and uncannily in the midst of the present, are concerns that clearly struck deeply into the poetic imagination of the most influential dramatist of the modern European theatre. The comment is perhaps even more appropriate if we recall that Ibsen's title for the play was *Gengangere,* meaning literally "those that come back again" (the French translation, *Revenants,* captures this concept much more successfully).

Relevant as this observation is to the works of Ibsen, one might expand this observation to remark that not only all of Ibsen's plays but all plays in general might be called *Ghosts,* since, as Herbert Blau has provocatively observed, one of the universals of performance, both East and West, is its ghostliness, its sense of return, the uncanny but inescapable impression imposed upon its spectators that *"we are seeing what we saw before."*[1] Blau is perhaps the most philosophical, but he is certainly not the only, recent theorist who has remarked upon this strange quality of experiencing something as a repetition in the theatre. Richard Schechner's oft-quoted characterization of performance as "restored behavior" or "twice-

behaved behavior"[2] looks in the same direction, as does Joseph
Roach's relation of performance to surrogation, the "doomed
search for originals by continuously auditioning stand-ins."[3] The
physical theatre, as a site of the continuing reinforcement of memory by surrogation, is not surprisingly among the most haunted of
human cultural structures. Almost any long-established theatre
has tales of its resident ghosts, a feature utilized by the French
director Daniel Mesguich in a number of his metatheatrical productions and by Mac Wellman, who summoned up the ghosts of
the abandoned Victory Theatre to reenact their stories in that
space in his site-specific 1990 production, *Crowbar.*

All theatrical cultures have recognized, in some form or
another, this ghostly quality, this sense of something coming back
in the theatre, and so the relationships between theatre and cultural memory are deep and complex. Just as one might say that
every play might be called *Ghosts,* so, with equal justification, one
might argue that every play is a memory play. Theatre, as a simulacrum of the cultural and historical process itself, seeking to
depict the full range of human actions within their physical context, has always provided society with the most tangible records of
its attempts to understand its own operations. It is the repository of
cultural memory, but, like the memory of each individual, it is also
subject to continual adjustment and modification as the memory is
recalled in new circumstances and contexts. The present experience is always ghosted by previous experiences and associations
while these ghosts are simultaneously shifted and modified by the
processes of recycling and recollection. As Elin Diamond has
noted, even the terminology associated with performance suggests
its inescapable and continuing negotiations with memory:

> While a performance embeds traces of other performances, it
> also produces an experience whose interpretation only par-
> tially depends on previous experience. Hence the terminology
> of "re" in discussion of performance, as in *re*member, *re*in-
> scribe, *re*configure, *re*iterate, *re*store. "Re" acknowledges the
> pre-existing discursive field, the repetition within the perfor-
> mative present, but "figure," "script," and "iterate" assert the
> possibility of something that *exceeds* our knowledge, that alters

the shape of sites and imagines new unsuspected subject positions.[4]

A parallel process can be seen in dreaming, which, as many dream theorists have observed, has distinct similarities in the private experience to the public experience of theatre. Bert States suggests that both human fictions and human dreams are centrally concerned with memory negotiation. "If something is to be remembered at all, it must be remembered not as *what* happened but as what has happened *again* in a different way and will surely happen again in the future in still another way."[5] The waking dream of theatre, like dreaming itself, is particula. well suited to this strange but apparently essential process. Both recycle past perceptions and experience in imaginary configurations that, although different, are powerfully haunted by a sense of repetition and involve the whole range of human activity and its context.

The close relationships between theatre and memory have been recognized in many cultures and in many different fashions. The founding myths and legends of cultures around the world have been registered in their cultures by theatrical repetition, and, as modern nationalism arose to challenge the older religious faiths, national myths, legends, and historical stories again utilized the medium of theatre to present—or, rather, to represent, reinscribe, and reinforce—this new cultural construction. Central to the Noh drama of Japan, one of the world's oldest and most venerated dramatic traditions, is the image of the play as a story of the past recounted by a ghost, but ghostly storytellers and recalled events are the common coin of theatre everywhere in the world at every period.

The retelling of stories already told, the reenactment of events already enacted, the reexperience of emotions already experienced, these are and have always been central concerns of the theatre in all times and places, but closely allied to these concerns are the particular production dynamics of theatre: the stories it chooses to tell, the bodies and other physical materials it utilizes to tell them, and the places in which they are told. Each of these production elements are also, to a striking degree, composed of material "that we have seen before," and the memory of that recycled material as it moves through new and different productions contributes in no small measure to the richness and density of the operations of theatre in general as a site of memory, both personal and cultural. The focus of this study will be upon such material and how the memories that it evokes have conditioned the processes of theatrical composition and, even more important, of theatrical reception in theatrical cultures around the world and across the centuries.

Of course, as anyone involved in the theatre knows, performance, however highly controlled and codified, is never exactly repeatable, an insight that Derrida used to challenge the speech-act theories of Austin and Searle, arguing that, while performative speech depends upon the citing of previous speech, the citation is never exact because of its shifting context.[6] As Hamlet remarks in that most haunted of all Western dramas, "I'll have these players / Play something like the murder of my father." That evocative phrase *something like* not only admits the inevitable slippage in all repetition but at the same time acknowledges the congruence that still haunts the new performance, a congruence upon which Hamlet, rightly, relies to "catch the conscience of the king" through the embodied memory of the theatre.

One of the important insights of modern literary theory has been that every new work may also be seen as a new assemblage of material from old works. As Roland Barthes observes in a widely quoted passage from *Image, Music, Text:* "We now know that the text is not a line of words releasing a single theological meaning (the 'message' of an Author-God) but a multi-dimensional space in which a variety of writings, *none of them original,* blend and clash. The text is a tissue of quotations drawn from innumerable centers of culture."[7]

This complex recycling of old elements, far from being a disadvantage, is an absolutely essential part of the reception process. We are able to "read" new works—whether they be plays, paintings, musical compositions, or, for that matter, new signifying structures that make no claim to artistic expression at all—only because we recognize within them elements that have been recycled from other structures of experience that we have experienced earlier. This "intertextual" attitude, approaching the text not as a unique and essentially self-contained structure but as an open-ended "tissue of quotations," has become now quite familiar. The dramatic script, as text, readily opens itself to analysis on these terms, though, as I will argue in the next chapter, it participates in the recycling of elements in a rather different and arguably more comprehensive manner than do texts created in the tradition of other "literary" genres.

Definitions and examples of the workings of intertextuality have usually discussed this phenomenon as Barthes does, as a dynamic working within the text or among a body of texts, usually with a corresponding de-emphasis of the individual author (or at least of the originality of that author). Such an emphasis somewhat obscures the importance of memory to this process, an importance that becomes much clearer when we shift attention from the text itself to its reception. All reception is deeply involved with memory, because it is memory that supplies the codes and strategies that shape reception, and, as cultural and social memories change, so do the parameters within which reception operates, those parameters that reception theorist Hans Robert Jauss has called the "horizon of expectations."[8] The expectations an audience brings to a new reception experience are the residue of memory of previous such experiences. The reception group that Stanley Fish has called the "interpretive community" might in fact be described as a community in which there is a significant overlap of such memory,[9] and the reception process itself might be characterized as the selective application of memory to experience.

This process occurs, of course, not only in the arts but in any human activity involving interpretation, which includes any human activity to which consciousness is brought, but the major feature generally separating a work of art from other activities of the consciousness lies in the particular way it is framed, as an activity or object created to stimulate interpretation, that is, to invite an audience to interact in this way with it. Their interaction will in turn be primarily based upon their previous experience with similar activities or objects, that is, upon memory. The primary tools for audiences confronted with new paintings, pieces of music, books, or pieces of theatre are previous examples of these various arts they have experienced. An audience member, bombarded with a variety of stimuli, processes them by selectively applying reception strategies remembered from previous situations that seem congruent. The process is a kind of continuing trial and error, since many interpretive possibilities are always present, and, as the reception experience continues, strategies remembered from a great many previous experiences may be successively tried in the search for the one apparently most compatible with this new situation. If a work requires reception techniques outside those provided by an audience's memory, then it falls outside their horizon of expectations, but more commonly it will operate, or can be made to operate, within that horizon, thus adding a new experiential memory for future use.

A familiar example of this process can be seen in the operations of genre. Although the term is most closely associated with literature, most of the arts offer groupings of material that could be called genres, and such groupings provide one important and traditional part of the horizon of expectations. Whether a literary genre is a very broad and flexible one, such as a comedy or romance, or one much more specifically defined, such as a classic detective story, the audience for a new work in the genre can be normally expected to have read other works in the genre and to apply the memory of how those works are constructed to the understanding and appreciation of the new example. In his perceptive recent study of the relationship between the concepts of genre and of drama Michael Goldman begins his discussion with a consideration of the dynamic of recognition, noting that "the first function of genre is that it be recognized" and that recognition, the awareness of witnessing something once again, has been a process particularly associated with drama from "the very beginning of dramatic theory."[10]

This process of using the memory of previous encounters to understand and interpret encounters with new and somewhat different but apparently similar phenomena is fundamental to human cognition in general, and it plays a major role in the theatre, as it does in all the arts. Within the theatre, however, a related but somewhat different aspect of memory operates in a manner distinct from, or at least in a more central way than in, the other arts, so much so that I would argue that it is one of the characteristic features of theatre. To this phenomenon I have given the name *ghosting*. Unlike the reception operations of genre (also, of course, of major importance in theatre), in which audience members encounter a new but distinctly different example of a type of artistic product they have encountered before, ghosting presents the identical thing they have encountered before, although now in a somewhat different context. Thus, a recognition not of similarity, as in genre, but of identity becomes a part of the reception process, with results that can complicate this process considerably. Of course, on the most basic level all arts are built up of identical material used over and over again, individual words in poetry, tones in music, hues in painting, but these semiotic building blocks carry much of their reception burden in their combinations. Certainly, these combinations can and do evoke memories of similar, and at times identical, use in particular previous works in all of the arts, but it seems to me that the practice of theatre has been in all periods and cultures particularly obsessed with memory and ghosting, a phenomenon that I propose to explore in various constituent parts of that art.

Freddie Rokem, who sees, as I do, Marcellus' question in *Hamlet*, "What, has this thing appeared again tonight?" as profoundly evocative of the operations of theatre itself, focuses upon its significance for theatrical representations of historical events, the theme of Rokem's book *Performing History*. "On the metatheatrical level," Rokem observes, this question "implies that the repressed ghostly figures and events from that ('real') historical past can (re)appear on the stage in theatrical performances. The actors performing such historical figures are in fact the 'things' who are appearing again tonight in the performance. And when these ghosts are historical figures they are in a sense performing history."[11] Indeed, this is true, and this ghostly reappearance of historical, and legendary, figures on the stage has been throughout history an essential part of the theatre experience. My own interest here is somewhat different, however, focusing not only upon what is being performed (or, better, performed again) but also upon the means of performance, not only the actors but all the accouterments of theatre, the literal "things" that are "appearing again tonight at the performance." These are the ghosts that have haunted all theatrical performance in all periods, whatever the particular subject matter of the presentation.

I propose to begin with the functioning of ghosting in the dramatic text, the widely accepted ground of theatre in many cultures, including our own. Although recent writings on intertextuality have called our attention to the fact that all literary texts are involved in the process of recycling and memory, weaving together elements of preexisting and previously read other texts, the dramatic text seems particularly self-conscious of this process, particularly haunted by its predecessors. Drama, more than any other literary form, seems to be associated in all cultures with the retelling again and again of stories that bear a particular religious, social, or political significance for their public. There clearly seems to be something in the nature of dramatic presentation that makes it a particularly attractive repository for the storage and mechanism for the continued recirculation of cultural memory. This common characteristic of the dramatic text will be the subject of my next chapter.

When we move from the dramatic text to its physical realization in the theatre, the operations of memory upon reception become even more striking. Because every physical element of the production can be and often is used over and over again in subsequent productions, the opportunities for an audience to bring memories of previous uses to new productions are enormous. Often these memories have been consciously utilized by the theatre culture, but, even when they are not, they may well continue to operate, affecting reception in powerful and unexpected ways. The most familiar example of this phenomenon is the appearance of an actor, remembered from previous roles, in a new characterization. The recycled body of an actor, already a complex bearer of semiotic messages, will almost inevitably in a new role evoke the ghost or ghosts of previous roles if they have made any impression whatever on the audience, a phenomenon that often colors and indeed may dominate the reception process. When the new character is of the same general type as the previous one, then the reappearance of an already known body operates rather like one of the variable recurring components that allow readers to recognize a genre. From this has arisen the familiar theatre and filmic practice of "typecasting," when an actor appears again and again as a rugged fighter or comic buffoon, in a character whose actions and gestures are so similar role to role that the audience recognizes them as they would the conventions of a familiar genre. But, even when an actor strives to vary his roles, he is, especially as his reputation grows, entrapped by the memories of his public, so that each new appearance requires a renegotiation with those memories.

A striking but not untypical recent example of this is provided by a review appearing in the *New York Times* in June 2000, written by that paper's leading drama critic, Ben Brantley, and concerning a current Broadway production of *Macbeth*. Not only is the review centrally concerned with the phenomenon of ghosting, but it even seeks to evoke in its own style something of the psychic disjuncture that the ghosting of an actor can evoke in the theatre. The opening paragraph, in full, reads:

> Across the bloody fields of Scotland, in the land where the stage smoke swirls and the synthesizers scream like banshees, strides a faceless figure in black, thudding along in thick, corpse-kicking boots. Who is this masked man, speaking so portentously about how "foul and fair" his day has been? At last he raises the gleaming vizard of his helmet and there, behold, is a most familiar wide-browed visage: hey, it's one of America's most popular television stars, and, boy, does he look as if he means business.

The popular television star in question is Kelsey Grammer, familiar as a very un-Macbeth-like character, an engaging, though ineffectual psychiatrist on the highly popular sitcom "Frasier." Brantley then goes on to consider why this well-known actor would choose to make a "semi-incognito first appearance" in the production and suggests, as one "quite legitimate" reason, that such an entrance

> forestalls that disruptive shock of recognition that might prompt some rowdy theatregoer to yell out "Where's Niles?" in reference to Frasier's television brother. It allows that actor's voice, most un-Frasier-like here as it solemnly intones Mac-

beth's opening line, to introduce his character without prejudice.[12]

The highly suggestive words *disruptive* and *without prejudice* suggest the powerful, troubling, ambiguous, and yet undeniable role
that ghosting can play in the reception process in theatre, a role so
powerful in this production (as in many) that Brantley chose to
make it the centerpiece of his review. Ironically, in so doing, he
has (unwittingly?) "blown Grammer's cover." If there were any
members in the preview or opening night audiences whose first
impressions of the "faceless figure" in black were not ghosted by
"Frasier" (advance publicity and program notes already having
prepared most of them for this effect), then that number was
doubtless considerably reduced by the association being stressed
in the most visible professional review of the production. An effect
of this sort of ghosting upon reception is by no means confined to
constant theatregoers such as Broadway reviewers. Almost any theatregoer can doubtless recall situations when the memory of an
actor seen in a previous role or roles remained in the mind to
haunt a subsequent performance. Despite its commonality, this
familiar reception phenomenon has been accorded very little critical or theoretical attention. The haunted body of the performer
and its operations will be the concern of my third chapter.

If the recycling of the bodies of actors has received little attention as an aspect of reception, still less attention has been given to
the interesting fact that these bodies are only one part of a
dynamic of recycling that affects almost every part of the theatrical
experience and that, in its extent and variety, is more central to
the reception operations of theatre than it is to any other art form.
In my fourth chapter I will examine these operations as they have
been manifested in the various production elements that surround and condition the body of the individual actor: costumes,
lighting, sound, and the rest of the production apparatus. I will
then move in my fifth chapter from these components of the performance space to the space itself, discussing some of the ways in
which reception memory operates in relation to the places performance takes place. Each, I will argue, is centrally involved, in all
theatre cultures, with the recycling of specific material, and the

ghosting arising from this recycling contributes, sometimes positively, sometimes negatively, but always significantly, to the reception process of the theatre as a whole.

All theatre, I will argue, is as a cultural activity deeply involved with memory and haunted by repetition. Moreover, as an ongoing social institution it almost invariably reinforces this involvement and haunting by bringing together on repeated occasions and in the same spaces the same bodies (onstage and in the audience) and the same physical material. To indicate the importance and ubiquity of this involvement I will present examples from a wide range of theatrical cultures. Yet, while I do hope to demonstrate that the operations of repetition, memory, and ghosting are deeply involved in the nature of the theatrical experience itself, I am fully aware that, just as the theatrical impulse manifests itself in a very different manner in different periods and cultures, so does the particular way in which these operations are carried out. Highly traditional theatrical organizations, such as those of classic Japan and China, are so deeply committed to the process of recycling of material that ghosting might well be considered as their most prominent reception feature. There is scarcely an element of the theatrical experience in these traditions that audiences cannot immediately recognize as having witnessed before. The same actors appear year after year playing the same roles in the same plays, wearing the same makeup and the same costumes, using the same movements, gestures, and vocal intonations, all of which are inherited by the successors of these actors. In such performance cultures the attempt to repeat the original has resulted in a codification of actions and physical objects so detailed as to be almost obsessive.

On the other hand, some theatre cultures, particularly in more recent times, have so prized innovation and originality that they have attempted (never with complete success) to avoid entirely the sort of performance citationality that characterizes the classic theatres of the East and, to a somewhat lesser extent, the major national performance traditions of the West. The passion of romantic artists and theorists for original expression and the genius who would repeat nothing of his forebears (an ideal now almost totally discredited by postmodern theory and thought) and the vogue for theatrical realism and the various avant-gardes that came in the wake of romanticism very much weakened the major traditions of citationality in Western theatre. Among them one might mention the traditional lines of business, the genealogies of performance, with certain gestures and patterns of movement handed down from actor to actor, and the common practice of using the same scenery, costumes, and properties in production after production, all of these normal practice in the pre-romantic European theatre and increasingly rejected in the wake of romanticism.

Neither romanticism's desire for the original nor its rejection of theatrical traditions in the name of the presumably more individual, even unique experiences of real life in fact removed the theatre from its close ties to cultural memory. Nor did they remove the performative memories that inevitably haunted its productions, the bodies of its performers, and the physical objects that surrounded them. In the major theatrical manifesto of romanticism, Victor Hugo's preface to his play *Cromwell,* the author condemns the traditional neutral chamber or peristyle used indiscriminately as the setting for countless French tragedies since Corneille and Racine and called, instead, for exact and specific settings, unique to each situation and free of the memories of a theatrical tradition."The place where this or that catastrophe occurred is an incorruptible and convincing witness to the catastrophe," Hugo argued, and the absence of this species of silent character would render incomplete upon the stage the grandest scenes of history.[13]

The romantic (and realistic) interest in the specific illustrated by this passage encouraged a trend in the Western theatre away from the tradition not only of the generic stock settings that Hugo would replace with settings unique to each event but the entire interrelated tradition of recycled material—in costuming, plotting, character types, and interpretive traditions. Nevertheless, the connections between memory and theatre went far deeper than these changes in performance practice, and, as first romanticism then realism strongly altered theatre practice, the operations of memory in this practice in some ways (but by no means all ways) shifted, yet they remained of central importance to the experience and reception of theatre.

Even the radical change in the attitude toward stage setting proposed by Hugo simply shifts the operations of memory and association in different directions. If in fact the "exact locality" that he proposes were to be achieved (as it never was in his own theatre but subsequently would be in certain "site-specific" theatre of the twentieth century), then the settings would be haunted not by the theatrical associations of their use in previous productions but by historical associations that, as Hugo notes, could be relied upon to produce "a faithful impression of the [historical] facts upon the mind of the spectator." Its operations, theatrically, still depend upon an audience's recognition of it as "restored" material.

The new approach represented by romanticism and realism in Western theatrical practice did not, moreover, ever really challenge certain of the most common and powerful traditions of recycled material, the most important of which was the body of the individual actor. For all his interest in unique and individual settings for each production, Hugo willingly, indeed eagerly, sought to use his favorite actors, such as Marie Dorval and Frédérick Lemaître, again and again, fully aware that they would inevitably bring associations from old productions to new ones. Indeed, in his afterword to the published text of *Ruy Blas* Hugo praises Lemaître precisely in terms of the associations he evokes. After noting that "enthusiastic acclamations" greet this actor "as soon as he comes on stage" (a practice still common even in the most realistic theatre and perhaps the most obvious sign of the audience's reception being haunted from the beginning by previous acquaintance with the individual actor in other works), Hugo proceeds to laud him for the acting associations he evokes. At his peak, says Hugo, "he *dominates all the memories of his art.* For old men, he is Lekain and Garrick in one; for us, his coevals, he is Kean's action combined with Talma's emotion."[14] For all of its passion for originality, the romantic theatre remained deeply involved with cultural memory for its subjects and theatrical memory for their enactment.

The particular manner in which memory, recycling, and ghosting has been utilized in the theatre has taken a distinctly different direction in the wide variety of theatrical and dramatic expression that may be generally characterized as postmodern. In a move that created a relationship between theatre and memory quite distinct both from the classical search for the preservation of particular artistic models and traditions and from romanticism and realism's search for unique and individual insight and expression, post-modern drama and theatre has tended to favor the conscious reuse of material haunted by memory, but in an ironic and self-conscious manner quite different from classical usage. The post-modern stage, one could argue, is as deeply committed to the recycling of previously utilized material, both physical and textual, as have been the traditional theatres of Asia and of the pre-romantic West. As Peter Rabinowitz has noted, "We live in an age of artistic recycling."[15] The actual manifestations of this commitment, however, reflect a very different cultural consciousness.

Theatre artists of the seventeenth and eighteenth century based much of their work upon what Derrida speaks of as citation, but rarely did they present it directly *as* citation. The postmodern theatre, on the other hand, is almost obsessed with citation, with gestural, physical, and textual material consciously recycled, often almost like pieces of a collage, into new combinations with little attempt to hide the fragmentary and "quoted" nature of these pieces. This is certainly true, for example, of the work of Heiner Müller, widely considered one of the central examples of a "postmodern" dramatist. In his study of Müller, Jonathan Kalb describes him as "a new kind of master author whose identity is a pastiche of other identities"[16] and speaks of Müller's "postmodern valuing of fragments."[17] This can be clearly seen in what is probably Müller's best-known text, *Hamletmachine*, which, as Kalb notes, is "packed with quotations and paraphrases from Eliot, cummings, Hölderlin, Marx, Benjamin, Artaud, Sartre, Warhol, Shakespeare, the Bible, Müller himself, and others, often strung together without connecting text."[18]

The conscious and calculated recycling of material, from one's own previous life and work as well as those of others, is widely recognized as one of the hallmarks of postmodern expression, not only in literary texts but in theatrical performance. Robert Simonson, in a brief essay on the actor Spalding Gray in the popular theatre publication *Playbill*, called Gray "a walking piece of masterful post-modernism," justifying this appellation by Gray's continual and highly self-conscious recycling of material, largely from his own life and work:

> Gray's drama never ends. One need hardly observe that his is hardly the unobserved life. The curtain rises when he gets up and falls with his head upon the pillow. Once onstage, relating the details of that existence, he is Gray the Performer in Gray the Drama. And, as an actor, in Gore Vidal's *The Best Man,* he is Gray the Performer playing Gray the Actor—a chapter in Gray the Drama, and a role he will no doubt dissect in his next monologue (as he did his experience in *Our Town* in the piece, *Monster in a Box.*)[19]

Gray was one of the founding members of what is probably the best-known experimental theatre company of the postmodern era, the Wooster Group, and that company also, like most companies around the world involved in experimental performance in the closing years of the twentieth century, has been centrally concerned with the process of recycling. In my final chapter I will focus upon the work of this group, not only because it is likely to be the most familiar postmodern experimental company for my readers but also because it provides so clear an illustration of the particular manner in which theatre's long-standing fascination with reappearance is being worked out in contemporary postmodern terms.

Although the Wooster Group may be, especially for Americans, the most familiar example of this process, an almost obsessive concern with memory, citation, and the reappearance of bodies and other material from the past is in fact widespread in the contemporary theatre internationally. It is indeed so widespread that one may be tempted to think of this concern as a particularly contemporary one. I hope to demonstrate, however, in the pages that follow that the theatre has been obsessed always with things that return, that appear again tonight, even though this obsession has been manifested in quite different ways in different cultural situations. Everything in the theatre, the bodies, the materials utilized, the language, the space itself, is now and has always been haunted, and that haunting has been an essential part of the theatre's meaning to and reception by its audiences in all times and all places.

two

The Haunted Text

As we undertake a consideration of the many ways in which the art of theatre utilizes the recycling of material to encourage particular structures of reception in its potential audiences, it seems most proper to begin with that aspect of the theatre that traditionally serves as the grounding for the rest, the dramatic script. In most theatrical cultures a preexisting text, written or orally transmitted, serves as the foundation for whatever sort of physical performance makes up the theatrical experience of that culture. Indeed, in the relationship between the preexisting dramatic text and its enactment onstage we can already speak of one kind of "haunting" that lies close to the structure of the theatrical experience, in which the physical embodiment of an action that is witnessed in the theatre is in an important sense haunted by a preexisting text, a phenomenon that is particularly apparent in those eras, such as the present, when audiences often bring an acquaintance with this preexisting text with them to the theatre. In later chapters I will consider some of the reception implications of this aspect of haunting, but, before moving on to an analysis of the physical theatre experience and its reception, it is necessary to point out how extensively recycling is involved in dramatic texts themselves. In several important ways dramatic texts, even before they enter the theatre, are so extensively involved with this process that some theorists have suggested it as one of the defining features of such texts.

Derrida and others have argued that all texts are in fact haunted by other texts and can be best understood as weavings together of preexisting textual material—indeed, that all reception is based upon this intertextual dynamic. Without disputing this more global view of every text existing in and built upon a network of other texts, I think it still may be argued that the dramatic text is distinguished in part by the extent and specificity of its relationship to previous texts, literary and nonliterary. Among all literary forms it is the drama preeminently that has always been centrally concerned not simply with the telling of stories but with the retelling of stories already known to its public. This process naturally involves but goes far beyond the recycling of references, tropes, even structural elements and patterns that intertextuality considers. It involves the dramatist in the presentation of a narrative that is haunted in almost every aspect—its names, its character relationships, the structure of its action, even small physical or linguistic details—by a specific previous narrative. Although the operations of recycling might be traced out in each of these elements, I propose to illustrate the process by considering some of the ways that it has functioned in the two closely related aspects of the dramatic text that demonstrate this feature most clearly: the recycling of specific narratives and the recycling of specific characters.

Already in classic times lyric poetry, focused upon emotion rather than plot, was much less tied to the specific received materials of history, myth, and legend than the epic or dramatic narratives, and, with the passing of time and the gradual replacement of the epic by the novel after the renaissance, the close association of the drama with such received materials became much more specifically associated with that genre. Although the novel could and did from time to time draw upon history and legend, its authors much more consciously from the beginning sought to tell "new" stories, even when they had historical settings. Indeed, it was in significant measure due to the growing interest in and popularity of the novel that the drama during the eighteenth and, even more, during the nineteenth century began to take a much greater interest in the sort of new stories that became the standard offerings of realism and naturalism.

The rise of romanticism and the fundamental challenge that its emphasis upon innovation, individuality, and uniqueness mounted to the classic tradition separated the drama in significant measure from its traditional concern with the retelling of familiar stories and brought drama closer to the novel in this respect (a genre much more suited to this new consciousness and moving at this time to replace the drama at the center of European literary consciousness). The rise of realism, similarly concerned with the new and "unique" story, emphasized this tendency. Yet it is important to remember that, despite the changes wrought by romanticism and realism, for most of its history the drama, East and West, has been based primarily upon the retelling of already familiar stories, so much so that many theorists have considered this one of the characteristics of this genre.

Although the Western theatre tradition will remain my major source of reference and illustration throughout this study, it is important to recognize that the particular importance of preexisting narratives to dramatic literature is not a specifically or primarily Western phenomenon but is characteristic of drama around the world. This can be seen from the very beginning of drama and of writing about the drama, in the way that every one of the world's great dramatic traditions has stressed from the outset the importance not of telling stories on stage but of retelling stories that are already known to their public. The three great grounding theoretical texts for the world's drama, both East and West—Bharata's *Natyasastra,* Aristotle's *Poetics,* and Zeami's writings on the Noh— take surprisingly similar positions on the importance of utilizing already existing stories for the creation of theatre. All three allow for both the retelling of stories and for the creation of new stories for dramatic purposes, but all three also consider the superior and more significant drama to be that in which the material is already familiar to the audience, drawn from a shared body of historic, legendary, and mythic material treating heroes, kings, and gods. For Aristotle these are the tragedies to which the vast majority of his treatise is dedicated. Even though he distinguishes poetry from history on the grounds that history deals with "the particular," Aristotle nevertheless recognizes, and approves of, the fact that writers of tragedies normally and preferably draw material from historical subjects and received legends.

The prominence that Aristotle gives to tragedy, Bharata gives to his most highly regarded type of drama, the *Nataka,* which is "the type of play whose subject is a well-known plot material, the hero equally well-known and exalted."[1] The *Natyasastra* is not concerned with eliciting the particular kind of emotional response favored by Aristotle but, rather, with drama that induces in its audience a play of emotions, the *rasas.* Nevertheless, like the *Poetics,* it recognizes that certain stories, certain situations, certain structures of action, are more naturally suited for this purpose than others, and the very familiarity and popularity of certain stories could be assumed to be due in large part to their success in stimulating these effects. The dramatist, in adapting these stories, would already have a certain measure of these effects at his disposal.

The earliest work by the Japanese Noh master, Zeami, *Fushikaden,* calls the written text the life of the art and asserts that "the very best Noh play is such as has an authentic source, novelty, a key point plus some elegant taste or flavour." Not only must the source material be "accurate and authentic," but, if possible, "the original source must be mentioned at the head of the piece, then a story well-known to the people must be described in a plain style." If the play concerns a place of scenic and historic interest, as many Noh plays do, then "some piece of poetry widely known about the place may be used to form the core of the piece."[2] Some twenty years later Zeami wrote an entire text on playwriting, the *Sando,* which contains a similar concern for recycling of material, not only whole stories but even familiar phrases, and for specifically calling them to the attention of the audience:

> In a play there should be a place where the original source is pointed out. If it is a famous place or a historical site, then you should take lines from well-known poems about the place, in Chinese or Japanese, and write them into concentrated points . . . In addition to this, you should work distinguished sayings and well-known Expressions into the *shite*'s language.[3]

Zeami and other masters of the Noh found their subject matter in history, legend, and folklore but especially in literary classics such as the *waka* poems of the seventh century, the ninth-century *Tales of Ise,* the eleventh-century *Tales of Genji,* and the thirteenth-century *Tales of Heike.* The Noh play is surely the most intensely haunted of any of the world's classic dramatic forms, since its central figure is often literally a ghost, who in the course of the play remembers and to some extent relives his story. If classic Greek and Indian drama may be said to be haunted by previous tellings of the same story, the Japanese Noh drama is doubly haunted, since the preexisting story is known not only to the audience but also to the central figure of the play, who now looks back upon it as a spirit. It is as if Oedipus were presented after his death, reflecting upon his fate while sharing with the audience a full knowledge of that fate.

The next major Japanese dramatic form was the *joruri,* a kind of play first created for the puppet theatre, the Bunraku, and then utilized as the literary basis for the live theatre, the Kabuki. *Joruri* drama is traditionally divided into two categories, used in Kabuki as well and based upon the "world" to which the hero belongs and the type of society that surrounds him. The first is the *jidaimono,* dealing with the deeds of warriors and princes; the second is the *sewamono,* depicting more everyday doings, particularly those of merchants and farmers. As might be expected, the *jidaimono* draw upon much of the same epic and legendary sources as the Noh, along with more recent work in the same spirit such as *Gikeiki* and *Taiheiki* from the era of Zeami himself and the later *Life of the Taiko* from the sixteenth century. The *sewamono,* although drawn from less literary antecedents, were nevertheless retellings of already known stories, in this case of actual current or recent events that were popular subjects of contemporary conversation. The concept of the "worlds" (*seikai*) in which plays are set is fundamental to Kabuki and deeply involved with the recycling of material. As Samuel Leiter explains in the *New Kabuki Encyclopedia:*

> The number of *seikai* was fixed, being derived for history plays from such historical narratives as the *Ise Monogatari, Masakadoki, Hogen Heiji, Gikeiki, Taiheiki, Heike Monogatari,* and

others. Their well-known characters and situations were borrowed by many playwrights. In the case of domestic plays, the worlds were generally chosen from famous incidents for which conventional characters' names were combined with the plot.[4]

The practice of returning to the stories of a few mythic houses, continued throughout the classic period of Greece and Rome, was paralleled in the reliance upon the great Hindu epics the *Mahabharata* and the *Ramayana* by the dramatists of India and Southeast Asia and upon the great cycles of legends such as the *Tale of the Heike* by the dramatists of Japan. Similarly, as the modern Arabic theatre developed in the nineteenth and twentieth centuries, its dramatists looked for subject matter not only to classic myths (Oedipus has been a particular favorite) but, even more centrally, to the collection of native narrative material offered by the *Arabian Nights*.

Before demonstrating how this recycling of narrative material has developed in theatre since classic times, it might be well to explore what considerations might have led both dramatists and theorists from our earliest records to privilege such material. Somewhat surprisingly, this question receives little attention from Aristotle, Zeami, and Bharata, although all three give prominence to already existing narratives in the creation of drama, and all are centrally concerned with the operations of reception. The focus in each, however, tends to be more upon the general and specific emotional effects sought by the drama and the various technical means in writing and production by which these effects are to be achieved. Little speculation is devoted specifically to the effects of recycling itself upon reception or to why dramatists should prefer to retell familiar stories rather than create new ones. The only substantial passage related to this matter is in Aristotle, in his comments on probability. The narratives most effective in stimulating the proper emotions for tragedy are those that the audience will accept as probable, and already known and accepted stories provide the least obstacle to audience belief and acceptance.[5]

In his discussion of how dramatic authors came to realize this, Aristotle follows his favored pattern of historical evolution. At first, he suggests, poets simply "recounted any legend that came in their way," relying on probability and the random effects of each story to move their audiences. Gradually, however, they came to realize that certain stories were more effective in producing the sort of emotional effects upon audiences they sought. These stories, he argues, were most effective because they had in common certain structural elements, which he analyzes in detail in his *Poetics* and which he felt were most effective in stimulating the proper tragic experience in audiences. Those few stories that came closest to the ideal tragic structure, stories like that of Alcmaeon, Oedipus, Orestes, and Thyestes, were returned to again and again.[6] Thus, while probability encouraged dramatists to look to already known stories, stories of a particular type, with a particular narrative shape or structure, were generally favored. The process is thus self-reinforcing, since these favored stories became the most familiar and the most likely to be selected for future retellings. Audiences would very likely already be familiar with the stories of Oedipus and Orestes from the mythological tradition, but this familiarity would be reinforced if the stories were often treated, as they were, by the country's dramatists.

This concern with believability, at least in terms of narrative content, is not nearly so important to Zeami or Bharata, whose concern with verisimilitude is more like that of Horace, directed toward the creation of certain types of dramatic characters who behave according to the expectations of their type. More ready acceptance by the audience is, in any case, only one and generally not the most important advantage a dramatist may gain by utilizing already known stories. Aristotle suggests another in his observation that certain stories are much more frequently retold than others, the most popular, he suggests, being those that have the shape most conducive to the pleasure of the tragic experience. Whether this "survival of the fittest" theory is correct or not, it is obviously the case that, amid the vast body of potential recyclable material offered on the one hand by the huge corpus of myths, legends, and historical writings and on the other by the welter of current and contemporary crimes, scandals, and other events of popular interest, certain stories or sets of stories in every era prove particularly attractive for retelling and for continued popular interest. It may be that, as Aristotle argues, these stories possess a particularly appealing narrative shape, but, whether that is the case or not, the very fact that they are familiar and popular means that the dramatist can turn to them with some assurance that his public will want to hear them again.

One must also consider, though Aristotle does not, that there are very practical advantages for a dramatist in taking already known narratives for his raw material. The theatre is a far more concentrated form than the epic or the epic's modern descendant, the novel, and dramatists have always sought ways to present their material and make their effects in the most efficient possible manner. Clearly, much less time has to be spent on exposition and explanation in the case of stories already known to the audience, allowing a dramatist to plunge directly into the action at or near a point of maximum interest. This strategy was so popular with the Greeks that the so-called late point of attack, with a large part of a story already completed when the play begins, was one of the most typical structural features of Greek tragedy. It is also central to the Noh, especially as developed by Zeami, whose warrior plays often begin with a point of attack even later than the Greeks, not shortly before the death of the hero, but afterward, so that the ghost of the hero, like the audience, can look back on the whole known arc of his story yet concentrate on the memory of a single incident, even a single moment, with all the rest only hinted at or implied.

The conditions of the theatrical event, enacted not only in a brief period of time but before a mass audience, provide none of the opportunity for reflection or even rereading offered by novels or lyric poetry and thus encourage the use of material already somewhat familiar to an audience for ease in reception. This consideration has often been stressed by theorists of populist and politically oriented theatre. Thus, the first recommendation in Romain Rolland's influential 1913 study of a theatre for the people stated: "the writer should choose only well-known historical themes which allow a quick rendering."[7]

This eminently practical encouragement for recycling operates for almost all drama of all periods, but it is often reinforced by other more specialized concerns. The assumption that drama was primarily concerned not with telling but with retelling stories was, for example, almost universal during the Renaissance. When dramatists began at that time to create a theatre based upon their understanding of Greek and Roman practice, their first attempts were simply translations and adaptations of specific classic plays, the most straightforward type of retelling. Then, as more original work began to be done, the favored subjects for dramatic treatment remained already known stories out of the classic tradition— the myths and legends already treated by classic authors or narratives drawn from historical figures, most often Roman but occasionally Greek or biblical. The general assumption of Renaissance aesthetics, that Greek and Roman practice should be followed as closely as possible, already encouraged the reworking of familiar material from antiquity, but this reworking was particularly stressed in the case of drama, since classic practice itself, as we have seen, stressed the continual retelling of a rather small number of favored narratives.

The French theorist Jacques Peletier du Mans in his 1555 *Art poétique* called for French dramatists to seek subjects from Sophocles, Euripides, and Seneca—advice that was widely followed by Renaissance dramatists throughout Europe.[8] Christian Biet, for example, counted more than thirty different retellings of the Oedipus story in France between 1614 and 1818.[9] Tragedy, the most highly respected of dramatic forms, was also the form most dedicated to the recycling of narratives, and it remained the favored domain of serious drama, particularly in France and Italy, until the coming of romanticism in the early nineteenth century.

The Quarrel of the Ancients and the Moderns and, even more important, the subsequent romantic movement encouraged an approach to art that did not depend upon the continued reuse of traditional materials, but the theatre's traditional association with cultural memory was not disrupted; it simply began now to be developed in other directions. The romantic dramatists of Germany, France, and elsewhere may have turned their backs on the long central myths, legends, and histories of classical antiquity, but this was often only to replace them with the myths, legends, and histories of their own particular culture. If anything, this new orientation demonstrated once again how central a role theatre has always played in a culture repeating again and again to its members its own particular stories.

Nor did the long-established and familiar classic myths disappear from the stage. Despite the infusion of national material in the nineteenth century, the old familiar stories of Electra, Oedipus, Medea, and others continued to stimulate important dramatic reworkings in almost every generation. Even in the twentieth century, after the triumph of realism, these stories are retold again and again, providing a familiar grounding upon which each new generation of dramatists can develop the concerns of their particular time. Among the countless twentieth century examples one might cite in the United States Eugene O'Neill's ambitious attempt at retelling the Electra-Orestes story in the Greek manner, in a tragic trilogy of plays, *Mourning Becomes Electra,* infused with an interest in Freudian psychology that marked much creative work of that period; or in France, the *Antigone* of Jean Anouilh, written under German occupation and reflecting the moral and intellectual tensions of that era; or in Germany, the abstract, experimental *Medeamaterial* of Germany's leading late-twentieth-century dramatist, Heiner Müller, which, like much of Müller's work, is haunted by a past surviving in sharp, disconnected fragments.

Many theorists have attempted to explain the continued attraction of the drama to already used material. C. R. Post, speaking of the phenomenon in the case of the comic tradition, and in particular of the predictability of narrative in Greek New Comedy and its successors, provides a strongly teleological explanation:

> The ideal of the past has been to repeat again and again the same subject until it has achieved perfect expression . . . the tragic poet utilizes the well-worn myths, the comic writer the familiar intrigues, each impressing upon the old matter his own individuality in the hope that his interpretation may prove the ultimate.[10]

This theory points in an interesting and useful direction, even though its strongly Aristotelian vision of each subject headed toward an ultimate "perfect expression" does not really accurately describe the actual ongoing dynamic of this process.[11] Attractive as this abstraction may be to an Aristotelian theorist, it seems unlikely that the primary reason New Comedy writers kept returning to the same basic plot or that for centuries serious dramatists have retold the stories of Electra or Medea was a desire to finally "get it right." It may be that a dramatist may dream of writing the "ultimate" version of some story, one that will drive all others from public memory and make unnecessary any further variations, but that is clearly not the way the process normally works. Even Sophocles' *Oedipus,* perhaps the single play that might be argued is the "definitive" version of the story, has not prevented subsequent dramatists from continuing to offer other reworkings; indeed, its prominence is surely one of the reasons that such reworkings continue to appear.

Post's theory does, however, suggest one important force for dramatic recycling, particularly in certain periods. The fact that Greek dramas were created to be presented in competition with one another may well have provided some encouragement for the repeated use of the same basic set of stories, since each recycling almost inevitably encouraged audiences to be alert to the particular features of the new version and to experience it in part as a contribution to an ongoing comparative process if not a direct competition. This spirit of competition is potentially present in all periods and in those in which reworkings are the norm has usually been highly prominent. Dramatists then sought, and were expected by their audiences, to measure themselves against work of the past or to establish their position within a tradition by producing their own version of standard narratives, even when there was no thought of any of these being the ultimate one. The dramatic career and reception dynamics of a neoclassic dramatist such as Voltaire, for example, can scarcely be understood without a recognition of the importance, and complexity, of the reuse of earlier dramatic material in his work. His first important success was one of the many French *Oedipuses,* and the extensive contemporary critical commentary on the play demonstrates clearly that a primary concern of its first audiences and critics, both positive and negative, was to compare it with previous versions of the story, particularly, of course, the most famous ones, by Sophocles and Corneille. Indeed, in the very selection of this subject Voltaire knowingly challenged such comparisons, and later in his career he undertook a whole series of plays, beginning with *Semiramis* (1746), *Rome sauvée* (1749), and *Oreste* (1750), each one based on the same story utilized in a play by Crébillon, the leading French tragedian of the previous generation, in a campaign designed specifically to eclipse the other dramatist. Once again, the sought-for effect in such drama relies primarily upon an audience's binocular vision— its members' familiarity with the previous treatment of this same material and their ability to draw comparisons between that and the new, rival treatment.

Even when direct competition or artistic rivalry is not involved, as it was in classic Greece or neoclassic France, dramatists have often utilized familiar stories to relate their work to a tradition or because the retelling of a familiar story allowed emphasis to be placed on subtle variations, thus providing the author with a convenient means of stressing certain matters of content and style that were of particular interest to him or her. Netta Zagagi, another critic of Menander, specifically takes issue with her predecessor Post on the motives for reworking familiar narrative material in the classic and neoclassic theatre. A spectator in these theatres, suggests Zagagi, "preferred to build up his expectations upon familiar territory, rather than grope in the dark in the mysterious world of a writer who is cut off from traditional patterns of thought, and creates his own situations from scratch." The goal sought by the author was not so much Post's suggested "ultimate" working of material but, rather, a rich and complex new presentation of it. Says Zagagi:

> variations on a given theme were far more likely to stimulate the imagination, and the more complex and comprehensive the link between the individual work and the literary tradition from which it sprang, the greater were the prospects of the writer winning praise and recognition for his work.[12]

One of the most important effects of drama's recycling of material is that it encourages audiences to compare varying versions of the same story, leading them to pay closer attention to how the story is told and less to the story itself. Thus, in a kind of paradox the author uses a familiar story to emphasize the originality of his contribution. In a sense every retelling of a story like Faust could be entitled, as Paul Valéry entitled his version, *Mon Faust*

(*My* Faust).[13] This is clearly not just a Western preoccupation, either, but has been an important part of the theatre experience for publics in many periods and most theatrical cultures. D. J. Crump, writing on the Chinese drama of the classic period, for example, observes that "the majority of Chinese plays are 'historical.' That is, they deal with men who lived, and deeds the Chinese themselves believe to have transpired in the past and *with which even the illiterate seem to have been astonishingly conversant* [italics mine]." This preexisting knowledge, Crump suggests, has a "magnifying effect on the playwright's plots and personification."

> He may, for example, deal gently with a well-known historical character—a cruel general, let us say—which may be in contrast with folk knowledge of him and produce effects which the Westerner may miss; more important, he can depend upon his audience to accept the extravagances of his lines, in prose or verse, in just the manner the playwright intends, since both audience and playwright share roughly the same view of the *dramatis personae*.[14]

In modern times, when the tradition of realism has on the whole discouraged dramatists, especially in English, from following the tradition of reworking familiar material, the comparison with previous treatments as an important part of the process of reception of new plays has much diminished in importance, but in many periods it was an important and in some periods a dominant element.

Ever since the Greeks one device, dependent entirely upon an audience's previous knowledge of the story they are watching, has been the use of irony. Indeed, many modern critics have argued that irony is so fundamental an aspect of drama that the two terms cannot really be separated. Kenneth Burke, for example, essentially equates *drama* and *irony* in *Grammar of Motives,*[15] and D. C. Muecke, in his book-length study of the ironic, argues that "irony is essentially both theatrical and dramatic" and further that "drama is at least typically ironic and perhaps essentially ironigenic, that is, productive of irony."[16] Bert States, following Burke, suggests that there is a "reliable (if intuitive) truth in our common habit of grouping the terms *irony, dialectic,* and *drama,* often using them to define one another."[17]

G. G. Sedgewick in his book *Of Irony, Especially in Drama* suggests that this particular association of the ironic mode with drama is related to the theatre itself, which he calls a "sort of ironic convention, whereby a spectator occupying a good seat, as it were, in the real world is enabled to look into a world of illusion and so to get 'a view of life from on high.'" The particular pleasure of the theatre is "the spectacle of a life in which, it is true, we do not interfere but over which we exercise the control of knowledge." As a result of the balance of superior knowledge and detached sympathy, concludes Sedgewick: "*The whole attitude of the interested spectator is ironic.*"[18] The full range of emotional reactions sought of the theatre, from the amusement felt in farce to the pathos felt in tragedy, rely to an important extent upon the audience having an understanding that the characters do not have of the future turns of the dramatic action or the real state of affairs onstage, a disjuncture Shakespearian scholar Bertrand Evans has called "discrepant awareness."[19]

There is a certain ironic element, as Sedgewick suggests, in the basic situation of being an unobserved and unparticipating observer, but the irony is much sharped and focused when the observer, by whatever means, is put in possession of knowledge that concerns the action being observed but which is not accessible to the participants. This establishes the doubled or dialectic condition necessary for irony, since "discrepant awareness" itself is not sufficient; the observer must be simultaneously conscious of what the characters onstage are aware of and also the presumed more complete and incompatible or contradictory state of affairs as she understands them.

The recycling of an already existing narrative, historical or imaginary, already known to the audience is by no means the only way to set up a drama that utilizes discrepant awareness, but it is one of the most common and effective ones and has been employed by serious and comic dramatists in every period since the Greeks and Romans. A major part of the dramatic effect of Sophocles' *Oedipus* depends upon this audience effect, to the extent that this central classic example of tragic art has also become a central example of the use of dramatic irony. The audience's assumed previous knowledge of this story is utilized for effect in every scene and often in almost every line, as in the famous moment when Oedipus pledges to seek the murderer of Laius:

> Since I am now the holder of his office,
> and have his bed and wife that once was his,
> and had his line not been unfortunate
> we would have common children—(fortune leaped
> upon his head)—because of all these things,
> I fight in his defense as for my father.[20]

Similar effects pervade the Noh dramas, in which the audience's knowledge of the play's action is almost always superior to that of the subordinate character, the *waki*, who begins the play and who must often learn what the audience already knows, the true identity of the central figure, the *shite*. Thus, in Zeami's warrior play, *Atsumori*, even though the *waki* is himself the warrior who killed Atsumori and who, now a Buddhist priest, is returning to the site of the fatal battle to pray for the spirit of his fallen foe, he does not at first recognize, as the audience does, that the grass cutter he encounters is in fact the spirit of Atsumori. His first sign of the approach of the grass cutter is the sound of a flute, a musical instrument, all the audience knows, especially associated with Atsumori and a courtly instrument quite out of keeping with this rural setting. Indeed, the *waki* remarks on this disjuncture, in an exchange filled with the same ironic use of discrepant awareness that is operating in the Oedipus passage just cited:

> *Waki:* About the flute I have just heard, is it played among you?
> *Shite:* Yes. The flute is played among us.
> *Waki:* How elegant! The performance is unbecoming for folks like you, but it is very, very elegant indeed, I should say.[21]

Like Oedipus, the *waki* inadvertently speaks more truly than he knows, to the delight of the observing audience, who understand, as he does not, the total situation.

Reliance upon this effect becomes if anything more striking in more modern versions of the story. French dramatists ever since the Renaissance have been especially attracted to the recycling of classic material, often in the twentieth century with a kind of whimsical self-consciousness. This attitude reaches a kind of apogee in Jean Cocteau's *The Infernal Machine,* which pushes narrative self-awareness almost to the point of parody. First, a disembodied "Voice" recounts the story, perhaps to add a note of ritual to the proceedings but also to insure that the audience will be prepared for the frequent ironic references that follow. The Voice describes the catastrophe thus:

> reeling from one monstrous discovery to another,
> drunk with his own misfortune, Oedipus is finally
> caught. The trap closes on him. Everything is now
> clear. With her red scarf Jocasta hangs herself.
> With the gold brooch, Oedipus tears out his eyes.

Such a passage assures that the audience, even in the unlikely event that they are unfamiliar with the original story, is prepared to revel in the irony of such interchanges as this, a few pages into the play, when Jocasta enters, her fatal scarf trailing behind her. Tiresias, following her, treads upon it and she cries out:

> *Jocasta:* Oh!
> *Tiresias:* What is it?
> *Jocasta:* Your foot, Zizi. You're stepping on my scarf.
> *Tiresias:* I beg your pardon.
> *Jocasta:* I'm not blaming you—it's the scarf. This scarf is against me. It's always trying to strangle me. One moment it catches in branches, another moment in the moving wheel of a carriage; then you step on it. I'm afraid of it, but I can't part with it. In the end, it will kill me.[22]

The familiarity and dominance of *Oedipus* has perhaps encouraged the impression that ironic exchanges of this kind are primarily the domain of the ruthlessly preordained "infernal machine" of classic tragedy, but the thrill of superior knowledge that discrepant awareness offers to audiences is so attractive that one finds it operating wherever the audience knows more than the characters. Previous familiarity with the story being told, or even with the type of story being told, has provided ample opportunity for the pleasures of dramatic irony in almost every period. The world of nineteenth-century crime melodrama is far removed from the high tragedy of classic Greece, but a passage such as the following, from Edward Fitzball's *Jonathan Bradford,* draws upon the same discrepant awareness, as the audience recognizes the ironic prophecy in the comments of the doomed Hayes:

> *Hayes (rising):* Host, with your leave, for I'm a man of regular habits, I'll retire for the night;—you know the chamber?
> *Bradford:* Oh, yes! The one above the bar; my wife will attend to the bed herself—Sally will light you up stairs.
> *Hayes:* That chamber, on my different journies [sic] from London to Oxford, I've slept in for fifteen years;—I, one night, dreamt that I died there.[23]

Although the performance of drama in classic times was generally tied to religious and political celebrations of various kinds and the material being presented, particularly in the serious drama, drew upon historical and mythological sources, there is little evidence of any attempt to use these vivid retellings of central cultural narratives for any specifically political or religious purpose (as the old Athenian proverb "Nothing to do with Dionysos" suggests).[24] In later periods, however, governments and other organizations, with varying degrees of consciousness, came to understand that the theatre's presentation of material in a vivid and public manner made it a valuable tool for inculcating, reinforcing, and celebrating particular social concerns. Recycling remained a major, sometimes the unique means of dramatic creation, but the material selected for recycling was selected for its educative or even propagandistic value. A notable example was the theatre that appeared in the West during the Middle Ages, developed within and naturally reflective of the beliefs and concerns of the medieval church. The subject matter of this dramatic tradition, while totally different from that of classic Greece and Rome, was equally firmly grounded in already existing and familiar narrative material—the stories of the Bible, the lives of the saints, the homilitic material of the Paternoster tradition. Thus, despite the enormous cultural differences between classic and medieval theatre audiences, they shared the basic reception experience of encountering in drama primarily not new narratives but narratives already known to them.

The leaders of the French Revolution saw theatre as an important instrument for building and maintaining public support, and they promulgated a number of decrees requiring theatres to present plays regularly retelling those stories, myths, and historical events that were best suited to achieve these ends.[25] During the French Revolution and the Napoleonic period scarcely any battle or public event, large or small, escaped dramatic treatment in a highly politicized and theatricalized culture, nor were the subjects exclusively French. The *Journal de l'Empire* in 1806 marveled at the theatrical popularity, for example, of the Prussian ruler Frederick the Great:

> Frederick is in all of our theatres; he has appeared in comedy, in comic opera, in vaudeville, in drama, in melodrama. Only in tragedy has he not yet made his appearance.[26]

The appearance of modern nationalism, which swept across Europe in the years immediately following the Napoleonic period, significantly involved the theatre in almost every new nation, and in each a central function of the theatre continued to be what French Revolutionary leaders had sought, a place where the legends and historical events were continually recirculated as a part of the process of developing a new national consciousness: the legend of Libussa in Czechoslovakia, the Hermann dramas in Germany, tales of the Foscari in Italy, Viking and bardic narratives from the Scandinavian nations, and countless other narratives of varying degrees of familiarity became the central fare of the new national stages.[27]

The rise of nationalism gave a new prominence to the dramatization of historical material in the nineteenth century, but the dramatization of such material was already a familiar practice. Although classic material provided the most common source for dramatic recycling in the renaissance and baroque theatre, it was by no means the only such source. More recent history, myth, and legend continued to provide material just as it had done for the Greeks, and certain stories, once in the dramatic repertoire, inspired countless dramatic reworkings, just as those of Electra and Antigone had done. One of the first was the story of Joan of Arc, whose first dramatic treatment appeared in a late medieval saint's play in Joan's own century, the *Mistère du siège d'Orléans.* The theatrical potential of this story was immediately apparent and was reinforced by the association of Joan with the rise of French nationalism. The classic bibliography of Joan of Arc material, appearing in 1894, cites more than two hundred dramatic works, French and foreign, that had appeared on this subject up until that date.[28]

Along with the stories of kings and heroes, common to dramatic retellings since classic times the world over, dramatists in more recent times have more and more commonly turned to dramatizations of well-known public events involving central characters of a more modest nature, with highly publicized scandals and crimes leading the way. The motive for retelling here was clearly not the encouragement of patriotism or national pride but the rather more mundane one of capitalizing on current sensations to attract audiences. The so-called domestic drama in England begins with the 1592 *Arden of Feversham,* the dramatization of a sensational and highly publicized crime of the previous generation in Kent. The same era saw the appearance in the theatre of two of the most durable theatrical myths presumably also drawn from real-life scandals, the stories of Dr. Faust in Germany and of Don Juan in Spain. Each story, like that of Saint Joan, soon joined the repertoire of continually recirculated theatrical narratives, retold hundreds of times on the stage and continuing to inspire ever-new variations (one of the most recent being the *F@ust, Version 3.0,* of the Barcelona experimental company Fura dels Baus, which placed the ancient story squarely in the computer era, even with its title).

Inoura and Kawatake, describing the domestic dramas of the great eighteenth-century Bunraku dramatist Chikamatsu, characterize them as "corresponding to many of the local news and feature items in our daily newspapers . . . dramatized versions of actual recent events."[29] This description could be applied not only to many of the most popular works of both the Japanese Bunraku and Kabuki theatres but also to a large number of European works of this same period and for more than a century afterward. George Lillo's *The London Merchant,* the most popular serious English drama of the eighteenth century, took a familiar crime for its narrative, as did countless popular melodramas in the next century, such as the immensely successful *Maria Martin or The Red Barn.* These sensational retellings of current and well-publicized murder cases clearly owed much of their appeal to the audience's knowledge of many of the details, actual or added by p_ _ular retelling, of the crime.

Not only sensational crimes but any story that caught the public imagination was likely, before the days of television, to be offered to the public in a theatrical retelling. In 1711, for example, Richard Steele, in the pages of his paper the *Spectator,* offered the moving, though largely fictional, tale of a young London merchant, Thomas Inkle, who reportedly traveled to Barbados, where he fell in love with and had a child by a native girl, Yarico, whom he later betrayed and sold into slavery. This pathetic story appalled and fascinated readers throughout the sentimental eighteenth century and inspired during that period more than fifteen dramatic retellings in a variety of languages.[30]

Most of the strategies of recycling so far mentioned, both East and West, have been utilized primarily in serious drama, if not actual tragedy in the Aristotelian sense. Both Aristotle and Bharata give greater latitude to the comic dramatist in creating new narratives than to the serious dramatist, and the practice of the comic Kyogen as opposed to the serious Noh within the Japanese classic tradition suggests the same orientation there. The dynamic of recycling is deeply embedded in the process of theatrical reception, however, and this apparent freedom of comedy from the kinds of narrative recycling often followed by serious drama by no means has freed it as a genre from this dynamic. Rather, the extremely varied comedic tradition in drama has developed its own strategies of recycling and has often assumed a pre-knowledge of material as important to reception as that expected by conventional tragedy, even if the material involved is of a generally quite different sort.

Before considering these alternative strategies, however, it must be noted that Aristotle's distinction between comic writers, who first construct plots and then "insert characteristic names," and tragic writers, who "still keep to real names,"[31] is a distinction that is valid only for the very limited cultural and historical period in which Aristotle was writing and in which so-called New Comedy was dominant. That comedy could, and did, utilize "real names" both of historical and legendary figures is amply demonstrated in the Old Comedy of Aristophanes, and, if we range more widely through the history of dramatic representation, we can even find a number of continually recycled specific comedic plots that correspond directly to those of tragedy, being drawn directly from parallel classic sources. The most notable example is probably the story of Amphitryon, whose considerable stage history is gently mocked in the title of Jean Giraudoux's fanciful *Amphitryon 38*, claiming thirty-seven previous versions of the story.

Aristophanes, however, points us to another comedic use of the same material recycled by tragedy, a use that is seen much more commonly in the whole tradition of dramatic writing from classic times to the present. This is the dramatic burlesque, or parody, which may draw directly upon the same subject matter as more serious drama but more often draws upon it indirectly, by reworking, in a comic manner, material previously presented on the serious stage.

Parody is a very ancient phenomenon. Almost as soon as stories began to be told, it appears, they became also the subject of parodic treatment. The first known use of the Greek word *parodia* is found in Artistotle's *Poetics,* in which credit for inventing this form is given to Hegemon the Phasian. His poetic narratives, says Aristotle, relate to Homer's epics somewhat as comedies relate to tragedies.[32] Homer apparently provided the sole inspiration for such works, yet not primarily as a source of narrative material but, rather, of meter, style, and vocabulary, which was then employed for lighter subject matter.[33] Parody is utilized in Western comedy from the very beginning, most notably in Aristophanes' *The Frogs,* with its parodies of the manner, matter, and general conventions of the Greek tragic dramatists.[34]

Whereas the serious retelling of preexisting narratives is particularly favored in drama, the comic reworking not only of preexisting narratives but of almost any preexisting cultural material is something that drama has shared equally with other literary genres, and indeed with art, music, and many aspects of popular culture. A variety of terms have appeared over time to describe this activity, and most writers on the subject are forced to begin their studies by sorting out the shades of meaning of parody, travesty, satire, burlesque, and so on, terms that have all appeared frequently (and often interchangeably) in the theatre. One common distinction, and the only one I would like to make at this point, is between burlesque and parody. In the words of Robert F. Willson in his study of English burlesque plays, parody "in the strictest sense deals with individual works," while burlesque "generally attempts to ridicule in a looser way some recognizable form, such as heroic tragedy, the opera, the epic or lyric."[35]

The best-known plays in the parody and burlesque tradition, such as George Villiers's *The Rehearsal,* Sheridan's *The Critic,* the comic operas of Gilbert and Sullivan, or Tom Stoppard's *The Real Inspector Hound,* all have echoes of specific previous works, but are all by Willson's distinction more accurately burlesques than parodies. The same tends to be true of the best-known literary satires, such as *Don Quixote* or *Northanger Abbey.* The Western theatrical tradition also, however, offers countless examples of dramatic parodies in Willson's "strictest" sense, that is, comic reworkings of specific serious works. This is especially the case in the period from the seventeenth through the nineteenth centuries, since the spread of neoclassicism in the European theatre carried the tradition of parody, a part of that inheritance, along with it. A number of theatrical capitals, Paris and Vienna in particular, contained theatres that made a specialty of works of this kind. In Paris this was the domain of the Comédie Italienne and the fair theatres. Almost as soon as the traditional Italian comedy in Paris began to incorporate the French language into its production, in the final years of the seventeenth century and the opening of the eigh-

teenth, one of the uses the language was put to was the presentation of parodies of familiar French classics, such as *Le Cid* and
Bérénice.[36] During the following century attention shifted from
such established classics to contemporary works, so that scarcely
any new play of any significance could appear at the Comédie
Française without inspiring one or more parody versions at the
Italienne or the popular fair theatres. One, or often several, parody versions soon followed new serious works by Voltaire and his
contemporaries, and the passing of neoclassicism caused no
decline in this practice. The most famous of the romantic dramas,
Hugo's *Hernani* at the Comédie, was almost immediately followed
by the parodies *Harlani* at the Vaudeville and *N.I. Ni* at the Porte-
Saint-Martin theatre. Indeed, parody versions of popular plays
remained fairly common in France for another century, producing such works as Yves Mirande and Gustave Quinin's *Le Chausseur
de chez Maxim* at the Palais Royale in 1920 and Gardel-Hervé's *La
Poule de chez Maxim* at the Cluny in 1927, both parodic versions of
George Feydeau's classic 1899 farce comedy, *Le Dame de chez
Maxim*.

The centers for dramatic parody in Vienna were the popular
suburban folk theatres, the Leopoldstädter Bühne, the Kärntner-
tortheater, and the Theater an der Wien, now best remembered
for premiering Mozart's *The Magic Flute*. Emanuel Schikaneder
(the first Papageno) and his fellow directors made a specialty of
parody drama at the beginning of the nineteenth century, and
their range was far broader than that of their French counterparts,
including works of the French neoclassic stage headed by Voltaire
and the leading Austrian neoclassic author, Grillparzer, the
tragedies of Shakespeare, the melodramas of Pixérécourt, the
tragedies of Schiller and Goethe, the popular contemporary German "Fate-tragedies," Greek tragedies, the dramas of Hebbel and
Kleist, the operas of Adam, Auber, and Gluck, even *The Magic Flute*
itself, parodied by two of the Viennese specialists in this genre,
Karl Meisl and Joachim Perinet.[37] The continuing popularity of
this form can be seen today in the ongoing success of the production *Forbidden Broadway*, a regularly updated parodic revue of many
of the most popular shows in New York, located in the heart of the
plays it is parodying, on Times Square, and so successful that it has

opened the new century boasting a longer continuous run than almost all of its changing targets.

Margaret Rose, in her study of parody, has argued that, historically, there have been two fairly distinct attitudes of the parody creator toward the work parodied. The first is mockery, in which the parody creator shows a certain contempt for the original material; the second is more sympathetic, even admiring, in which the parodist imitates in order to write in that style.[38] Certainly, in the rich tradition of theatrical parody both motivations can be seen, although in most cases I am not sure that one can make so clear a distinction between mockery and celebration. More recently, Linda Hutcheon has discussed this distinction in more general, and I think more useful, terms, speaking of the "conservative" side of parody, which "stresses sameness and stasis," and the "subversive" side, which "stresses only difference," and she suggests that, especially in recent uses of this device, parody both reinscribes and subverts.[39] What I would like to stress is that, however individual uses of this device may mix such concerns as mockery and celebration or reaffirmation and subversion, parody in the theatre has in all periods functioned as a device to further reinforce the collective and ongoing nature of the theatregoing community. In order to enjoy a theatrical parody the audience must be essentially composed of a community that shares a common theatrical history of attending the work being parodied. A great deal of the pleasure derives from the shared recognition of the parody's references, in their exaggerated or distorted form, and also of the fact that the recognition *is* shared. The laughter, as is normally the case in the theatre, is reinforced by its collectivity. The parallel response by our fellow audience members is evidence that they share our memory of the material whose comic iteration we are witnessing. Surely one of the reasons that parody, from the beginning, has been a particularly popular theatre form, is that in the theatre it is so directly involved with the theatre's ongoing involvement with collectivity, history, and memory.

Even though parody has been in all periods one of comedy's most favored devices, it has by no means been the only way in which comedic drama has followed the practice of more serious theatre in re-presenting already familiar stories. What has very frequently occurred is that comedy has found its own, quite different narrative sources for dramatic reworking, the sources offered not by history or legend but by popular or folk material. In certain periods this practice has been so common that one could even argue a kind of parallel between the use of "high" literary sources such as myth and legend as source material for high drama such as tragedy and the use of "low" literary sources such as popular folk and fairy tales for low drama such as comedy. Well-known folk or popular tales have been utilized to provide subjects for dramatization at least as familiar, and for more democratic audiences probably more familiar, than the more learned material from classic or historical sources favored by traditional tragedy.

A significant number of medieval plays dramatized familiar proverbs, a form giving a shape to a narrative while allowing considerable freedom in its actual execution. The medievalist Eugènie Droz, in a review of Gustave Cohen's major 1949 edition of French farces of the fifteenth century, notes that at least a quarter of the fifty-three pieces are in fact dramatizations of proverbs,[40] a tradition revived in the nineteenth century by Alfred de Musset. Another medieval scholar, P. Toledo, has suggested that many other farces are dramatizations of other widely known examples of folk literature, the *fabliaux* and *novelles,* written consolidations of folk material that were then recirculated in oral form by *jongleurs* and other professional entertainers.[41] Most of these short plays, like the dramatizations of proverbs, deal with a single situation, a trickster tricked, a braggart exposed, a simpleton who misunderstands or takes too literally instructions given him, but the situation itself is so familiar as to be instantly recognized by its audience and thus to provide a familiar shape for reception. Perhaps the most common of all these situations is the erotic triangle of husband, wife, and would-be lover (a triangle equally familiar in the more literary courtly romances of the period). "Especially typical," notes Grace Frank, "is the triangle, faithless wife, philandering priest, and cuckolded husband."[42] The generic nature of this repeated structural pattern is emphasized by the fact that the characters who participate in it are generally not provided with specific names but identified only as "the wife," "the husband," or "the priest." The predictability of the dramatic relationship between a group of characters so designated is so great, then, that from a reception point of view one can speak of a relationship between character names and action in such plays as almost as well established as that in a classic drama that offers the names and accompanying actions of, for example, Oedipus, Jocasta, and Tiresias.

An even closer parallel to tragedy's dramatic reworking of classic myth has been comedy's dramatic retelling of fairy and folktales. This is a process that some literary critics have traced back to Aristophanes, most of whose comedies clearly suggest a folktale background even though few traces of ancient Greek fairy and folktales remain.[43] Fairies and sprites from the world of folktale appear in occasional plays of the Renaissance (most notably in the comedies of Shakespeare) and even in the late Middle Ages (as in Adam de la Halle's *Jeu de la feuillée*), though the specific retelling of complete folktales onstage, as George Peele does in his *The Old Wives Tale* (ca. 1593), remains uncommon until late-seventeenth-century France, when an enormous vogue for this presumed popular form developed in aristocratic circles. Louis XIV had a lifelong interest in hearing fairy tales, a taste shared by many in his court, and the reading, writing, and dramatic presentation of this material gained great popularity.[44] Horace's twofold purpose of poetry, to delight and to instruct, was considered fundamental in the neoclassic period, and the civilizing and cultivating function of these tales was always foregrounded, as can be seen even in the title of the most famous and influential collection from the period, Charles Perrault's 1697 *Contes du temps passé de ma mere l'oye: Avec des morales* (Tales of Times Past by My Mother Goose: With Morals).

Although the writing and telling of fairy tales in seventeenth- and eighteenth-century France remained primarily a literary activity, the influence of this vogue was felt on the stage, not in major literary drama, in which this "popular" material would have been quite unacceptable, but in the more fanciful realm of court ballets and spectacle dramas (an early example being Molière and Corneille's 1671 *Psyche*), in which social content gave way to spectacular display. This interest in fairytale subject matter as an excuse for spectacular visual effects remained central to such entertainments for the next two centuries in France and subsequently elsewhere in Europe as well, with the French *féerie* (fairy tale) and the British pantomime being probably the most familiar examples.

The nineteenth century was the golden age of the dramatic retelling of folk and fairy stories. At the beginning of the century fairy tales such as *Tom Thumb* and *Sleeping Beauty* alternated with and were often written by the same authors who provided the spectacular new melodramas for the minor theatres of Paris and who favored such stories because their fanciful backgrounds encouraged the sort of scenic display that was a specialty of these theatres. Within a few years this rather exotic interest in the dramatization of folk material was supplemented by an even stronger cultural force with the coming of romanticism.

Much of the intellectual groundwork for the European-wide movement of romanticism was laid in Germany, and no art was more affected in all of its aspects than the theatre. Closely related to the rise of romanticism was the rise of nationalism, particularly in Germany, where the establishment of a German nation-state became now a matter of the greatest political import. In the theatre, as in other arts, this meant a new interest in German subject matter. One result, as we have already noted, was the replacement of the neoclassic tragedies on Greek and Roman themes with dramas and tragedies based on local history and legend. Another, closely related, was a new interest in local popular and folk culture, especially as opposed to the aristocratic, high culture emphasis of neoclassicism. In sharp contrast to Perrault's consciously literary reworkings of folktales, the German Grimm brothers presented in 1825 the first edition of their *Kinder- und Hausmärchen* (Nursery and Household Tales), purportedly presenting material directly out of the oral peasant tradition. This collection, containing such classic tales as *Cinderella, Snow White,* and *Little Red Riding Hood,* was itself read throughout Europe and inspired a European-wide interest in the collecting and publishing of similar material.

The sudden interest and widespread availability of this new body of narrative material provided the nineteenth-century stage with a major new source of stories for dramatic reworking. What had attracted organizers of court entertainments to this sort of material in the seventeenth and eighteenth centuries was less the stories themselves than the opportunities they offered for spectacular scenic and costume display, and this continued to be the case in the nineteenth century, although the primary audiences were now more socially diverse. Probably the best known of these spectacle traditions were the *féeries* of France and the British pantomimes, which, despite their title, were well provided with spoken and sung dialogue during their peak period, the mid-nineteenth century. In the later years of the century the emphasis on spectacle declined, but the tradition of popular dramatic recycling of folk material continued, especially in the English pantomime. Thelma Niklaus, a historian of European popular entertainment, points out the importance of traditional narrative material even as spectacle diminished:

> By 1870, authors of pantomime had not only abandoned extravaganza, they now restricted themselves to only a few of the many themes of fairy mythology. To this repertoire England contributed *Dick Whittington, The Babes in the Wood, Robinson Crusoe, St. George and the Dragon, Gulliver's Travels,* and *Goody Two Shoes,* based on a nursery tale by Oliver Goldsmith. From France via Perrault came *Cinderella, The Sleeping Beauty, Red Riding Hood, Bluebeard,* and *Puss in Boots. The Arabian Nights' Tales,* first translated into English at the beginning of the Eighteenth century, yielded *Aladdin, Sinbad the Sailor* and *Ali Baba and the Forty Thieves.*[45]

The British pantomime, with its traditional characters and folk and fairy narratives, maintains a distinct if somewhat tenuous position still in the British theatre, particularly in the Christmas season, but the major domain of the dramatic recycling of material of this sort has shifted in the twentieth century to an important new form emerging in Europe and America, the children's theatre. Today these familiar stories are still receiving almost continual retellings in the theatre on stages, live and puppet, focused on youthful audiences. Occasional new retellings do still appear on other stages, however, Elizabeth Egloff's *The Swan* and Stephen Sondheim's *Into the Woods* providing two recent English-language examples.

Into the Woods may serve to call our attention to a type of contemporary theatre that is particularly dedicated to the recycling of narrative material—the musical comedy. Not surprisingly, Walt Disney productions, whose film recyclings of fairy and folk tales are among the best known of twentieth-century films, have continued this recycling as they have expanded from films into musical theatre with such contributions as *Beauty and the Beast* and *The Lion King*, but, in creating new musicals from old narrative material, they are merely following the general practice of this genre. Recent musical successes, both original works and revivals, in New York and London illustrate clearly both the range and the ubiquity of this practice, utilizing novels (*Les Misérables, Jekyll and Hyde, Ragtime, Jane Eyre, The Phantom of the Opera*), ballads and poems (*Cats, Sweeney Todd, The Wild Party*), and, of course, plays and operas (*Rent, The Scarlet Pimpernel, Kiss Me Kate*).

The theatre's reuse of already familiar narrative material is a phenomenon seemingly as old as the theatre itself and developing along with the theatre, from the enactment of sacred texts to the contemporary Broadway musical. Highly diverse in its manifestations, it has involved retelling stories from sacred and secular writings, from ancient history, myth, and legend and from notorious recent crimes and scandals, from epic and from folk sources. It has worked with every possible style, from the high seriousness of Greek tragedy and Japanese Noh to the slapstick and burlesque of the Viennese popular stage or the British pantomime.

Important as the practice of narrative recycling is to the dramatic text, however, it is rivaled in ubiquity and versatility by an often closely related type of recycling used by such texts, that of specific characters. Like narrative recycling, character recycling is not unique to drama, but it is equally widespread within the tradition and distinctly more common in it than in other literary forms. Certainly, there are many cases of literary sequels or series books, and popular forms, such as detective fiction, have traditionally utilized repeating characters in a number of narratives, but the ubiquity and extent of such recycling is distinctly greater in the theatre tradition. In the case of recycled characters the audience is expected to bring to its experience not a knowledge so much of such a specific narrative line but, rather, of the character traits of one or more familiar figures, who continue to demonstrate those already known traits within changing situations. When, as has often been the case, a group of recycled characters appear together in a variety of narratives, not only individual traits may be repeated but also ongoing relationships. What results is a much looser kind of narrative recycling than in, for example, a new version of the *Electra* story, a recycling in which the parts are familiar although they may be put into different combinations. The most familiar example of this blend of character and narrative recycling in the Western theatre is surely the *commedia dell'arte*. In the classic *commedia* a complicated and shifting set of familiar characters reappeared in varying combinations but with a basic stability of relationships and type characteristics in innumerable dramatic treatments. This process was already apparent in even earlier comedic forms, the Atellan farces of the Roman countryside. Although the evidence concerning these early popular entertainments is fragmentary, it is clear that one of their basic features was the use of stock characters repeated from play to play. Four rustic types were particularly popular: the lustful Maccus, the talkative Bucco, the foolish old man Pappus, and the greedy Dossennus.[46] A recent study of this form by Elaine Fantham notes that "the plots hinged on the mutual deceptions of this quartet, and titles indicate that plays usually started from an impersonation or change of trade and worked through the humor of trickery or exposure."[47] The similarity of this practice to that of the later *commedia,* and indeed the similarity of certain of the earliest standard *commedia* characters to the four rustic Atellan clowns, have led many historians to posit a direct link between the two.[48] Much argument has surrounded this claim, but for our purposes it is necessary only to note that both popular forms utilize the same general strategy of recycling characters and character groupings, as fundamental and widespread a practice in the drama as that of recycling specific narratives or narrative structures.

The earliest known examples of the *commedia dell'arte* regularly involve four basic clown figures—two servants, most often the whimsical Arlecchino and the wily Brighella, and two masters, most often the foolish old man Pantalone and the pedantic Dottore—and a basic pair of lovers, whose union provided the serious or romantic element of these plays. The importance of the love intrigue moved the *commedia* away from the knockabout Atellan farce and closer to another highly formulaic and predictable comedic structure, the Greek and Roman New Comedy as developed by Menander, Plautus, and Terence. The Greek New Comedy illustrates clearly the frequently close relationship between recycled narrative and recycled characters. Although the comic theatre, unlike the tragic one, did not generally recycle specific stories, its narratives were nevertheless so formulaic that one early-twentieth-century writer on Menander was driven to complain of his "almost perverse narrowness" and "almost identical plots."[49] Most writers on this tradition are more sympathetic, but none denies the predictability of a standard New Comedy narrative, which is described in the following terms by one editor of Terence:

> the action depicted the efforts of a youth to obtain possession of his mistress, often in the face of determined opposition of a parent or guardian, and with the assistance of a tricky slave. The heroine, who at the start was supposed to belong to the class of courtesans of *heterae* (regarded as aliens), was eventually discovered to be a well-born maiden and an Athenian citizen, and her marriage to the hero of the play was the necessary and suitable conclusion.[50]

How close this narrative structure came to a standard *commedia* plot, or at least to a standard *commedia* set of character relationships, may be seen by comparing it with a description of such a plot by a *commedia* historian:

> typically a domestic intrigue centred on the young lover and his apparently unsuitable beloved and his frustrations at the hands of a skinflint father, a cruel slaveowner or an arrogant soldier rival; intrigues in which the real hero is not the ineffectual bourgeois youth but his flamboyant servant, an exhibitionist, disrespectful, unscrupulous and bibulous slave of dubious age and origin.[51]

Another *commedia* historian puts the formula more simply: "Whatever the story, the lovers were always opposed to cantankerous and eccentric old men and served by comic or greedy valets."[52]

It may seem a bit odd to speak of the narrative structure of a traditionally improvised form, but some sort of story, however whimsical or disjointed, was sketched out from the beginning in the scenarios that provided frameworks for the improvised sequences, and it is in the early scenari that we find the structures here referred to. The highly predictable narrative structure of New Comedy unquestionably played a part in the development of the *commedia,* as indeed it did in the work of Molière and of countless other writers in the Western comedic tradition, so much so that this structure provides in the comic tradition a model almost as firm in its specificity and predictability as the continuing recycled specific mythic stories in the tragic tradition.

Such recycling of groups of characters with established relationships that remain essentially unchanged from play to play, even though the details of the situation or even the basic narrative in which they appear may alter, can be traced in popular theatre through every succeeding period. It survives in its most familiar form today in the television sitcom, from the broad traditional farce of a show like "Gilligan's Island" to the more sophisticated urban humor of one such as "Seinfeld." The pre-knowledge that audiences bring to dramatic works in this tradition is not that of a particular story or even, necessarily, of a particular *type* of story but, rather, of particular characters and of how they will act in particular situations and in relationship to other characters.[53] In his book *Liveness* Philip Auslander calls Spalding Gray's monologues "televisual" in that, like television serials, they involve "the continuing adventures of a small group of central characters whose essential traits never change."[54] In fact, however, although television offers the most familiar example of this recycling today, it has been a familiar practice in the theatre for centuries.

As the *commedia* developed in popularity and sophistication, other narrative and structural devices provided increased competition with this standard form, though the principle of using recycled material remained constant. The number and diversity, especially of the servant clowns, steadily increased, allowing for individual actors to put an individual stamp (and often a unique name) on a single servant type, thus contributing to the tradition of the recycled character tied to a particular actor and flourishing in a single generation, but other characters were handed down from one generation to another. Equally important, the *commedia*, as it developed and spread, turned away from the traditional structure of the New Comedy tradition and turned more in the direction of burlesque and parody, allowing characters such as Arlecchino (or Arlequin or Harlequin) to carry out his subversive antics within almost every sort of traditionally recycled dramatic material, within the narratives of classical mythology (*Arlequin Mercure Galant* [1681], *Arlequin Aneé ou la Prise de Troyes* [1711], *Arelequin Deucalion* [1722], *Arlequin Phaéton* [1743], *Harlequin Neptune* [1775]), within those of popular legend (*The Harlequin Dr. Faustus* [multiple versions], *Harlequin and Guy Fawkes* [1835], *Harlequin and William Tell* [1842]), and, finally, and especially in England, within the highly popular domain of fairy and folk material (*Harlequin and Cinderella* [1841], *Harlequin and Jack the Giant Killer* [1845], and *Harlequin Jack Horner and the Enchanted Pie* [1925]).

In Harlequin we have a particularly clear example of a recycled character who has broken free of the cluster of relationships and narrative frameworks that originally accompanied him and can move freely through an almost infinite variety of other relationships and narratives. Obviously, audience memory is still essential to his effectiveness, but now it is memory only of the character and his way of being in the theatrical world, unrelated to any specific narrative thread. The dizzying complexity of the popular eighteenth- and nineteenth-century adventures of this figure, especially in England and France, where a whole variety of narrative and character material from both high and low culture and from an enormous variety of sources is continually recirculated, is a particularly impressive but by no means unique illustration of the drama's continual interest, one might almost say obsession, with presenting again material with which its public is already familiar.

Like the recycling of narratives, the recycling of characters is based upon an assumption that the theatre audience is itself recycled, an assemblage of people who, like the ghostly king, are "appearing here again tonight" and thus carrying in their collective memory the awareness that drives the theatre experience. In the highly concentrated form represented by drama there are very practical advantages to this ability to rely heavily upon a remembering public. Offering an already familiar character to such a public, just as offering an already familiar narrative, allows a dramatist to cut down on lengthy orientation. In the case of a recycled character such as Harlequin, however, a motive much more important than dramatic economy is the prospect of attracting audiences to see further adventures of a character or characters that they have enjoyed seeing in previous stage presentations. Probably the most famous instance involves Shakespeare's writing of *The Merry Wives of Windsor*. Nicholas Rowe reports in his 1709 edition:

> Queen *Elizabeth* had several of his Plays Acted before her, and without doubt gave him many gracious Marks of her Favour ... She was so well pleas'd with that admirable Character of *Falstaff*, in the two Parts of *Henry* the Fourth, that she commanded him to continue it for one Play more, and to shew him in Love. This is said to be the Occasion of his Writing *The Merry Wives of Windsor*.[55]

Over the centuries many enthusiastic playgoers have shared the desire of Queen Elizabeth to see further adventures of certain popular figures, and in almost every era when the theatre has depended for its prosperity on a large populist audience playwrights have responded to this interest or sought to capitalize on it by bringing back a popular character or characters in a series of sequels, as, for example, Beaumarchais did with Figaro and indeed the whole Almaviva household.

When recycled characters appear without a specific accompanying recycled narrative, audiences are encouraged to focus not so much on changes in the new versions but, on the contrary, on what has not changed, that is, on the predictable quirks, characteristics, and interpersonal relationships of the character or characters being recycled. This makes the movement of recycled dramatic elements, which requires important alterations as times and cultures change, easier in the case of recycled narratives, which accommodate such alterations fairly comfortably, than in the case of recycled characters, whose inflexibility makes this more difficult. Although many periods of theatre history offer popular characters who appear in a whole series of plays, only in a few cases do these characters survive, like Harlequin, to carry on their dramatic careers in further sequels in changed circumstances. Even Beaumarchais's enormously popular and apparently highly flexible Figaro, created in the rapidly shifting culture of the French Revolution, was not able successfully to fit into that changing world, and the third Figaro play, *La Mère coupable,* has never come near the appeal of its predecessors.

Nor is this inflexibility solely a matter of shifting social circumstances. A single character or group of characters utilized in a series of plays has very often been the creation of a single dramatic author and of a single actor or group of actors and is so closely tied in the public imagination with the style and approach of that author and those actors and with a particular cultural moment that their vogue, however great, rarely lasts more than a decade. So we have, for example, a whole series of plays by J. Aude during the Napoleonic era about each of the popular characters Cadet Roussel and Madame Angot, both largely forgotten today. The early- to mid-nineteenth-century American theatre was particularly rich in characters of this sort, offering a variety of ethnic and social types—the Yankee, the Irishman, the Dutchman, the Negro, the New York "Bowery b'hoy." They appeared not only as type characters in countless popular plays but also often as a particular named character, whose vogue normally lasted only for a few years, before another personification was established by another actor or dramatist. Thus, the stage Yankee appeared in a number of plays as Jonathan in the 1820s, Jedediah Homebred in the 1830s, Deuteronomy Dutiful in the 1840s, and Hiram Hireout in the 1850s.[56] Probably the best remembered of these ephemeral recycled characters of the nineteenth-century stage is the roughneck Bowery fireman, Mose, who appeared in no less than four different plays on the New York stage in the single season of 1848–49.[57] The often close association between a reappearing character and a particular actor will be further explored in the following chapter, which will consider the memory evoked by particular performing bodies.

The many examples so far given, drawn from classic to modern times and from theatrical cultures around the world, have, I hope, demonstrated how important this interest has been in the history of dramatic scripts. A number of practical and artistic advantages have been suggested for the continuing appearance of this interest, but I would like to suggest that a more fundamental concern lies beneath the drama's continuing attraction to recycling. There appears to be something in the very nature of the theatrical experience itself that encourages, in this genre more than others, a simultaneous awareness of something previously experienced and of something being offered in the present that is both the same and different, which can only be fully appreciated by a kind of doubleness of perception in the audience.

The kind of double vision that is encouraged by the recycled dramatic text has its parallels in every aspect of the theatre experience and, indeed, is so fundamental to certain aspects of theatrical performance (as opposed to the preexisting text) that it seems to me very likely that the proclivity for the recycling of material that we have been tracing in the dramatic text has been encouraged if not occasioned by this basic characteristic within the structure of performance itself and of its close association with the processes of personal and cultural memory. The two major sorts of textual recycling that I have discussed have close ties to certain aspects of the performance, and I will consider each of them in a separate chapter. The recycled character, as I have already suggested, is often tied to a single actor, and this phenomenon, among others, will be the concern of "The Haunted Body." The recycled narrative, of course, concerns not a single actor but the group work of a company, and some of the implications of recycling on this level will be further considered in the chapter "The Haunted Production."

three

The Haunted Body

While the dramatic text has traditionally been considered a kind of founding element of theatre, that text does not in fact become theatre until it is embodied by an actor and presented to an audience. Although there have been many instances of theatre being created by actors without a conventional preexisting text and occasional (though very rare) examples of an actorless text being presented to an audience, the conventional basic elements of theatre are text and actor. Eric Bentley, in *The Life of the Drama,* suggests that "the theatrical situation, reduced to a minimum," occurs when "A impersonates B while C looks on,"[1] the *B* in most cases being provided by a preexisting dramatic text. Having now considered some of the ways in which the text that traditionally provides this *B* is ghosted, let us now turn to the operations of *A*, the actor, where we will find a rather different but often even more powerful set of ghostings that condition, in very significant ways, the "looking on" of *C*, the audience.

The common view of theatrical production as the embodiment of a preexisting literary text tends to take the actor as a more or less transparent vehicle for that text, physically congruent with the stated requirements of the text and possessing adequate vocal and physical skills to deliver the text effectively to the audience. This simplified view, however, does not take into account what the actor creatively adds to the literary text, nor does it take into account the central concern of this chapter, the major contribution of the actor to the process of theatrical recycling and its effect upon reception. Within any theatrical culture audience members typically see many of the same actors in many different productions, and they will inevitably carry some memory of those actors from production to production. The operations of that sort of recycling, the recycled body and persona of the actor, will be the focus of this chapter.

In every culture in which theatre is developed as an ongoing cultural activity, a group of specialists in that activity appears, the actors. In theatre traditions East and West the most common arrangement is for groups of actors to gather into ongoing associations for the production of dramatic works. The theatre is normally a social occasion on both sides of the curtain. Bentley speaks of A, B, and C as if they were individuals, but in fact they are almost invariably groups—a group of audience members assembles to watch a group of actors impersonate a group of stage characters. This gathering of actors into ongoing groups naturally encourages the association of particular actors with particular types of roles in production after production. This is not just a matter of assigning parts that are congruent with the age and gender of each actor but also a matter of the particular skills or inclinations each actor possesses—a particular physical build or quality of voice may seem to suit an actor for darker or heavier roles, a natural grace and handsome features may propel another toward romantic roles, while more irregular, even grotesque features or a gift for physical or verbal dexterity may lead yet another toward character and comic work. One of the earliest extended treatises on the art of acting, Sainte-Albine's *Le Comédien* in 1749, remarked that, although many physical types were acceptable on the stage, actors, whatever their ability, could not depart far from audience expectations of the type of roles they were playing—heroes must have imposing bodies and lovers attractive ones; actors must look the proper age for their roles and have the natural vocal qualities suitable for their characters.[2]

The highly formalized and yet flexible *commedia dell'arte* provides one of the best examples of the combined workings of the recycling of characters and the recycling of individual actors. Within a typical *commedia* company certain actors would continually play the same basic traditional characters—the young lovers, the comic servants, the foolish old men, the ridiculous pedants or flamboyant soldiers—all types well-known to their audiences and reappearing in countless scenarios. But individual actors could also put their own mark on a traditional character, even create a new name for that character, and thus appear again and again in a part uniquely their own and recognized and anticipated as such by their audiences in each new incarnation. In every generation of *commedia* performance, audiences went with a foreknowledge of traditional characters and character relationships and often with previous experience of a particular company, in which a memory of the physical characteristics and acting style of particular actors playing the same type in play after play reinforced the anticipation of how that type would be experienced in each new production.

The *commedia dell'arte* provides a particularly clear example of a close relationship between actors and types of roles that can be found, in varying degrees of organizational complexity, in theatre companies throughout history and around the world. We are perhaps most familiar with this custom in connection with the stock roles in nineteenth-century melodrama, but long before the rise of melodrama actors specialized in noble fathers, male romantic leads, tyrants, soubrettes, and ingenues. Nor is this a peculiarly European phenomenon. The classic Sanskrit theatre manual, the *Natyasastra,* contains lengthy descriptions of a great array of traditional stock character types, and Japanese Kabuki contains carefully delineated traditional role categories. Actors perform in the same category throughout their lives, the few who change (such as Ichinatsu Sanokama I in the eighteenth century, who began playing young men and changed to villains in later life) causing considerable amazement.[3]

In theatrical cultures in which theatre companies have operated under detailed and specific rules of organization, this close relationship between actors and predictable types of roles played is often embodied within the organizational legislation of the company. The best-known Western example is surely the neoclassic theatre of France, whose organization served as a model for the leading professional European theatres from the seventeenth through the early nineteenth centuries. The French national theatre provided a detailed and fairly rigid system of acting roles, called *emplois,* with each actor assigned to a certain type of role. Pougin's monumental 1885 dictionary of the theatre provides for the Comédie Française a list of thirteen *emplois* for the men (*premier rôles, jeunes premiers, fort jeunes premiers, seconds amoureux, grands raisonneurs, pères nobles, seconds pères, pères non chantants, financiers, manteaux, grimes, paysans, comiques,* and *rôles de convenance*) and ten *emplois* for the women (*premier rôles, grandes coquettes, jeunes premières, jeunes amoureuses, secondes amoureuses, troisième amoureuses, mères nobles, ingénuités, soubrettes* or *utilités.*)[4] The subtlety of these distinctions may be suggested by Pougin's definitions of *ingénuités* and *soubrettes.* The former is "a very young woman in love, whose heart has barely opened to the emotions and accents of passion, and who retains the purest candor and innocence" (the naïveté is what separates her from the various *amoureuses*), while the latter is a "young comic woman, frank, vivacious, and gay." In Molière's *Tartuffe* the daughter, Marianne, would be played by an *ingénuité* and the maid Dorine by a *soubrette.* Small companies could double up the *emplois,* if necessary (Pougin remarks that this is often done with *grimes* and *financiers,* since they are both character old men),[5] but they were normally considered quite distinct by actors, audiences, and theatre administrators. In the famous *Moscow Decree* in which Napoléon drew up the legislative rules to govern the Comédie Française, one entire section is devoted to the "Distribution of *Emplois,*" which notes, in part, that "no actor or actress can be the primary holder of two different *emplois* without a special authorization from the superintendent, which should be given only rarely and for the most pressing reasons."[6]

A British commentator in the *Quarterly Review* reported on this legislation shortly after, noting that in France the official connection of actor with *emploi* "is so well understood, that each actor and actress is obliged to make a selection of a particular *rôle,* from which these decrees forbid them afterwards to depart . . . The *Père Noble* cannot become *Comique,* whatever be his vocation this way; and the *Ingénuité* must not look to be the *Jeune Première,* whatever ambition she may feel for playing the heroine." The reviewer uses this occasion to praise, by contrast, the more flexible English theatre, in which "all this foolery would be impossible. We represent not *Jeunes Premiers,* nor *Ingénuités,* but *men and women,* with all their various and changeable feelings, humours, and passions."[7] The fact is, however, that the British stock system, already well in place when this review was written and the dominant form of theatrical organization in Britain throughout the century, created a system there that, while not legislated in the French manner, was just as rigid in the delineation and predictability of types. As in any theatrical culture, certain actors often became associated in the public mind with certain types of roles, and this universal tendency was reinforced in a theatrical culture, in which many plays were mounted in a very short period of time, and neither actors nor dramatists had either the time or the incentive to strike out in significantly new directions. In England, and in the English-speaking theatre, the practice of "lines of business," in fact closely parallel to the French system of *emplois,* was almost universal.

The popular dramatist Dion Boucicault drew up a list of British lines of business that compares favorably with the detail and complexity of the contemporary French system. According to Boucicault, a "first-class theatrical company" should consist of "a leading man, leading juvenile man, heavy man, first old man, first low comedian, walking gentleman, second old man and utility, second low comedian and character actor, second walking gentleman and utility, leading woman, leading juvenile woman, heavy woman, first old woman, first chambermaid, walking lady, second old woman and utility, second chambermaid and character actress, second walking lady and utility lady."[8] Dutton Cook, who reproduces this list, further comments that, even without French-style legislation, British actors in fact rarely departed from their accustomed lines of business. As in France, a player once associated with a particular line tended to remain within it.

> The light comedian of twenty is usually found to be still a light comedian at seventy: the Orlandos of the stage rarely become its old Adams. The actresses who have personated youthful heroines are apt to disregard the flight of time and the burden of age, and to the last shrink from the assumption of matronly

or mature characters—Juliets and Ophelias, as a rule, declining to expand into Nurses or Gertrudes. And the actor who in his youth has undertaken systematically to portray senility finds himself eventually the thing he had merely affected to be.[9]

At first glance the tradition of the *emploi* or the line of business would seem to be based on a desire for verisimilitude—attractive young performers playing stage lovers, wiry acrobatic actors playing clowns, and older actors, especially those with grotesque or less attractive features, playing character roles. Surely, this natural sort of division lies at the basis of role assignment in the theatre and today dominates the more naturalistic genre of film, in which casting according to physical type is the normal practice. In the theatre, however, in which the fundamental organizational unit has frequently been an ongoing established group of actors known to a continuing public, other forces in casting have proven more powerful than the demands of verisimilitude.

We in the United States, as members of a theatrical culture that, unlike most others, has provided little social or economic encouragement for the establishment of ongoing companies and one that, moreover, places particular stress upon verisimilitude, tend to be amused by or even contemptuously dismissive of the common practice in cultures with such companies to keep the same actors in the same roles or types of roles for most or all of their careers. We are perhaps willing to accept an actor who spends a career in the portrayal of "character" roles, like the *commedia* masks—simpletons, villains, or comic old men or women—but we tend to dismiss as grotesque or foolish an actor who similarly maintains youthful roles into advanced age. In the case of a highly stylized theatre, such as Japan's Noh, in which convention reigns and all female parts are in any case taken by men, we may be more willing to accept the possibility of an actor even of advanced years still successfully portraying youthful maidens, but, when we read of an actress such as Mlle Mars, the leading lady of the Comédie Française at the beginning of the nineteenth century, still playing romantic heroines until the end of her lengthy career, we tend to dismiss this as a product of vanity and possessiveness of good roles and to pity the audiences who were forced to tolerate this grotesque affectation. Doubtless, vanity has been a factor in such cases, but, before we simply dismiss the common phenomenon on those grounds alone, we must take into account the importance of the audience's memory and associations.

In the operations of traditional theatre, East and West, in which audiences are normally accustomed to relatively stable companies of actors who offer the same plays over and over again, they become accustomed to seeing certain actors appearing again and again in specific roles or in specific types of closely related roles and soon come to associate those actors with those roles or types of roles. Before we too hastily condemn the apparent folly and vanity of an aging actor still playing youthful roles, we must recall that every new performance of these roles will be ghosted by a theatrical recollection of the previous performances, so that audience reception of each new performance is conditioned by inevitable memories of this actor playing similar roles in the past. The voice that might seem to an outsider grown thin with age may still to a faithful public echo with the resonances of decades of theatregoing, that slightly bent body still be ghosted by years of memories of it in its full vigor.

Joseph Roach describes precisely this process in the case of the aging Betterton, who at the age of seventy still was preferred by his public to all others in the portrayal of youthful roles. That public, suggests Roach, looked past the infirmities of his physical body to his "other body, the one that existed outside itself in the fact of his performance of it. Transcending the body of flesh and blood, this other body consisted of actions, gestures, intonations, vocal colors, mannerisms, expressions, customs, protocols, inherited routines, authenticated traditions—'bits.'" Unlike the physical body, "the actions of this theatrical body could not be invalidated by age or decrepitude."[10] The power of performance memory, reinforced by the repetition of familiar gestures, intonations, and mannerisms, here proved more powerful than the actual physical appearance of Betterton himself; the ghost had a greater performative visibility than the body it haunted.

In the case of well-known and highly celebrated actors a phenomenon that in some ways is even stranger is not uncommon. Even new audiences, for whom a performance cannot possibly be ghosted by fond personal memories of previous high achievement, may be affected by the operations of celebrity itself to view and experience a famous actor through an aura of expectations that masks failings that would be troubling in someone less celebrated. It would be an oversimplification to assume that an audience that apparently excessively admires a famous actor well past his prime when seeing him for the first time are simply hiding their feelings of disappointment out of social pressure, fearful of saying that the emperor has no clothes. It is quite possible that their reception has been in fact significantly conditioned by the actor's celebrity, ghosting their reception even in the absence of previous theatre experience. A similar effect has long been known to psychological researchers, the so-called halo effect, by the operations of which teachers prepared for certain levels of performance from particular students tend to experience the work of the students according to those expectations.

In a traditional and basically stable theatrical culture in which actors are employed and cast according to certain culturally defined *emplois,* or types, or lines of business, even a young actor never before seen by the audience will appear onstage already ghosted by the expectations of the role type in which he appears. As time passes, however, and the audience experiences them in a variety of roles, most actors begin to develop audience expectations about their particular approach, even in the highly conventionalized and traditional theatres, like the Japanese Kabuki or Noh. Before many appearances most actors, consciously or not, develop associations with particular ways of portraying even the most codified *emplois* and so appear in new roles with a double ghosting, the cultural expectations of the *emploi* itself overlaid with those of the actor's own previous appearances.

This dynamic can be clearly seen even in the *commedia dell'arte,* the most familiar example in the West of stable companies with character types repeated in generation after generation of theatrical production. Despite the apparent solidity of these early examples of lines of business, when they are looked at not in general but in the actual operations of specific companies and individuals, we find, not surprisingly, that in every generation the familiar general types were developed in infinite variations, according to the skill and popularity of individual performers. Instead of there being a standardized servant mask like Brighella or an old man mask like Il Dottore, in which the individuality of the actor disappeared, these masks were continually adapted, often to the extent of creating new masks that combined or varied features of the old ones. These in turn inspired yet other individual variations in an endless series while keeping the idea (and the audience foreknowledge) of the type. Thus, the great early *commedia* actor Francesco Andreini was best known for his particular version of the flamboyant Spanish captain, Il Capitano Spavento, played "with a verve and *braggadocio* that set the pattern for all future players of the part," but he also created his own special variations of another traditional mask, Il Dottore, with the Dottore Siciliano and Falcirone the Magician, each featured in many popular productions. Locatelli, a leading *commedia* performer in early-seventeenth-century France, created an Arlecchino variant called Trivelino, making adjustments to both character and costume that were unique to him and also influential to other, Arlecchinos, Tivelinos, and still newer variants that followed.[11] Niklaus, a historian of the *commedia,* suggests the complexity of a single such variation, the Arlequin of Biancolelli, a disciple of Locatelli:

> Where Locatelli had created a variant in which was more of Brighella than of Arlecchino, Biancolelli achieved the fusion of the two Bergamasque clowns. His Arlequin looked like Arlecchino, practised all the traditional *lazzi,* played the same role: but he behaved with the bold cunning of Brighella. Brighella's mind entered Arlecchino's body. Then Biancolelli enriched that mind with his own wit and wisdom, his own culture, and shaded it with a little of his own sadness.

After Biancolelli, this more whimsical, emotional, and deft Arlequin was widely imitated, as was the throaty, croaking voice that Biancolelli added not as a matter of choice but because of a laryngeal defect.[12] But the character continued to change and evolve, with actors in each new generation making their own Arlequins, repeated with a combination of generic and individual features in production after production. A highly ghosted role such

as Arlequin provides a particulary clear example of what Joseph
Roach has called "effigies fashioned from flesh," which manifest
themselves in performance and which "consist of a set of actions
that hold open a place in memory into which many different people may step according to circumstances and occasions."[13]

In the *commedia* the responsibility for developing and maintaining this living body of recycled material remained in the hands
of the actors, well aware, as theatre professionals have always been,
of the public's interest in seeing a particular actor in a particularly
appreciated role or type of role. In theatres utilizing written scripts
this process has also been traditionally reinforced by playwrights.
They also, in most historical periods, have created new works with
particular existing companies in mind and, whether the theatre
was committed to some system of lines of business or not, have
naturally designed characters to suit the proven skills and specialties of the actors that would create these roles. Goethe and Schiller
conceived their productions with the specialties of Weimar actors
in mind, Voltaire for the actors of the Comédie Française, Molière
for the company in which he was the leading player. Even a playwright like Ibsen, with very tenuous ties to his major producing
organization, is revealed through his letters to be quite concerned
with the specific actors that would perform his roles and with what
associations and physical and emotional characteristics they would
bring to the roles, certainly predictable concerns in any dramatist
who writes with an eye toward stage realization.

Thomas Baldwin's study of the organization of acting companies in the time of Shakespeare finds that in fact, as in British companies three centuries later, "each of the major actors had his particular 'business.'"[14] As in the *commedia,* actors became associated
in the public mind with certain types of roles, but, also as in the
commedia, popular actors created certain idiosyncratic ways of performing those types, establishing an echo effect in role after role
to which both public and dramatists responded. Historians of the
Shakespearean stage have often noted how sharply the clown roles
in Shakespeare changed in 1599 when Will Kemp, associated with
a particular type of clown, left the company and was replaced by
Robert Armin, who specialized in a very different style. A recent
study of the Shakespearean clown summarizes the change thus:

During Kemp's residency, the clown parts were created to allow for much improvisation; with his talents for jig dancing and quick repartee, Kemp could be trusted to make the most of any opportunity given him. For him were created the down-to-earth bawdy clowns, those with much wit and great hearts, if not always great intelligence: busy Dogberry, bumbling Bottom, and that mountain of flesh, Sir John Falstaff. Armin brought to the company a talent for subtle acting and a flair for music. For him were written clown parts with lyrics to sing, and he was given openings for elegant tumbling. He inspired the beloved court jesters, Touchstone, Feste, and Lear's Fool.[15]

In most periods of theatre history certain popular "types" have emerged in the dramatic writing: the witty maids of Molière's comedies; the fops of the English Restoration; the noble fathers of the eighteenth century; the outlaw heroes of the romantic era; the honest British sailors, aristocratic villains, and persecuted maidens of nineteenth-century melodrama; the grotesque spinsters in the Gilbert and Sullivan operettas; and so on. Most of them, like the traditional *commedia* masks, appeared in repeated clusters of recycled characters, while others appeared in new situations and new relationships in different plays, but all, like the masks, became associated with particular actors, and these actors, like their *commedia* forebears, inevitably introduced specific variations that marked their individual use of the stock type. Thus, a new production by an actor specializing in fops, witty maids, or noble fathers would be ghosted not only by memories of performances of that stock type by a number of actors but also by memories of previous performances of the type by that particular actor.

When, as has become increasingly common in the Western theatre during the past two centuries, major actors pursue their careers outside the operations of traditional repertory companies and their associated collective memory of a particular group or performers related in similar ways in production after production, the effect of what might be called *emploi*-ghosting is lessened, but the phenomenon of ghosting itself remains as powerful in its effect upon reception as ever. Even more basic to the theatre experience than ongoing theatrical organizations with relatively stable companies of actors is the devotion of the audience itself to the theatre experience. The majority of theatregoers in any theatre culture are repeating theatregoers, so that, even when there is not a highly organized ongoing specific theatre organization, such as a national repertory theatre, there is a nonorganized but fairly stable ongoing collection of devoted theatregoers, who singly and collectively carry to each new theatre experience a substantial memory of previous experience. This continuity is paralleled, on the other side of the footlights, by a relatively stable body of actors, who, even in the absence of permanent established theatre companies, will be seen by a regular theatregoing public in play after play. It is these two continuities, more than that of any specific producing organizations, that primarily guarantees the operations and importance of ghosting.

In nineteenth-century America, when the theatre experience was dominated by popular star actors and when stock characters and character types were more common and more broadly drawn than in more modern times, the association of specific actors with specific types of roles was particularly clear and often operated in a manner very similar to the development and elaboration of the traditional *commedia* masks, except that in the later period playwrights also contributed significantly to this process. The "Stage Yankee," for example, became as familiar to American theatregoers of the early nineteenth century as a figure like Brighella had been to their Italian predecessors three centuries before. The Yankee, like the *commedia* mask, was particularly associated with certain actors, some of whom even, like *commedia* players, took on their character name, such as George "Yankee" Hill (1809–48).[16] The Yankee, also like a *commedia* mask, possessed certain general qualities but in the case of the best-known actors would take on special features associated with that particular interpreter. One of the most popular Yankee actors was Dan Marble (1810–49). Although Marble appeared in a variety of Yankee plays, among them *Sam Patch, the Yankee Jumper* and its sequels, *The Maiden's Vow, or The Yankee in Time* and *The Vermont Wool Deal, or The Yankee Traveller,* written by a variety of different authors and using a variety of names of Marble's character—Sam Patch, Jacob Jewsharp, Deuteronomy Dutiful, Lot Sap Sago—nevertheless all of these stage figures were recognizably the unique Marble Yankee, a variation on George Hill's character with a distinctly Westernized, Kentucky feel.[17] Once again a close relationship may be seen between the reuse of a stock character type by one or often a whole series of dramatists and the reappearance of one or a whole series of actors specializing in this type. We have already noted the popularity of stage types, such as the Yankee or Irishman, on the nineteenth-century American stage as an example of textual recycling, but here again we must note that this phenomenon invariably involves the recycling of specific actors as well.

Although the echoes of previous characters in new creations is by far the more common phenomenon, the theatre, of course, also offers many examples of actors who literally appear as the same character in a number of different narrative contexts. The specific reappearing sequel or series character, like the more general type of stock character, is a common feature in dramatic literature, as I have already noted in my comments on the haunted text, and is, of course, a feature of nondramatic literature as well. The status of drama as a performed art, however, gives an extra impetus to this practice. The desire of readers, especially of popular fiction, to follow the adventures of popular characters through additional narratives has made sequel or series narratives a major part of that tradition, so that Arthur Conan Doyle, to take a famous example, was forced quite against his will to produce more and more Sherlock Holmes stories for a dedicated public. In the theatre this popular enthusiasm for a character may be created by or reinforced by the work of a particular actor (as, indeed, the American actor William Gillette did for the character of Sherlock Holmes), so that sequels may be created not necessarily because of an interest in the adventures of the character but to repeat the pleasure of once again seeing a specific actor appearing as this character. Thus, we have the phenomenon of the actor who becomes associated with a particular role, as the popular mid-nineteenth-century American actor Francis S. Chanfrau was with Mose, the "Bowery b'hoy," or the leading French actor of almost the same period, Frédérick Lemaître, with his colorful outlaw Robert Macaire. In the popular mind these actors and characters became almost indistinguishable. New plays were written in which the already familiar characters could appear, but so strong was the identification of character with actor that no rival interpretations ever achieved any appreciable popularity. In the twentieth century television has largely taken over this aspect of popular theatre, but one may still get an idea of the appeal of the recycled actors and characters in the enormously popular series television shows, either serious, like the ongoing soap operas, or comic, like the vast array of family sitcoms.

Many of the great actors of the eighteenth and nineteenth century became particularly associated with a single role, even when they appeared with success in many other parts. Thus, for example, Coquelin, after his creation of Cyrano de Bergerac, was forever after associated with that role, as Tommaso Salvini was with Othello and Sarah Bernhardt with Camille. A late-nineteenth-century biographer of Edwin Booth remarks on precisely this quality in Booth's rendering of Hamlet and notes its similarity to other actor/character bondings in these terms: "Booth's impersonation of Hamlet was one of the best known works of the dramatic age. In many minds the actor and the character had become identical, and it is not to be doubted that Booth's performance of Hamlet will live, in commemorative dramatic history, with great representative embodiments of the stage—with Garrick's Lear, Kemble's Coriolanus, Edmund Kean's Richard, Macready's Macbeth, Forrest's Othello, and Irving's Mathias."[18]

In each of these famous cases, so dominant was the public association of actor with character and indeed with the whole pattern of action represented by the dramatic narrative in which this character appears that these characters were not even transferred to successful sequels in the manner of Mose or Robert Macaire. Many great nineteenth-century actors had their "signature roles," permanently associated with their names, like James O'Neill's Count of Monte Cristo or Joseph Jefferson's Rip Van Winkle. As one of Jefferson's biographers observes: "He was Rip and Rip was he. It might be said that the play was an incident, more or less important, in the life of every other player who had performed it, but that, comparatively speaking, it was Jefferson's whole existence."[19] The nineteenth-century emphasis on the star encouraged this sort of association, of course, but so did the related phenomena of widespread touring and frequent revivals of the "vehicles." An interested theatregoer of this period would very likely see an actor like Jefferson many times and would moreover most likely see him many times in the same role, reinforcing both the associations and the ghosted memories of that interpretation.

The close connection between a popular actor and an often-revived vehicle role is less common in the twentieth century, particularly in the American commercial theatre, in which the nineteenth-century practice of frequent revivals has been replaced by the single long run. This has certainly not meant, however, the end of the often powerful bonding of a particular actor to a particular part. Very often the actor who creates a particular role in a popular success or in a major revival that overshadows the original production will create so strong a bond between himself and that role that for a generation or more all productions are haunted by the memory of that interpretation, and all actors performing the role must contend with the cultural ghost of the great originator. Anthony Sher's study *The Year of the King,* perhaps the best book ever written by an actor about the process of creating a role, returns again and again to the tension between this creation and the inevitable ghost of the most famous modern interpreter of the role, Lawrence Olivier. The struggle begins with the very opening speech, as Sher observes:

> "Now is the winter . . ."
>   God. It seems terribly unfair of Shakespeare to begin his play with such a famous speech. You don't like to put your mouth to it, so many other mouths have been there. Or to be more honest, one particularly distinctive mouth. His poised, staccato delivery is imprinted on those words like teeth marks.[20]

Not infrequently, the public memory of the original is so powerful and so entrenched that younger actors fear to attempt the role, since they can neither present a totally realized embodiment of the remembered interpretation, nor can they reasonably hope to displace it by something distinctly different. This is almost always the case when the first production of a play is a particularly powerful and memorable one, with strong actors who are either well-known before the production or become well-known as a result of it and thus remain forever associated with it. Of the many examples in the American theatre, one might cite Lee J. Cobb as Willie Loman in *Death of a Salesman,* Marlon Brando as Stanley Kowalski in *Streetcar Named Desire,* Mary Martin as Nellie Forbush in *South Pacific,* or Joel Grey as the Master of Ceremonies in *Cabaret.* For the rest of the century a major revival of any of these plays could hardly be mounted without reviewers comparing the new interpreters with these famous originals, a comparison surely made by many in the audience as well.

Even when actors are not associated in the public (and media) mind with a certain specific role or even a certain 'ock type, it is difficult, perhaps impossible, once their career is under way, for them to avoid a certain aura of expectations based on past roles. The actor's new roles become, in a very real sense, ghosted by previous ones. H. L. Mencken describes this phenomenon in his usual acerbic manner. In the course of a career an actor, he suggests,

> becomes a grotesque boiling down of all the preposterous characters he has ever impersonated. Their characteristics are seen in his manner, in his reactions to stimuli, in his point of view. He becomes a walking artificiality, a strutting dummy, a thematic catalogue of imbecilities.[21]

Bert States, to whom I am indebted for this entertaining quote, provides his own much more sympathetic gloss on this same theatrical phenomenon:

> We do not think of an actor's portrayal of a role as being sealed off in the past tense, but as floating in a past absolute, as it were, like the role itself, outside time. Not only is it preserved in the communal memory as part of the history of the play, leaving its imprint (for a time) on the text, but due to the repetitive element in all style, remnants keep popping up in the later work of the actor. For example, certain mannerisms of Olivier's Othello—the darting glance, the emphasis on certain kinds of values, the deft economy of gesture—remind one of the "younger" Hamlet. Of course, this is only Olivier repeat-

ing himself, but it is Hamlet who is fleetingly remembered. There is *still* a Hamlet in Olivier.[22]

A typical example of this process in the American theatre is the romantic actor Edwin Forrest, whose favored roles would seem to have little in common (especially as compared with the narrow historical and geographical range of the Kentucky Yankee or the Bowery b'hoy): Metamora, an American Indian; Spartacus, a Thracian gladiator in classic Rome; Oralloosa, an Incan prince in the time of Pizzaro. In fact, however, each of these roles (all in plays created especially for the actor) involved mental and physical attributes that were particularly favored by Forrest and expected in any of his new roles by his audience. As his biographer Richard Moody observes: "Forrest found the noble Thracian [Spartacus in *The Gladiator*] an ideal role. The play offered abundant opportunities for muscular exertion, ferocious passion, and reiteration of the freedom-loving sentiments he held so dear."[23] Each new Forrest creation, seemingly so disparate, was thus strongly ghosted by his previous ones. The whole tradition of what has been called the vehicle play, a work constructed precisely to feature the already familiar aspects of a particular actor's performance, is based upon precisely this dynamic. One may think of the variety of regal and exotic queens Sardou created for Sarah Bernhardt or the neurasthenic, ethereal heroines D'Annunzio created for Eleanora Duse or, perhaps most strikingly, Rostand, who, after the actor Coquelin had achieved a stunning success in his creation of Cyrano de Bergerac, created for the same actor a Cyrano de Bergerac in feathers, as a heroic rooster in the folktale fantasy *Chantecler*.

The modern American theatrical culture offers few examples of the sort of ongoing theatrical establishments with comparatively stable companies of actors and often associated playwrights that have been common elsewhere in the world. The most familiar example of American professional theatre is much more ad hoc, with a company assembled for a particular production whose members may never work together again and with no guarantee for a playwright that any particular actor she may have in mind for a particular part will in fact be available or be used. This lack of institutional stability and predictability, however, does not affect the basic process of theatrical reception, however, nor its heavy reliance upon audience memory and association. Even though audiences are less likely to associate certain actors with a constellation of other particular actors, as is the case in an ongoing theatre organization such as the great national theatres of Europe or the traditional classic theatres of China and Japan, individual actors, often even relatively minor ones, still carry with them memories of their work in previous productions, and audiences are at least as often attracted to a new production by their previous acquaintance with the actors that are appearing in it as they are by the name of the dramatist.

One need only look at the advertisements and advance publicity for the plays in any new season on Broadway to see the power of this dynamic at work. The leading actors commonly receive the major attention, often even above that of the play or playwright and almost certainly above that of the director or any other contributing artist. Moreover, even though the contemporary American culture does not look favorably upon formulaic work either in acting or playwriting, any actor familiar enough to be featured in the advance advertising will inevitably bring associations to the minds of a potential audience. Every well-known actor brings to the mind of the theatregoing public memories of certain productions or types of production, sometimes even of a specific dramatist or dramatic school. The actor Joe Mantegna, strongly associated with the plays of David Mamet, or John Malkovich, with those of Sam Shepard, bring associations of those dramatists and their styles to a new production even if that production is in fact the work of some other dramatist. The same thing is more generally true of dramatic style or tonality; most actors have strong associations with certain types of play—high comedy, farce, serious family drama, and so on. Alan Schneider in his autobiography, *Entrances,* describes the catastrophe that resulted when audiences at the first American production of *Waiting for Godot* came expecting to see Bert Lahr in a traditional burlesque comedy (an expectation encouraged by publicity that billed the play as "the laugh riot of two continents") and left in irritation and confusion when they could not fit the experience with those expectations.[24]

The process of recalling previous roles while watching the creation of new ones is clearly deeply involved in the process of reception, but it is also institutionally encouraged in the United States and elsewhere by the rather odd practice of providing in theatre programs actors' biographies listing previous roles, a practice so honored in the American theatre that this information is offered even in the absence of almost any other background information on the play or production. Indeed, I have even seen programs in which professional biographies of all the actors in the production appeared but without a word about the playwright, if he happened to have the misfortune to be dead.

In the case of actors who appear on television or in films as well as in the live theatre, the mass circulation of these other media makes it highly likely that even an active theatregoing public may bring to an actor's newest theatrical creation associations drawn more for that actor's work in the mass media than onstage. Often this ghosting is actively encouraged by the production's publicity program, hoping to draw to the theatre audience members who have enjoyed the work of a particular actor on television or in films. The advertising for the 1997 revival of the musical *Grease* on Broadway regularly mentioned that its star, Lucy Lawless, was well-known on television as the adventure heroine Xena, "Warrior Princess." Indeed, some advertisements mentioned only Xena, not the actress's name, or showed her in her Warrior Princess costume. Thus, both casting and advertising relied upon and clearly encouraged a ghosting of the warrior princess upon the role of the 1950s cool teenager, Betty Rizzo, a ghosting that was almost grotesquely inappropriate in terms of the musical itself, however successful it may have been in terms of stimulating ticket sales.

The combination of the appeal of the mass media in comparison to theatre, the importance of advertising and publicity, and the emphasis in the contemporary commercial theatre, especially in the United States, upon the star means that the most common publicity practice is some variation of that attempting to market the *Grease* revival by drawing upon the popularity of Xena the Warrior Princess. In February 2000 I received a mailing that is typical of the practice. A revival this spring of Sam Shepard's *True West* is hailed in this flyer as "Hollywood comes to Broadway," and its two stars (whose head shots provide the only illustrations in the flyer) are identified as "Philip Seymour Hoffmann (*Magnolia, The Talented Mr. Ripley*) and John C. Reilly (*Boogie Nights, Magnolia*)." All three of these films were then among the most popular running in New York, and the advertisers clearly hoped that the opportunity to see these actors again, and live, would be at least as powerful as any wish to see this fairly well-known play itself. To the extent that they were correct, this revival was strongly and not necessarily positively ghosted by these current films, especially by *Magnolia,* in which both actors appeared. An almost comic concatenation of evoked roles was offered by the magazine *Playbill* in the opening sentence of its report on the then upcoming production of Neil Simon's *The Dinner Party:*

> Eve Harrington, Sweeney Todd, Baroness Else Schraeder, Jack Tripper, Flora the Red Menace and "Fonzie"—these are the past lives of the actors who've assembled onstage for *The Dinner Party,* which opens at the Music Box Theatre on October 19.[25]

A recent, more complex play of ghosting could be seen in a 1991 New York production called *Bon Appetit!* The premise of this unusual production was already a remarkably ghosted one, in which an actress studied a single television program on how to prepare a chocolate cake by the well-known television personality Julia Child and then precisely recreated this program onstage, scrupulously imitating every gesture and intonation of the original. I have already remarked, in speaking of dramatic texts, on the particularly close relationship between ghosting and parody. Clearly, the same observations can be applied to acting. Dramatic parody has been an important part of the theatrical experience since classic times, and, although there is little direct evidence that, for example, the actors in Aristophanes' parodies of Greek tragedy physically imitated the performance style as well as the content of those plays, the humor of the imitation would surely depend heavily upon this. Certainly, in later eras the physical ghosting of theatrical parody was usually even more important to the entertainment of the audience than the ghosting of the written text. Thus when Gherardi, a popular Arlequin of the late eighteenth century at the Comédie Italienne, appeared in a parody of Corneille's classic *Le*

Cid, there was little critical comment on the literary side of the parody but much admiration of Gherardi's imitation of the leading tragic actress of the time, Mlle Champmesle, in the role of Chimène. As one chronicler reported, he "imitates in his walk Mlle Champmesle, whose inflections he also imitates in his delivery."[26]

The existence of the videotaped TV program doubtless provided actress Jean Stapleton with the opportunity to create an even more detailed imitation of the gestures and vocal inflections of her subject, Julia Child, but the reception of her creation was further complicated by the fact that Stapleton herself came before audiences with an associated television personality probably as distinct in the public mind as that of chef Julia Child; this was Edith Bunker, the long-suffering and somewhat loopy wife in the television comedy series "All in the Family," probably the most popular such series of its period. An item in New York *Newsday* on the day the play opened provided an unusually clear insight into the resulting overlaying of personae. It began: "Three of the most-loved women in America will be on stage together tonight. There's actress Jean Stapleton. There's Julia Child, as played by Stapleton. And there's the invisible but inevitable presence of Edith Bunker, the lovable Queens housewife Stapleton created for *All in the Family.*"[27] Although Jean Stapleton is a stage actress of considerable experience and ability, any role she plays at this point in her career will for much of the audience be ghosted by the "invisible but inevitable" presence of Edith Bunker. The invisible but inevitable ghosting of previous roles in the theatre as well as in television and films has certain parallels to the phenomenon of intertextuality in reading and, like literary intertextuality, may be a source of distraction, a valuable tool for interpretation, or a source of enrichment and deepened pleasure in the work.

It is not only the operations of publicity that seek to capitalize upon audiences' associative memories and thus increase the reception power of theatrical recycling. Directors and producers, and of course the actors themselves, are also well aware, as they have always been, of the importance of an audience's previous experience with an actor in conditioning their reception of him or her in a new role. Normally speaking, the way that this process works is that an actor is cast who will bring to a new role audience associations with a certain type of character or certain style of the-atre, but the association can be much more specific, with a partic-ular previous and well-remembered role in a particular produc-tion. A striking and powerful example of this could be seen in the fall 1993 season in Paris, when Jorge Lavelli staged Tabori's *Mein Kampf* at the Théâtre de la Colline. In Tabori's dark, surrealistic farce a mysterious elegant woman, Madame La Mort, appears, who, as her name suggests, turns out indeed to be a personifi-cation of death and who takes under her tutelage the youthful Hitler. In this role Lavelli cast Maria Cesares, who was recognized at once by French audiences as the actress who in her youth cre-ated the memorable personification of Death in Cocteau's classic film *Orphée*. The recognition of this connection in Tabori's play with the older and darker version of death provided a stunning effect. Rosette Lamont, reviewing Lavelli's production, aptly char-acterized Cesares as a "living quote."[28]

This kind of ghosting can sometimes have unexpected effects. When Greg Mosher cast Spalding Gray as the Narrator in a 1988 revival of *Our Town* at Lincoln Center, this was reportedly not for commercial reasons but to give a more contemporary "feel" to the play, since audiences could be expected to associate Gray with such material. This succeeded all too well. The New York audi-ences most familiar with Gray's work thought not only of his recently released film *Swimming to Cambodia* but also of his con-nection with the Wooster Group and the parodic treatment of *Our Town* in the Wooster Group production, *Routes 1 and 9*. Thus, when Gray delivered such a line as "Nice town, y'know what I mean?" the ghost of his flip modern persona converted it into a modern, ironic, cynical put-down, and the sentimental nostalgia that drives the play was constantly disrupted.

In a period when the long run has become an established part of theatrical culture, another variation of this inevitable compari-son with the ghosts of past interpretations has also appeared. Often when a production has an extended run one or more of its leading actors, and sometimes the entire cast will, sooner or later, move on to other engagements. Nineteenth-century revivals were very often concentrated on a particular star, and when that star stopped appearing, for whatever reason, the production stopped as well. Certainly, long runs in the modern theatre can also be based on the attractiveness of their leading performers, but normally the attractiveness of the production is somewhat more dispersed, and it is in any case very much in the interests of the producing organization to keep the production running as long as possible, even if leading players must be replaced. When this occurs, the new performer steps into a production in which the haunting is particularly concentrated and immediate. The surrounding actors, the already established public reaction to the production through reviews and word of mouth, and, to some extent, the specific memories of audience members who are returning for a second look all work together to make negotiations between the new actor and his or her predecessor particularly complex and the haunting particularly clear to the public. A new actor undertaking Macbeth or Othello may escape comparison in the reviews of his production with various predecessors in these roles (though it is rather unlikely). An actor who takes over a leading role in a long-running production, however, can be absolutely certain that critics and public alike will begin their reception and analysis of his interpretation by a comparison with the actor he has replaced. The result is a strange hybrid, not exactly a new interpretation, since the production apparatus, the scenery and lighting, the direction, and perhaps all of the cast except the new actor remain the same, but not exactly a repetition of the old interpretation either, since the new figure will inevitably bring a somewhat different coloring and perhaps somewhat different motivations to the role.

When it was announced in the fall of 1991 that Howard McGillin was replacing Mandy Patinkin as the gloomy uncle in *The Secret Garden* on Broadway, this was rarely reported without a critical opinion, before McGillin ever appeared in the play, as to what his interpretation of the character would be and how it would compare with Patinkin's. The *New Yorker* placed its comparison of the two in a welter of intertextual reference, drawing upon memories of previous theatrical experience but also upon film and literature, suggesting something of the variety of potential ghosts hovering about the reception of the new actor:

Mr. Patinkin excels at projecting just the wrong sort of gothic depression—he's more Young Werther than Mr. Rochester. The kind of brooding that Mr. Craven (the uncle) goes in for—and he's a haunted sort of man—leads to self-loathing rather than self-absorption. Think of the lugubrious way Herbert Marshall addressed the little girl in the 1949 movie. McGillin has exactly that quality.[29]

It would not be unreasonable to suggest that the theatregoing public in a city like New York inevitably views any new creation by an actor with some experience not only ghosted by previous roles but by an interpretive persona developed and maintained, as in the case of Patinkin and McGillin, by the institutional structures of media and publicity, which offer for all but the most obscure productions a complex interpretive matrix, often even before the play opens.

A particularly delicate balance must be maintained by the advertising and publicity, now major factors in the reception process, when such a shift occurs. On the one hand, the publicity cannot simply suggest that a new actor will simply imitate the departed one, since that would suggest a somewhat inferior copy. On the other hand, it must in some way counter the feeling that an established and successful interpretation is being replaced by a new but untested and unfamiliar one. The normal compromise is to replace a departing leading player by another who comes to the role (like Jean Stapleton or Lucy Lawless) with some familiar acting persona already established, often in film or television. Whenever possible the advertising then stresses how this already familiar background will bring an interesting new dimension to the role. Examples could be found in any season, but here is a typical one from February 2000. At that time a new leading actor, Jack Wagner, was announced as assuming the title role in the long-running Broadway musical *Jekyll and Hyde*. Wagner was not a familiar figure to New York theatregoers, but he was well-known to television audiences as a leading player in two of television's most popular serial dramas, "Melrose Place" and "General Hospital." With particular reference to the latter, the large newspaper ads, showing

Wagner looking at a test tube, were headed "There's a New Doctor in the House!" The ad continued "Beginning January 25, the star of *Melrose Place* and *General Hospital* injects some new blood into Broadway's hottest thriller."[30] Actually, the Victorian Dr. Jekyll and the medical figures played by Wagner on television had scarcely anything in common, even professionally, but the desire to sell a familiar face was far more important than providing an accurate image of the production itself.

A quite different dynamic operates in what might seem to be a very similar situation, when because of illness or other problems a leading player cannot perform and his or her place must be taken by a stand-in. Stand-ins are an essential part of the modern system of long runs and large advance sales, but they operate quite differently from the replacement stars just discussed. A stand-in is normally physically and vocally suited to the role, but an actor of much less reputation, who normally fills a smaller role in the production and so is familiar enough with it to step into the lead with little notice. No commercial theatre could afford to hire stand-ins with the kind of established reputation that regular replacements almost invariably have, so audiences rarely have much previous knowledge of these actors. Moreover, as last-minute replacements, stand-ins have neither the time nor the authority to put any significant stamp of their own upon the role, as replacement leads are accustomed to do. Therefore, strangely enough, the work of a stand-in is frequently ghosted to a significant degree, not by his or her own past work but by that of the actor being replaced. This is true not only because the stand-in, for the unity of the production, is expected to imitate the timing and details of action of the actor being replaced but also because the audience, which is normally not informed of the replacement until they have arrived in the theatre, have come with the expectation (if they have any expectation about this role at all) of another, more familiar actor in it.

This situation is a fairly familiar one to any regular theatregoer, but I would like to illustrate it with an example from December 1993, when the combined operations of ghosting and reception became particularly interesting and complex. The production in question was Neil Simon's successful Broadway comedy, *Laughter on the 23rd Floor,* based, as all reviews and press releases on the production noted, on the author's experiences as a gag writer for the popular television personality Sid Caesar. When I attended, on December 28, the star of the production, Nathan Lane, was absent, and he was replaced by his understudy, Alan Blumenfeld. Lane is one of New York's most popular actors, having appeared the season before this as Nathan Detroit in *Guys and Dolls* and having won in 1992 the Obie Award for Sustained Excellence. Blumenfeld, though he has had a long television career, is not particularly familiar to New York theatre audiences, and in any case his movement, even his gestures and comic "takes," were so closely modeled on those of the absent Lane, an extremely familiar stage presence, that in Blumenfeld one could often "see" Lane, ghosting a part in which he had never been seen by this audience. This kind of "absent" ghosting is, in fact, not uncommon when understudies replace a familiar actor with a fairly recognizable style.

What made this particular experience of *Laughter on the 23rd Floor* much more complicated, and interesting, was that the ghosting did not stop there. At another level the character Max, normally played by Lane and this evening by Blumenfeld, was closely modeled on Sid Caesar, whose mannerisms, extremely familiar to audiences from his television appearances, were imitated by Blumenfeld and Lane, opening another level of ghosting. And, beyond this, one of the high points of the evening was a sequence in which Max and his writers rehearsed a skit in which Max imitated Marlon Brando in his famous "Method" interpretation of Brutus in the film *Julius Caesar*. Max added to the complexity of this moment by not only parodying Brando's style in general but actually introducing lines of *A Streetcar Named Desire,* which, as I have already noted, is the most familiar and recognizable example of the Brando style. Thus, at this moment we witnessed Blumenfeld ghosted by Nathan Lane ghosted by Sid Caesar ghosted by Marlon Brando playing Brutus ghosted by his interpretation of Stanley Kowalski. The wave of laughter and huge outburst of applause that was stimulated by this sequence provided clear evidence that the audience not only recognized but also vastly enjoyed this complex web of intertextual acting references.[31]

Surely, the most familiar example of ghosting outside the operations of the traditional established company is that which occurs when an actor who has developed a certain degree of public recognition undertakes a well-known role, a major role, for example, from one of the national playwrights—Schiller in Germany, Molière in France, or Shakespeare in England or the United States. Here two repositories of public cultural memory can and often have come into conflict, with potentially powerful dramatic results as they negotiate a new relationship, either a successful new combination or a preservation of a duality. The most familiar example of this in the Western theatre is the role of Shakespeare's Hamlet. Of course, in Hamlet we have one of the major repositories of Western cultural memory, as in Faust, but, while Goethe's version dominates that tradition, it is a tradition that allows, even encourages, new literary interpretations in almost every generation. Hamlet operates in a different manner. Here new literary retellings of the story are extremely uncommon, but new theatrical embodiments are innumerable, and so we have in every generation new embodiments of Hamlet onstage, each seeking to reshape the cultural memory of the character according to its own abilities and orientation. Each seeks to establish "*My* Hamlet" as Valéry, in literary terms, sought to establish "*My* Faust."

As both Bert States and Herbert Blau have noted, *Hamlet* is not only the central dramatic piece in Western cultural consciousness, but it is a play that is particularly concerned with ghosts and with haunting. In addition to the profound ways in which these two major theorists have demonstrated how the image of haunting appears within this complex and provocative drama, however, *Hamlet* is involved with haunting in quite another dimension: the temporal movement of the work and its accompanying theory and performance through history. Our language is haunted by Shakespeare in general and *Hamlet* in particular, so much so that anyone reading the play for the first time is invariably struck by how many of the play's lines are already known to her. Even more experienced readers (or viewers) can hardly escape the impression that the play is really a tissue of quotations. Our iconic memories are haunted by *Hamlet*. Who does not immediately recognize, in whatever pictorial style he may appear, the dark habited young man gazing contemplatively into the sightless eyes of a skull he is holding (and who, seeing that image, can keep from her mind the phrase, "Alas, poor Yorick")? Our critical and theoretical memories are haunted by *Hamlet,* as Shakespeare in general and *Hamlet* in particular have occupied a central position in critical thought for the past two centuries, a situation that has not changed at all even with the development of the most recent, most iconoclastic critical approaches, such as feminist theory, queer theory, new historicism, and cultural materialism. And, finally, our theatrical memories are haunted by *Hamlet,* surely the most often produced classic, the dream and ultimate test of every aspiring young serious actor in the English-speaking theatre and to a significant extent outside it as well.

The very thing that makes *Hamlet* so attractive to a young actor, the density of its ghosting, culturally, theatrically, and academically, also, of course, makes it a formidable, even daunting challenge. Rare indeed would be the actor who would attempt this role as his first major serious part (rarer still, probably, would be the producer or producing organization that would provide him with such an opportunity and expose themselves to such a risk). Much more normally, an actor attempts *Hamlet* only when he has already developed a strong individual style and achieved a sufficient level of success and reputation to test himself against the role generally accepted as the hallmark of the art. Thus, every new major revival of *Hamlet* is doubly haunted, on the one hand, by the memories of the famous Hamlets of the past (some within the living memory of audience members, others known only through historical reputation) and, on the other hand, by memories of the new interpreter, who comes with his own particular style and technique, in most cases also familiar to the audiences. The successful new Hamlet will add his unique voice to the tradition and join the ghosts with whom Hamlets of the future must deal.

In *Cities of the Dead* Joseph Roach employs the useful term *surrogation* to characterize this process. Surrogation, suggests Roach, occurs when "survivors attempt to fit satisfactory alternates" into "the cavities created by loss through death or other forms of departure." The fit, of course, can never be exact. "The intended substitute either cannot fulfill expectations, creating a deficit, or actually exceeds them, creating a surplus."[32] A new actor attempting so haunted a role as Hamlet seems to me a particularly complex and interesting example of this process, since he is attempting to act as surrogate for a whole host of departed predecessors, against whom he will inevitably be compared, to his advantage or disadvantage.

This dynamic has long been recognized by actors, audiences, and reviewers alike and is one of the features that makes each new major production of the play an interesting cultural event. It is most consistently recorded in reviews of and reports on each new production, which will almost inevitably make comparisons between the new Hamlet and others, living and dead. Occasionally, however, in the metatheatrical mode of the late twentieth century, directors have called attention to the dynamic within productions of *Hamlet* itself, especially in the already metatheatrical scenes with the Players. Thus, Daniel Mesguich, in his 1995 revival in Lille, France, had the famous "To be or not to be" speech delivered in several historical styles, along with commentaries on interpretation from Stanislavsky, Meyerhold, and Brecht. Similarly, Andrei Serban, in his 1999 revival at the Public Theater in New York, accented Hamlet's advice to the Players with a sequence filling the stage with actors carrying large reproductions of famous Hamlets of the past, many of them from the Public Theater itself but also including a few particularly memorable historical Hamlets, such as Sarah Bernhardt, and dominated by a poster of the present Hamlet, Liev Schreiber.

Occasionally, a single actor has come to *Hamlet* with so powerful and attractive an interpretation that he achieves for his generation the ideal fusion of the two ghosts, that of the role and that of the interpreter, making it extremely difficult for young actors in that particular generation to challenge this dominant image. This could certainly be claimed for Edwin Booth in late-nineteenth and John Barrymore in early-twentieth-century America and for a number of great British actors. Hamlet is so complex and so popular a role, however, that in most generations there have been a number of competing interpretations, so that the reception experience for regular theatregoers has not normally involved comparing a new Hamlet with one specific famous predecessor, as has often been the case with other famous roles, but with a number of competing ghosts, some from the past and others of the present.

Hamlet is surely the role in the English language tradition that evokes the most crowded field of ghosts. Most of the great roles of the traditional repertoire, those plays that undergo regular revival, share in this dynamic to a certain extent, but a part of the cultural memory of Hamlet has become that it is a kind of "test" for aspiring young actors, creating a special reception paradox wherein an important part of the audience expectation has become what the new actor will do to establish *his own* Hamlet. Here the comparisons inevitably made with the interpretations of the past take on a particular urgency and specificity.

Although the particular theatrical and cultural positioning of Hamlet makes the operations of ghosting and of cultural memory particularly obvious in this role, the memory of the bodies, the movements, the gestures, of previous actors haunts all theatrical performance. As Joseph Roach has observed in *Cities of the Dead:* "Even in death actors' roles tend to stay with them. They gather in the memory of audiences, like ghosts, as each new interpretation of a role sustains or upsets expectations derived from the previous ones."[33] Modern American theatre audiences are probably less conscious of this important part of the process of theatrical reception than audiences in almost any other theatre culture, past or present, for two reasons. The first is that, as I have already noted in relation to the reuse of dramatic textual material, the turn toward realism in the modern theatre diminished the overt recycling of such material that has characterized most theatre of the past, both East and West. The second is that the regular revival of older, especially classic works, is much more uncommon in modern America than it is almost anywhere else in the world, and so the opportunity of recalling previous interpretations of particular works is much reduced.

Until fairly recent times even in the United States a large number of familiar plays were regularly revived, and with them came a whole repertoire of actors' movements and gestures, reinforced on the one hand by the memories of the audience and on the other by the traditions of the acting profession itself. Lawrence Barrett, a popular American actor and manager in the late nineteenth century, clearly summarized the prevailing practice of that era:

The so-called "business" of nearly all the commonly acted plays has been handed down through generations of actors, amended and corrected in many cases by each performer, but never radically changed. New readings of certain passages have been substituted for old, but the traditional "points" have been preserved, personal characteristics and physical peculiarities finding ample expression within the old readings of the plays.[34]

This attitude toward acting and performance memory may seem a bit odd, even unnatural, to a theatregoer in modern America, within a theatrical culture that places relatively little value on either memory or tradition, but in the great majority of theatrical cultures, past and present, something akin to what Barrett is describing has been the performance norm.

The Japanese Kabuki theatre provides an excellent example of this dynamic at work. The entire performance of Kabuki is governed (as indeed are all theatrical performances, whether they foreground this or not) by a set of fundamental conventions of the form, in Japanese called *yakusoku*. Within each performance these conventions work themselves out through a series of discrete actions called *kata*, which Kabuki historian Samuel Leiter has called "the bones or building blocks of kabuki performance." We may speak of *kata* associated with a single actor, such as those of Ichikawa Danjuro IX, or those of a family, such as the *narikomaya kata*, the *otowaya kata*, and so on. Some *kata* are particularly associated with certain roles, while there are also many that may occur in a wide variety of plays. Thus, it is possible to speak of walking *kata*, crying *kata*, running *kata*, laughing *kata*, and so on, for the representation of all emotions and modes of deportment.[35] By definition an action does not become a *kata* until it is set and repeated a number of times, to the point where it becomes a recognizable entity and is handed down to posterity. Today in Japan, as in the West, a desire for innovation is pitted against the forces of tradition, but Kabuki actors have found an interesting compromise. A contemporary Japanese actor seeking innovation will rarely attempt to create a completely new *kata*. He will much more likely restore to the stage old *kata* that are no longer in common use, just as Euripides did not so much create new versions of traditional mythic material as to restore to public consciousness less familiar earlier variants. The father's ghost is passed over but only to summon the ghost of the grandfather.

The normal lineage and recycling of action and gesture has traditionally been handled somewhat differently in the West. Up until the last century a more or less conventional interpretive tradition was established within each country for commonly revived plays, often descended more or less directly from the originator of the role in that country. This process was particularly clear in the case of plays that revived with some frequency, such as the major works of Shakespeare in England or Molière in France. Augustan theatre historian John Downes, praising Thomas Betterton's performance of King Henry VIII, notes that Betterton had been "instructed in it by Sir *William,* who had it from Old Mr. *Lowen,* that had his instructions from Mr. *Shakespear* himself."[36] Downes provides a similar performance genealogy for Betterton's Hamlet, which, unlike that for Henry VIII, is clearly incorrect,[37] but even in that case, as editors Milhous and Hume note, "however spurious the interpretation of the role, the anecdote indicates respect for a performance tradition."[38] Joseph Roach recounts a telling anecdote from Thomas Davies's *Dramatic Miscellanies* (1789) concerning the importance of performance memory to the dramatic practice of this period. During a revival of Nathaniel Lee's *The Rival Queens,* Betterton "was at a loss to recover a particular emphasis of Hart, which gave force to some interesting situation of the part," when another actor, recalling Hart's interpretation, "repeated the line exactly in Hart's key," thus gaining Betterton's hearty thanks and a coin "for so acceptable a service."[39]

The practice suggested by these examples resulted in a performance tradition that remained fairly stable for a number of generations in the European theatre unless, as occasionally happened, an actor appeared with a new interpretation that was so striking, original, and popular, that for a generation, or perhaps for several generations, it haunted all subsequent interpretations of that role. A famous example in the British theatre is Charles Macklin's noted eighteenth-century reinterpretation of the character of Shylock in *The Merchant of Venice.* The play had often been revived in the period of more than a century since its creation, but before Macklin the character of Shylock had been traditionally played by one of the comic actors of the producing company—indeed, the most famous previous interpreter had been Thomas Doggett at the opening of the century, an actor who specialized in low comedy and broad farce. Macklin, who was still building his career when he first played Shylock in 1741, was associated with no particular type of part—he had played fops and young lovers, comic old men and burlesque transvestites. To the public, however, he was better known for his life outside the theatre, as a quick-tempered brawler, the subject of a famous trial for the murder in a heated quarrel of a fellow actor in 1735.

In this case audience reception of Macklin was potentially ghosted not only by the two traditional, and in this case mutually reinforcing, associations—his previous theatre appearances in a variety of basically comic representations and the traditional interpretation of Shylock as a comic figure by Doggett and others—but also by a third association, his public persona outside the theatre as a rather unstable and dangerous figure. Had Macklin presented Shylock in a conventionally comic manner, he would have reinforced the audience's ghosting of that performance by memories of his previous theatrical work, but, instead, he presented a revolutionary new reading of the part, not sympathetic but emphasizing the dark and dangerous side of Shylock, thus, consciously or unwittingly, encouraging the ghosting of his new interpretation not by his theatrical but by his public associations. Toby Lelyveld's performance history of the play suggests that Macklin's audiences "recalled his violent disposition and associated it with the character he now portrayed."[40] From this time onward public and theatrical impressions of Macklin coalesced in the character of Shylock. It became his signature role, played throughout his career, and, as one of his biographies observes, became itself the source of ghosting throughout that career:

> For almost fifty years he played the role. Indeed, most of his best parts were, in some degree, variations on it. Sir Gilbert Wrangle in *The Refusal,* Lovegold in *The Miser,* and his own creations, Sir Archy Macsarcasm and Sir Pertinax Macsycophant, are all cut from the same cloth. So closely associated was he

with the role that he became, for many of his contemporaries, particularly those who disliked him, Shylock Macklin.[41]

The case of Macklin's Shylock not only provides an example of one strategy by which an actor can challenge and to some degree replace the ghosts of past interpretations in the public consciousness (often thereby producing a new ghost to haunt future interpretations) but also introduces another element in the haunted body to which we must now turn our attention.

So far we have spoken, especially in the case of well-known and often revived roles, of the two sometimes contradictory, sometimes reinforcing ghostings provided by previous interpretations of that role and previous roles created by that actor. Macklin's Shylock, however, calls attention to a third source of ghosting, which in this case proved even more important than either of the others. This is the haunting of a new interpretation by the audience's knowledge of or assumptions about the actor's life outside the theatre. The operations of this sort of ghosting have been given almost no attention by theatre theorists, even by those centrally concerned with reception, despite the fact that in today's theatre culture (and indeed often in the past) the "private" lives, real or imagined, of famous actors and actresses have been a source of great interest to the theatregoing public and have unquestionably affected that public's reception of the artists' work. The only study that I know of devoted specifically to this phenomenon is Michael Quinn's pioneering 1990 essay, "Celebrity and the Semiotics of Acting."[42] Quinn, strongly influenced by the procedures of semiotic analysis, bases his comments upon the analysis of acting carried out by members of the Prague School, especially Jiří Veltrusky, who divided acting into three formal aspects, each with its own function. These three aspects Veltrusky calls the performer, which is the acting body itself; the stage figure, which is the image created by actor, playwright, director, and designers; and the character, which is the image as it is interpreted by the audience. The major function of the first is expressive, of the second, referential, and of the third, connotative.[43]

In the traditional post-romantic Western theatre, Quinn suggests, the second function, the referential, dominates. To it the performer's expressive function is subordinated, and upon it the audience's connotative activity is based. In what Quinn designates as "celebrity" performance, however, the actor reaches across the referentiality of the play to express directly to the audience something about himself personally that will affect their reception but, because it is not involved with the play's own referentiality, can often operate quite independently of it. Celebrity performance can take many forms, from the intimate experience of seeing a neighbor or a member of one's one family in a school or community play to the general experience of seeing on the professional stage some person we have never met but whom we know from wide exposure of them in magazines, newspapers, or on TV. In each case the public perception of the performer dominates the expressive function. As Quinn describes it, celebrity actors "bring something to the role other than a harmonious blend of features, an overdetermined quality that exceeds the needs of the fiction, and keeps them from disappearing entirely into the acting figure or the drama. Rather, their contribution to the performance is often a kind of collision with the role."

Quinn places the celebrity actor in direct opposition to the system of stage types, in that in the former case the "newest young ingenue" is "by definition excluded from enduring fame, because the extent to which she exemplifies her type will correspond to the rate of her disappearance."[44] Clearly, this is indeed the opposite of the celebrity actor, whom the audience precisely recognizes on the basis of qualities outside the theatrical establishment. On the basis of this opposition Quinn argues for an inevitable clash between celebrity and referentiality, but their relationship is, I think, much more complicated than that. Certainly, celebrity works against the illusion of theatrical naturalism, and Quinn rightly notes its close relationship to the workings of Brecht's *Verfremdungseffekt,* but it may be debated whether within a theatrical context the pure illusion sought by naturalism has ever really been achieved, and in any case the vast majority of theatre has not sought such an illusion but has frankly accepted and even emphasized the audience's parallel awareness of illusion and reality, of the character and the actor. In terms of reception, and indeed of illusion, the question seems to me not so much one of whether or not an actor's celebrity affects an audience's reception of a role (surely it normally does) but, rather, whether an actor's celebrity is naturally congruent to the role or, in a case like that of Macklin, can persuasively be made congruent. In Quinn's example of the ingenue, for example, it seems to me that if celebrity is congruent with the stage character being depicted this would be no more potentially disruptive to an audience's experience of the role than the parallel memory of the predictable stage type. Whether an audience member experiences an actress's work in a new role with the foreknowledge that a certain actress traditionally plays the ingenue parts or with the foreknowledge that the same actress has just won the Miss America beauty contest, the foreknowledge in either case ghosts the reception process and is, indeed, assumed to do so by an alert theatrical producing organization. In both of these cases the ghost reinforces the "illusion," but one could easily imagine cases, both involving the actress's stage career and offstage celebrity, that would be similarly challenging to the illusion. If, on the one hand, an actress known to the public for portraying comic old women or villainesses would suddenly decide to appear in an ingenue role, this ghosting would present a potentially serious reception problem, as would the audience's knowledge that this actress had just been involved in a major sexual scandal or a public morals charge outside the theatre (one might wonder, parenthetically, why Lillie Langtry, widely known to be the mistress of the Prince of Wales, scored such a success as Shakespeare's chaste Rosalind, but in fact the celebrity was reinforced by the opportunity *As You Like It* offered to see the rather scandalous Miss Langtry in tights).[45]

Freddie Rokem in the epilogue to his engaging study of theatrical memory, *Performing History,* discusses the use of two veteran German stage and film actors, Curt Bois and Heinz Rühmann, who near the end of their careers appeared in Wim Wenders's two filmic meditations on the history of modern Berlin, *Wings of Desire* and *So Far and So Close.* Both appear as melancholy oral historians. Bois, a Jewish actor who fled to the United States during the Nazi period, appears as a homeless vagabond, roaming through the rubble near the then desolate Potsdamer Platz. Rühmann, who had a successful career under the Nazis, plays an old chauffeur who served the Nazis faithfully and is now hiding somewhere in the ruins of Berlin with his old car. Rokem perceptively observes:

> Bois and Rühmann do not only *play* characters who are survivors/historians in the two respective films; like all actors, through their individual biographies as actors and human beings, they are also historians who represent certain aspects of the past. *Their biographical and professional pasts have in a sense become inscribed in their bodies,* as something which exists as an extension of their direct presence on the screen.[46]

Actors appearing onstage in full acceptance of their celebrity can in fact be traced far back in theatre history. In 1276 Adam de la Halle appeared in propria persona, along with several of his Arras friends and neighbors, in his comedy *Le Jeu de la Feuillée,* and well-known persons appearing as themselves were a fairly common feature of nineteenth-century popular entertainment. One notable example was William F. Cody ("Buffalo Bill"), who played himself in countless stage and later film reenactments of his scouting days and fights with the Indians. Clearly, in these performances the "real life" and "theatrical" performances were not in conflict in the audience's minds but, in fact, were mutually reinforcing. Toward the end of his career Cody added to the regular attractions of his touring company a reenactment of the Battle of San Juan Hill, which featured as one of its attractions soldiers who had actually taken place in that battle wearing (at least according to the company publicity) the very uniforms they had worn on that famous occasion.

Thus, the operations of celebrity do not necessarily subvert the authority of the dramatic role or even that of the production ensemble, as Quinn argues, although they clearly have the potential to do so. All depends upon the congruence or lack of congruence between the previous knowledge of the celebrity the audience brings to the production and the referential goal sought by the production. In both the United States and Europe in recent years theatres have sought to attract audiences by featuring well-known TV or recording personalities as stars, often with only the slightest concern with how well the public personae of these figures would fit the stage characters they were assigned. The results, such as the featuring of recording star Sting as Mack the Knife in Brecht's *Threepenny Opera* or putting cultural icon Madonna in a relatively minor role in Mamet's *Speed-the-Plow* was that their already established personae simply did not fit into the rest of the dramatic structure, creating precisely the sort of disjuncture and distraction Quinn describes. Even actors who have not sought to build a strong public persona outside the theatre may be caught up in unplanned public events that become an inescapable part of their theatre image. The famous French pantomimist Debureau at the peak of his career gave a fatal beating to a man who insulted his wife. He was acquitted by a jury and enthusiastically welcomed back to the stage by his public, but he never after was able to inspire the same spirit of carefree abandon in his audience. The critic of *Le Monde dramatique* made it clear that his performances were thereafter haunted by this extratheatrical event:

> Debureau might find his costume on the same hook, his ceruse on the same pad, but he would never again encounter the same laughter or the same fervour—because he who normally lashed out with his foot had struck a blow with his hand, and instead of making people cry with laughing, he had made somebody weep with sorrow.[47]

In terms of dramatic illusion, ghosting can clearly work in either a positive or negative way, and celebrity provides a particularly powerful example of this.

Two long-standing traditions in the theatre provide central situations for the foregrounding of celebrity. The first is the frequently encountered audience applause that greets the first entrance of the evening's star performer or performers, even, oddly enough, within a realistic production. Since the actor has done absolutely nothing at this point to merit any such sign of approbation other than to arrive onstage without falling down, what is being manifested is obviously the expression of a positive collective memory of the artist's previous work or his celebrity. In the nineteenth century it was common for such applause to be acknowledged with a bow, further disrupting the illusionistic flow of the performance, but, even though this acknowledgment of the audience tribute is now rarely seen, the applause, especially in productions that foreground a particular actor, still persists.

The other, much more universal locus for such interaction is, of course, the curtain call, a site where memory is particularly celebrated, primarily the short-term memory of the production just witnessed and now being recalled and acknowledged, but also, in many cases, the longer-term memory of past enjoyment of these actors or this company. No one has written more perceptively on the phenomenology of the curtain call than Bert States, and it is striking how central to his analysis are the operations of audience memory and, indeed, even the specific metaphor of ghosting:

> For obvious reasons, the actors remain in costume but not in character. Or, not exactly in character; for it often happens that an actor, if not the entire cast, will deliberately retain traces of his role, as in the continuance of mannerisms, or *lazzi*, for comic effect . . . or, in heavier plays, a general gravity of mood in which, say, the actor who played Hamlet remains vaguely Hamletic beneath a "house" smile. But this is taken by both audience and cast as evidence of the fanciful power of the play to outlast itself. As Bergson would say, it has encrusted its spirit on the actors who have just performed it.

Even more strikingly, States continues:

> There is also an unintentional, and far more interesting, sense in which the actor remains in character—or, to put it a better way, the character remains in the actor, like a ghost. It is not at all a clean metamorphosis . . . What we see now is not the unvarnished actor, fresh from Hamlet, but the real side of the Hamlet phenomenon . . . the actor has now annexed Hamlet, like a colony, to himself.[48]

Much of States's seminal study on the phenomenology of theatre deals with one or another aspect of what I have called ghosting. At one point, in speaking of recurring images and conventions, he astutely observes that "once the theatre is armed with a paradigm it will not be satisfied until it has tried out every available content."[49] Thus, for example, upon the particular ghosting machine of the curtain call may be grafted a higher level of ghosting, as any curtain call itself is ghosted by memories of previous curtain calls and their repertoire of expectations. This is how, for example, the curtain call for Mary Chase's 1944 Broadway comedy *Harvey* could conclude with the opening and closing of a stage door left followed shortly by the opening and closing of a stage door right, a sequence that the delighted audience, relying upon the ghosts of other curtain calls, rightly recognized as representing the final "appearance" of the invisible rabbit for whom the play was named. One might balance this famous "invisible" curtain call with the most famous one that conferred visibility upon its participants. In the 1941 comedy classic *Arsenic and Old Lace* the thirteen victims of the homicidal sisters, never seen in the play, came out of the onstage door to the cellar/crypt to appear for the curtain call, a striking reversal of the curtain call's normal function of representing a return to "reality" as well as an unusual literal representation of the "ghosts" of the production.

So popular was this device that it was continued, and it increased in complexity (as ghosted conventions in the theatre often do), when there appeared among the displayed "corpses" first the play's producers, Howard Lindsay and Russel Crouse, and then a variety of other well-known New York personalities. Thus, instead of the normal curtain call ghosting of actors by their stage personae that States notes, patrons were offered bodies ghosted by the operations of extratheatrical celebrity. Subsequent professional revivals of this popular classic have often followed this curtain call tradition, so that *Arsenic and Old Lace* has developed its own particular and complex ghosted curtain call. A London revival in 1966 featured among the bowing corpses such familiar stage figures as John Gielgud, Ralph Richardson, and Michael Redgrave, none of whom had any other connection with the production.

In this interesting variation well-known actors appeared encrusted not with the spirit of the play just seen but with that of a host of previous plays that had developed the stage figure of each of these familiar actors. Yet another variation appeared in the New York revival of the play in 1986, when former mayor John Lindsay, a familiar public figure, was observed among those emerging from the cellar. The *New York Times* article that reported this appearance placed Lindsay in the tradition of such noted earlier *Arsenic* corpses as Gielgud and Richardson,[50] showing that at least in the experience of some viewers Lindsay was ghosted not only by his political celebrity but by the performance tradition of this particular curtain call.

Gielgud and Richardson also introduce us to the last type of celebrity that I wish to mention. Like the others, it has an inevitable and quite distinct effect upon the process of reception and its operation is perhaps the most interesting of all such effects. One of the most powerful and positive experiences in the theatre arises from seeing a series of creations by those great actors in every theatre generation who in addition to creating memorable roles gradually take on a special aura of achievement, becoming in a sense indexes of the art itself, celebrity, if you will, but celebrity of a particular kind, based not so much on public notoriety but on a reputation for theatrical achievement. John Gielgud and Ralph Richardson are two obvious modern examples, as were Sarah Bernhardt and Eleanora Duse a century ago and David Garrick a century earlier. Once such actors have established themselves at the pinnacle of their profession, their appearance in each new role, or in each major revival, is ghosted not only by memories of specific past performances but, perhaps even more important, by a general audience awareness of the significance of the achievement represented by those performances. This effect is, of course, further heightened when the artist is nearing the end of a distinguished career. When John Gielgud plays Prospero, as he has done several times in recent years, the audience's view of the character is powerfully conditioned by ghosts of this great actor's own career, and Gielgud can draw upon that phenomenon to achieve an almost unbearable poignancy in his final "Now my charms are all o'erthrown / And what strength I have's mine own,— / Which is most faint." Similarly, when the aging Olivier played the aging James Tyrone in O'Neill's *Long Day's Journey into Night*, he created an unforgettable moment when the miserly Tyrone climbs on the table to turn off an overhead light and pauses a moment, looking out into the audience with the light sharply defining his features. In that instant the fictive Tyrone achieved a stunning fusion with the awareness of Olivier as actor and as an index for the art of acting itself.[51] In such moments it becomes difficult, perhaps impossible, to determine how much of the enormous impact that such a moment can have on an audience is the result of the skill of the actor and how much is the weight brought to this moment by the actor's evocation of the powerful ghosts accumulated throughout one of the greatest acting careers within the memory of the assembled public.

The tradition of the star performer and the growing importance, especially in the United States, of companies of actors assembled for a particular production and then dispersed have both served to focus the process of ghosting in acting upon the individual actor, but a broader view of the theatre in different periods provides many examples of two or more actors who so frequently appeared together that the ghosted memory of their relationship was carried from production to production in a manner identical to the memory of personal associations of an individual actor. Even in the more individualized plays and productions of recent times, particular repeated combinations of actors and relationships can easily summon up echoes of sequences in other dramas. The pairing of two male comics of contrasting physical types and intellectual acuity is a theatrical device that goes back at least as far as the *commedia* and arguably to Plautine comedy, with its clever and stupid servants. In the twentieth century this pairing became much more evident in films, with such famous and popular pairs as Laurel and Hardy or Abbot and Costello, who would play different characters in different films but rely on the audience's ghosting of each new film by the memory of their relationships in previous films. The Marx brothers provide a three-way example of the same phenomenon. Male comic pairs were less important on the live stage in the twentieth century (except in the burlesque/vaudeville tradition) than in films, but some of the best known and most loved actors of the century were male/female pairs such as Hume Cronyn and Jessica Tandy in the most recent generation or Alfred Lunt and Lynne Fontanne in the previous one. Certainly, it would be a misrepresentation of these distin-guished actors to suggest that they played essentially the same characters in most of their coappearances (as one might argue in the case of the traditional male comics), but what makes their careers even more interesting, from the point of view of ghosting, is that, even though they presented very different characters from play to play, each new incarnation stimulated in their faithful audi-ences memories of past work that deepened each new individual production. The fact that both of these prominent teams were also known as happily married couples in private life added the useful extra dimension of real-life reinforcement to the ghosting.

By the later years of their careers these acting teams were able to call upon the same kind of accumulated audience memories as could venerated single actors such as Gielgud or Olivier. When in the late 1970s Cronyn and Tandy appeared in a production of *The Gin Game,* dealing with two elderly inhabitants of a retirement home, it had been a quarter-century since their first major success together, in another well-known two-person play, *The Fourposter.* The emotional effect of *The Gin Game* was much increased by the audience's awareness of a career-long relationship between these actors, even though, in fact, the play itself assumes no previous con-nection between the two characters. There was, indeed, an inter-esting symmetry between these two two-person vehicles early and late in this dual career, since, if the reception aesthetic of *The Gin Game* drew significantly upon a backward awareness on the part of the audience, the first major Cronyn/Tandy vehicle, *The Fourposter,* seems more prophetic in retrospect, since it concerns the relation-ships of a couple over the entire course of their marriage.

The ghosting encouraged by two or more actors repeatedly appearing together, parallel to the ghosting of individual actors, is of course much more common in theatres such as the national theatres of Europe in which the acting companies, following the model of the first great national theatre, the Comédie Française, remain together for years and thus inevitably provide examples not only of personal but of group ghosting, sometimes consciously created by the director and sometimes occurring by chance. A good example of this process at work could be witnessed in a pro-duction of the late 1990s of Ibsen's *The Wild Duck* at the National

Theatre of Norway. Director Stein Winge and his actors created a powerful and original interpretation of the sequence when Gina confesses to Hjalmar that he may not be Hedwig's father. The actor playing Hjalmar reacted violently, pursuing Gina about the stage and then giving his unresisting wife a series of blows. This reaction is itself unusual and striking, but the experience of it was clearly colored, audience members and critics alike reported, by the memory of a recent *Hamlet* at this same theatre in which the actor now playing Hjalmar had played Hamlet and in the bed-chamber scene very similarly attacked Gertrude, played by the actress now playing Gina. We are not dealing here with as clear a conscious stimulation of audience ghosting as the corpses in *Arsenic and Old Lace;* indeed it is possible, though not likely, that director Winge may not have intended this effect at all. But, whether consciously intended by the director or not, the ghosted pattern of physical interaction created a reception relationship between two plays and two scenes that has, to the best of my knowledge, never been linked in critical commentary. In such cases one might speak of a kind of performance intertextuality, based not on literary but on performative echoes, since the literary texts of these two scenes have very little in common.[52] Like the invisible presences of the past roles of individual actors, past inter-actions of actors may be a calculated part of the production apparatus or may arise unexpectedly in the minds of the public, but in either case they may work equally strongly to condition the reading of a scene and perhaps of an entire production.

four

The Haunted Production

The strong tendency of the drama, in all theatrical cultures, to return again and again to the same narratives and the appearance of the same actor in a variety of character roles are probably the most familiar examples of theatrical ghosting, since most theatregoers attend the theatre primarily either to see a particular text or to see a particular actor or actors. Nevertheless, ghosting is an equally powerful component of reception in other, perhaps less widely considered aspects of the theatre experience, such as the production as a whole and its many and varied nonliving elements.

The previous chapter, "The Haunted Body," considered the reception dynamic involved when an audience sees a new actor appearing in a role already clearly associated in the public mind either with a particular previous actor (often the case when the previous actor was the first to play the role, enjoyed a great success in it, and thereby placed her "stamp" on the role) or with a series of previous actors (commonly the case with the great national classics, the most obvious example being the role of Hamlet in the English, and for that matter in the German performance tradition). As I have already noted, when a new actor undertakes an established role, this almost always involves a negotiation on the part of both audience and actor between two ghostly backgrounds,

96

that of the previous incarnation or incarnations of this role and that of the previous work of this new actor.

This chapter will first broaden the scope of this process to consider how it operates on the theatrical production as a whole, then turn to considerations of its implications in the elements of the production that surround the body of the actor, such as costume, scenery, and properties. To begin, then, at the global level of the theatrical production as a whole, we must first note that, important as the process of recycling narratives, such as those of the Greek myths or Saint Joan or Faust, has been in the history of theatre, even more important has been the recycling of specific retellings of these and other stories, that is, the continual restaging by different groups of actors of the same specific dramatic scripts. Any devoted theatregoer will in a lifetime of such activity probably see at least as many reinterpretations of the same plays as performances of new scripts, and certain standard works she may see dozens, even scores, of times. Some of them may be totally new productions of the same play, others may be the same play with everyone changed but the leading character, yet others may be revivals or returns to a long-running production in which all or most of the actors remain the same. Obviously, in each of these cases the effects of ghosting will be felt on the reception process but in an even more complicated manner than that of seeing a familiar story retold or viewing a specific actor in a new context, since here the entire production apparatus of the dramatic event is potentially involved.

The long run, seen at its most extreme in the modern American commercial theatre, or the production kept for years in the repertoire of one of Europe's major national theatres provide opportunities for audience members to return a number of times to what, in terms of overall concept and visual impression, is the same production, each new experience adding to the layering of memory. When the production runs for a truly extended period of time, however, the operations of ghosting become more complex and more interesting, since the physical bodies of the performers cannot be stabilized in the same way that their costumes, properties, and lighting can. I have already mentioned in connection with the individual actor the particular kind of ghosting that haunts the stand-in or understudy, but a different, though related process is set in motion in the case of the production that runs for years, or sometimes even for decades, such as the musical *The Fantasticks* in New York or Agatha Christie's indestructible thriller, *The Mousetrap,* in London. Here, although it may be that the contributions of individual actors will continue to affect subsequent viewings (I will never entirely forget Jerry Orbach as El Gallo in *The Fantasticks,* the first actor I saw in this role), it is more likely that a repeating audience will bring to their experience memories more associated with the production in general, with configurations or entire sequences (the blackout scenes and the whistling of "Three Blind Mice" in *The Mousetrap,* for example, or the "Round and Round" number with its staged commentary on illusion and reality in *The Fantasticks*). Clearly, the role of memory and ghosting contributes significantly to the pleasure and motivation of the young theatregoer who returns repeatedly to a popular production such as the musical *Rent,* in which almost every element of the production ensemble remains the same for the repeated viewings, but a subtler form of the same phenomenon operates when a theatregoer returns to a long-running production many months or even years after first seeing it, when one may have the sometimes uncanny experience (as I have had with both the productions here mentioned) of seeing a production in which everything—costumes, scenery, lighting, even basic blocking and gestures—has remained essentially the same but with a totally new set of bodies in place.

In certain theatrical traditions, the Japanese Noh being the most familiar example, this preservation of physical detail across time and the physical bodies of individual actors has become an established part of the form. Even in the more variable Kabuki, actors will traditionally follow the interpretation of a particular acting tradition or famous family. In speaking of the actor, I mentioned the importance of the traditional movements and gestures called *kata,* but what is handed down from actor to actor is not only a set of established business and vocal inflections but often the entire interpretation of a role, which includes the use of a specific inherited wig, costume, and makeup, down, for example, to the very facial mole used for the character Nikki Danjo in *Mei-*

boku Sendai hagi if the actor playing that part is following the *kata* created for that role by Matsumoto Koshiro V.[1]

A much more common theatre experience today, however, is that of seeing the same play on different occasions interpreted in quite varied ways by new actors, director, and designers. Here ghosting operates in a related but somewhat different manner. The echoes evoked by the performance are not of previous experience with the same basic configuration of stimuli but of the same grounding literary text and its implied patterns of action conceived by a different interpretive ensemble in different ways. The mental comparison of different actors appearing in the same role—Hamlet, Juliet, or Willy Loman—is one of the most familiar features of theatregoing, as has been noted, but there is a closely related and less obvious dynamic involving the comparison of relationships, sequences, or scenes. Audiences may, in fact, compare the particular interpretations of the Ghost in the opening scenes of Hamlet by different actors in different productions, but they are more likely to compare how the director or the production ensemble chose to portray the Ghost—as an ethereal, almost insubstantial shape, as a solid body, as a disembodied voice, as a group of several complimentary figures—all of which I have experienced. Sometimes a directorial choice will leave such a strong memory of a particular scene that an audience member's future experience of that scene will be as powerfully haunted by that choice as it sometimes is by the particularly memorable interpretation of a single actor. In Andre Serban's rather whimsical production of *Hamlet* at the Public Theater in New York in 1999, the director took literally Hamlet's amused description of Osric as "this water-fly" and played the scene with the foolish courtier literally flying about above the heads of Hamlet and Horatio. So striking and bizarre was the image that I am certain I will never see this scene again or hear Hamlet's line about the water-fly without Serban's image, for good or ill, ghosting any future experience of this scene. When in the case of well-known or often revived plays, actors, directors, and designers can assume that their audiences will remember certain key interpretive moments from previous productions, they will often build upon that memory to achieve a particular contrasting effect whose power lies largely in the contrast with its ghostly predecessor or predecessors. A good example of this was the production of Ibsen's *A Doll House* at the Arena Stage in Washington in 1990. Probably no stage direction or sound effect in the modern theatre is better known than the slam of the door at the end of the play as Nora leaves her doll house to find herself in the outside world, and that slam may be assumed to be ghosted in the memory of any informed audience member almost as firmly as the visual memory of the contemplative Hamlet regarding Yorick's skull. The Arena Stage, being a theatre-in-the-round and not a conventional proscenium theatre, staged this production, as it does many, with realistic furniture in the central area and doors in the four corners of the set, with audience members in blocks of seating between the doors on all four sides of the stage. When Nora left the stage for the final time, she shockingly left the door behind her open, and then after Torvald's final line there was a moment of silence. Then silently, without any apparent human agency, the three other doors swung open. Instead of the normal image of Nora closing the door behind her on her doll house, the audience was offered a counterimage of her action of moving out to freedom. This striking effect, however, was clearly based on the supposition that this unconventional stage effect would be ghosted, and thrown into relief by, the slamming door of countless previous productions of this familiar work.

In the twentieth century, with the rise of the director as an independent creative artist, it became increasingly common, especially in the European theatre, to see productions that very much mark this work as the creation of a particular director. Just as in earlier periods playwrights would demonstrate their skill by their personal retellings of familiar narratives, creating their own Oedipus, their own Saint Joan, their own Faust, so in the modern European theatre directors have demonstrated their skill by their personal retellings of the familiar classics: Shakespeare, Chekhov, Ibsen, Schiller. As has traditionally been the case with playwriting, this directorial process depends largely upon the processes of ghosting, since the innovation and imagination of the director's new interpretation requires that a significant part of the audience be aware of the interpretive tradition that is being both carried on and challenged.

Just as a part of the pleasure of seeing a new *Saint Joan* depends upon the ghosting of previous versions of the narrative and that of a new actor appearing as Hamlet depends upon the ghosting of his illustrious or not so illustrious predecessors, so the revival of a familiar classic in a new interpretation inevitably and often quite consciously evokes the ghosts of previous interpretations. One may even note, in recent times, the directorial equivalent of the famous acting rivalries of the past, when leading players would calculatedly mount competing productions of the same play challenging audience comparisons, such as the rival Romeos of David Garrick and Spranger Barry in eighteenth-century London, the rival Macbeths of Forrest and Macready in the romantic period, and the rival Marguerite Gautiers of Duse and Bernhardt in late nineteenth-century Paris. Such comparisons continue in our own times, of course, but the rise of the director and a corresponding greater attention to the totality of the individual productions has encouraged comparison and challenge on that level as well. The Duke of Saxe-Meiningen's *Julius Caesar,* with its detailed realism and huge crowd scenes, or Harley Granville-Barker's *Twelfth Night,* with its art deco simplicity, were particularly effective in their revolutionary impact at the dawn of the modern era because these works were already so familiar to their audiences but in a very different performative tradition. Today rival directors, especially in Europe, will often seek to mark out their distinctive approaches by rival productions of the same familiar play, just as virtuoso actors did a century ago. In 1990 the radical young Berlin director Frank Castorf mounted a production of Ibsen's *John Gabriel Borkman* that, like all of Castorf's work, was a thoroughgoing attack on traditional production approaches to the work. Castorf's production was in turn "answered" by a rival *Borkman* staged in 1991 in Munich and Paris by Luc Bondy. Bondy sought, by a detailed naturalistic approach stressing psychological acting, to demonstrate that, contrary to Castorf's claim, this tragedy of a failed capitalist could still be effective in traditional terms. In order for Bondy's challenge to have its effect, one has to assume an audience that would view his new interpretation both through the lens of Castorf's deconstructive reading and the tradition Castorf was rejecting and Bondy attempting to reinstate.

A similar but much more complex interplay of tradition and innovation informed another prominent pair of even more recent German rival productions, this time involving Chekhov. In the early 1990s the leading German director Peter Stein mounted at his theatre, the Schaubühne in Berlin, one of the most highly praised and influential Chekhov productions of the decade, a staging of *The Cherry Orchard* that, following decades of radically modern reinterpretations of the Russian author by other German directors and by Stein himself, returned to a production approach self-consciously imitating in scrupulous detail Stanislavsky's original interpretation, stressing in acting style, sound effects, lighting, costuming, and setting, the sort of detailed realism that was particularly associated with Moscow Art Theatre productions in general and with productions of Chekhov in particular. Ironically, coming out of a tradition of powerfully antirealistic stagings, this return to realism operated as a powerful innovation and was followed immediately by a vogue of neorealistic stagings by other directors in subsequent seasons.

In 1996 Stein was followed at the Schaubühne by Andrea Breth, who, as often has happened in theatre history, declared her independence from her famous predecessor by a production that directly challenged one of his. Her 1997 production of Chekhov's *The Sea Gull* was a perfect choice, since it contained within it the foundations of just the counterinterpretation that would be most useful to her. As any student of theatre history knows, the most significant and striking alternative to Stanislavsky's approach was mounted by Meyerhold, who began at the Moscow Art Theatre but then split with Stanislavsky to develop an approach far less dedicated to psychology and realism and more to theatricality and physical actions. In the dramatic schools of the time Stanislavsky became associated with realism, later socialist realism, and Meyerhold first with symbolism and subsequently with other antirealist reactions. Echoes of these historical tensions are embedded in *The Seagull,* especially in the first act, in which Chekhov offers an amused but sympathetic look at the young visionary Treplev (played by Meyerhold), who is attempting to present a kind of symbolist drama to a largely unsympathetic and uncomprehending audience. Breth, whose productions have often utilized large, open, abstract settings and nonrealistic touches, created a *Seagull* that carried on this experimentation in a manner that strongly reinforced her debt to the nonrealistic tradition represented by Meyerhold and the symbolists, ingeniously replaying the historical relationship between the two famous Russian directors in modern terms to place her own directorial stamp on this major German theatre. The texture of ghosting operating here is highly complex, involving not only familiarity with the previous work of both Stein and Breth but also with the history of Chekhovian production both in Germany and Russia. Obviously, in the case of the specific Russian productions we are not dealing with memories of audience members in the 1990s (though ghosting from specific memory may be longer than is generally supposed, the author of this book having a fairly clear memory of a production of Chekhov's *The Three Sisters* presented by the Moscow Art Theatre in the 1950s with a cast including several actors who had performed the play under Stanislavsky's direction), but the institutional and theatrical heritage of those productions is so strong, especially in Europe, that they still are readily accessible for psychic reference.

In the modern theatre, especially in Europe, where directors not infrequently dominate a theatre experience in the same way that actors or playwrights did in earlier periods, a new production by a director, once his or her career is established, will almost certainly be ghosted by that director's previous work in almost as strong a manner as a new role undertaken by a well-known actor is ghosted by that actor's previous work. This is particularly true in the case of directors, as it is in the case of actors, with a particularly striking or individualistic style. The majority of the public that attends a new production by directors such as Peter Brook, Peter Stein, Patrice Chereau, Giorgio Strehler, Julie Taymor, especially when the director is associated with an entire production apparatus, will inevitably bring to the experience memories of earlier productions by these directors and view each new work in part in its relationship to a developing oeuvre. This dynamic can be traced from the very beginnings of the modern tradition of directing, from the meticulously controlled productions of Germany's Duke of Saxe-Meiningen, whose revolutionary attention to the details of crowd scenes and personal sketches of stage compositions gave to his productions a unique look that international audiences soon learned to associate with his work.

Although any major director, like any major actor, will through a series of productions build up an inevitable bank of remembered previous work in the minds of spectators that will bear upon their expectations and their reception of subsequent work, certain directors clearly create with this process in mind, while others, though no less affected by it, seem not to have built it into their personal aesthetic. The highly individualistic visual, aural, and narrative style of an artist such as Richard Foreman guarantees that any audience member who has attended more than one of his productions (and the majority of the audiences for an experimental director such as Foreman are in fact regular viewers of his work) will inevitably recall previous Foreman productions in watching each new one. Foreman has to some extent acknowledged this process by grouping certain sets of his plays into cycles, clustering around common themes and mutually illuminating to the audience member who has seen all of them. Certain directors, like certain playwrights, calculatedly link together in a variety of ways a number of different plays or productions, encouraging audiences to allow one play or production to enrich the experience of another through the operations of ghosting. So we have, for example, the continuing Epidog cycle of Lee Breuer, a work that will almost certainly never be presented in its entirety but which is gradually building up a structure of interlocking memories as audiences experience each new element of the work haunted by the experience of previous elements. Perhaps the most self-conscious modern example of this dynamic was the great Polish director Tadeusz Kantor, whose late works might almost be called memory machines, weaving together powerful combinations of the author's autobiography, the memories of Europe's dreams and nightmares, and the remarkable production history of Kantor's own works. The concept of ghosting took on a special and personal meaning in Kantor's final work (1990), poignantly entitled *Today Is My Birthday*. Michal Kobialka has suggested something of the web of ghosted bodies and objects revived from earlier art and theatre works by Kantor and appearing again in *Today Is My Birthday:*

a mouldering book from the "Emballage Manifesto" and *The Dead Class;* a stove with a chimney from *The Silent Night;* a series of paintings from the different stages of Kantor's artistic journey; a family photograph and a family portrait from *Wielopole, Wielopole;* recent paintings "I Am Leaving this Painting"and "Infanta Margarita Came to My Room One Night"; a Cleaning woman from *The Dead Class, Let the Artists Die,* and *I Shall Never Return;* a human emballage; the custodian, Pedel, from *The Dead Class;* a figure which assumed a posture of Dr. Klein in this production, but was already present in *The Water-Hen, The Dead Class, Wielopole, Wielopole,* and *I Shall Never Return;* the soldiers, the generals, the politicians and dignitaries as well as their monuments and machines of power from *Wielopole, Wielopole, Let the Artists Die,* and *I Shall Never Return;* the grave diggers and their crosses from *Wielopole, Wielopole, Let the Artists Die,* and *I Shall Never Return;* a family table from *Wielopole, Wielopole.*[2]

To such production ghosting, which had long been a central part of Kantor's artistic vision, an extra dimension was added in this final production. Kantor died during the final rehearsals of *Today Is My Birthday,* and as the production toured the world after his death it featured an empty chair downstage, where the director had invariably sat in both rehearsals and performance. Kantor himself had joined the ghosts of the last representations of his memory machine.

Other major directors, although apparently much less self-consciously building up an oeuvre each new contribution to which evokes past contributions, nevertheless clearly participate in this process. A striking example is the recent work of Ariane Mnouchkine, with its strongly Orientalist flavor. Mnouchkine was already one of France's most highly respected directors when she began experimenting with visual referents from the Japanese Kabuki theatre in three Shakespearean productions, *Richard II* in 1982 and the subsequent *Twelfth Night* and *Henry V.* These unusual combinations of the classic theatres of two non-French traditions, one East and one West, were enormously successful and substantially increased Mnouchkine's reputation. They also increased Mnouchkine's interest in Asia, which she now often referred to as the birthplace of theatre. After her "Japanese" Shakespeares, she undertook two major epics based on recent Asian history, *Sihanouk* and *The Indiade*. Her next major undertaking, *Les Atrides*, returned to the classic Western theatre with a tetrology composed of Euripides' *Iphigenia in Aulis* and Aeschylus' *Oresteia*, but, as with the earlier Shakespeares, the Greek dramas were presented in a style evoking Asian performance, this time the Indian Kathakali, in costumes, makeup, and performance style. In the spring of 2000 Mnouchkine premiered a major new work written by Hélène Cixous, *Tambours sur la digue*, a Brechtian-style "parable" set in an imaginary China. Continuing her experiments begun with Shakespeare and the Greeks, Mnouchkine took as her visual style of this production the Japanese puppet theatre, the Bunraku, and her actors all gave astonishingly effective imitations of the movements of these puppets, complete with black-robed manipulators aiding them from behind.

For the audience member familiar with the Japanese form (and the Bunraku is one of the most familiar and widely traveled of the Japanese performance traditions), this production was of course continually ghosted by memories and images of that form, but for those familiar with Mnouchkine's previous work, and this would surely include the vast majority of those who attend her theatre, the primary interpretive contextualization of this new work was not the Bunraku itself, nor even a specific or generalized impression of Oriental performance (as Jean Alter convincingly argued was essentially the case with Mnouchkine's first "orientalist" project, *Richard II*),[3] but, rather, the now almost two decades–long Mnouchkine orientalist project, whereby an audience attending *Tambours sur la digue* likely found that its brilliant puppet-actors stirred memories not so much of the Japanese Bunraku tradition upon which they were based but of the equally brilliant Indian Kathakali figures in *Les Atrides* or the Kabuki warriors in *Richard II*. The primary haunting of a new Mnouchkine production, like that of a new role by a famous actor, has become the artist's own previous work.

Much the same dynamic can be observed in recent productions of the other best-known director of the contemporary French stage, Peter Brook. Although Brook was much involved, especially during the 1970s and 1980s, with attempting at his Research Center to create a kind of transcultural theatre, speaking in a voice unique to no specific group but attempting to express something essential in the human experience in a manner immediately accessible to viewers from any culture, he in fact produced during those years a theatre that continued to repeat certain images and techniques that, like Mnouchkine's orientalism, came to become a hallmark not of some universal expression but of the modern "Brook" style—dirt floors, Indian musical instruments, rugs, earth colors, poles and banners, and so on. Brook's *The Tempest* or his *Cherry Orchard* looked very much like *The Mahabharata* and for most audience members inevitably summoned up ghosts of that famous production, not because each drew upon some precultural repertoire of basic human images but because all drew upon the visual and aural vocabulary and used most of the same actors as all recent Peter Brook productions.

Further evidence that the well-known directors of the past century often developed approaches so individualistic that they became part of the expectations and thus the reception of their works is provided by the fact that distinctive directing styles, like the distinctive styles of certain actors, have been the inspiration for those most self-conscious sorts of ghosting, the quotation and the parody. The particular combination of abstract, stylized, and repetitive movement with equally abstract and stylized settings that characterizes the work of Robert Wilson has been delightfully parodied in David Ives's one-act *Philip Glass Buys a Loaf of Bread,* and Karen Beier, in her 1995 multicultural interpretation of Shakespeare's *Midsummer Night's Dream,* demonstrated a variety of interpretive approaches during the rehearsal scenes of *Pyramus and Thisbe,* with parodies of, among others, the style of Stanislavsky, of Meyerhold, of Brecht, and of Grotowski.

There is little evidence that directors such as Brook or Mnouchkine have consciously sought to capitalize on the effect of repeated similar or identical material repeated in different productions, but a number of other modern directors and companies have quite consciously recycled elements of their previous productions, clearly in the expectation that audiences would recognize this ghosting and make it a part of their reception. Tadeusz Kantor, as I have noted, continually introduced in his later works conscious echoes of previous ones, utilizing the same actors, the same images, sometimes even the same entire sequences, with the result that his final compositions offered a deeply moving evocation of years of theatrical experience for those in his audience, by this time a clear majority, who had seen a number of his works. Giorgio Strehler's 1992 *Faust* similarly drew upon images from the director's past work, most notably in the opening scene of the second part, in which the Ariel from Strehler's version of Shakespeare's *Tempest* appeared now as Goethe's Ariel but played by the same actress in the same costume and utilizing the same flying apparatus. The fact that Strehler himself, the director of both productions, appeared as the unconscious Faust revived by this Ariel, added to the foregrounding of the artist and his double role as creator of this image.

France's Daniel Mesguich has offered particularly complex examples of this sort of activity, often quoting both his own and other's works in his productions. His staging of Victor Hugo's *Marie Tudor* utilized a visual vocabulary (most strikingly books that spontaneously burst into flame) and even a particular and highly distinctive scenic rhythm that referred unmistakably to his earlier *Titus Andronicus,* while characters and images from his first production of *Hamlet* reappeared both in his subsequent *King Lear* and *Romeo and Juliet* along with characters and images from other plays by other directors. A particularly complex and intriguing example of this was the ball scene in Mesguich's 1985 *Romeo and Juliet.* In this scene Mesguich costumed the ball guests as participants in other theatrical stories of frustrated love and, moreover, directed them during the ball sequence to perform brief excerpts from their "home" plays, in the style of those plays most familiar to French theatregoers. Thus, Juliet appeared as Nina in Chekhov's *The Seagull,* while other actors played the Lady Anne scene from *Richard III,* the rejection of Nero from Racine's *Britannicus,* a lovers' quarrel from Marivaux, and the scene between Hamlet and Gertrude in the Queen's bedchamber, a scene that Mesguich has always seen in deeply Freudian terms. Some of these scenes were performed for the entertainment of other guests, like charades at a party, but at other times several scenes were played simultaneously on different parts of the stage, their lines interlocking and seemingly commenting on one another. Romeo, the outsider, participated in none of this, playing only his real party scene (the pilgrim speeches) with Juliet. He was last seen by Juliet amid the thwarted lovers of Chekhov, Marivaux, and Racine, gathered upstage, each acting out his or her agony to an absent lover, while downstage "Hamlet" tried in vain to make Gertrude see this intertextual version of his "ghost."

The complex sequence shows how intricate the reliance on ghosting may become in the work of a postmodern, self-reflexive director such as Mesguich. In order to make sense of such a scene, audiences must recognize visual and textual references to a wide range of previous theatrical experience, experience that the director assumes them to have had and, in this case, very little of it in previous productions of his own. Mesguich's parallel scenes demonstrate that specific theatrical situations and sequences may not only be ghosted by the audience's experience with those situations and sequences in previous interpretations of the play at hand but also by similar situations and sequences in other plays entirely.

This recycling of particular building blocks of performance was particularly highly developed in the classic *commedia dell'arte*, in which certain sequences, known as *lazzi* or *burle*, were memorized as interchangeable units of comic action that, like the set speeches of certain characters, could be placed in a wide variety of dramatic narratives as comic elaboration. Through the more literary comedies of dramatists such as Molière, Goldoni, and Beaumarchais, this style of humor lived on in the theatre after the *commedia* had largely disappeared, and an important part of the experience of comedy is the recognition that a production has entered into a familiar comedic pattern of action, such as hiding a series of characters in various places of concealment all over the stage or the closely related scenes of eavesdropping from within convenient closets or behind convenient screens. The balcony scene in Rostand's *Cyrano de Bergerac* draws much of its considerable power from its almost certain evocation in the audience's memories, on the one hand, of that most famous of balcony scenes, in *Romeo and Juliet*, that provides an association with star-crossed love and, on the other, with the countless balcony serenades in the tradition of

Spanish romantic comedy, which Rostand gently parodies by requiring Cyrano to provide words to Christian.

When Christoph Marthaler assumed directorship of the Schauspielhaus Zurich in the fall of 2000, he inaugurated his administration with a new work of his own creation called *Hotel Angst*. The production was full of echoes and quotations from Swiss culture but also from the directing career of Marthaler himself, a native of Switzerland who achieved his first major successes here and then created a major international reputation in Germany and Austria before returning to his homeland. The title and setting of Marthaler's new piece was surely inspired at least in part by Ödön von Horváth's 1926 play *Hotel "Zur schönen Aussicht,"* which Marthaler directed for the Salzburg Festival in 1999 and which was subsequently performed in Zurich. In the setting (the decaying lobby of a once grand hotel), and many lines and situations, the new play quotes the old, but one scene in *Hotel Angst* actually brings in a character from the earlier play in the manner of Mesguich. In the earlier play a young female backpacker comes into the lobby/hotel restaurant when it is full of the male habitués. They treat her in so sexist and abrasive a manner that she flees the room. In Marthaler's play the same young woman (indeed, the same actress, Olivia Grigolli, in the same costume) suddenly appears in this alternative hotel, much to the amusement of the Zurich audience, and receives the same treatment from the male habitués of the Hotel Angst, with the extra joke that they are now harassing her not only because she is an attractive young woman but because she is not Swiss.

This ghosting of a sequence in a particular production by memories of a sequence or sequences in other productions, perhaps of other plays entirely, is especially common when a group of actors continue to perform together over a significant period of time. In such cases, which were typical of the major theatre traditions in both East and West until quite recent times, an audience's reception was normally conditioned not only by previous experience with certain individual actors but also, and perhaps even more significantly, by previous experience with groups of actors in certain relationships. The already mentioned formalized *lazzi* of the *commedia dell'arte* were clearly only particularly obvious examples of what is an important part of the performance experience in any situation in which the same actors will be repeatedly seen together, as, for example, in the eighteenth- and nineteenth-century stock companies or, indeed, in the ongoing established companies of today. Just as the noble father, the ingenue, and the jeune premier of the stock companies repeated predictable structures of relationships in the written texts of play after play, the actors who regularly appeared in these conventionalized roles also soon came to be ghosted not only by their personal lines of business but by the network of relationships in which these lines were embedded, so that audiences could use their memories of past performances of these actors to orient themselves to the interplay of characters in each new production. When the audience of the Comédie Française attended the first production of Molière's *The Miser* in 1668 and the curtain rose to reveal the actor La Grange and the actress La Brie engaged in intimate conversation, this audience knew at once that these were the young lovers whose temporarily thwarted attraction to each other and whose eventual uniting would be the major plot concern of the play. They had, after all, already seen the same actors (sometimes even with the same character names) engaged in this same relationship in many previous plays, both by Molière and others.

The examples given so far have focused upon the ghosting effects of performance sequences, the interrelationships of actors, and the stamp of a director's style, all quite common contributing elements to the reception process and all involved with the recycling of previously displayed theatrical material, that is, with what I have earlier characterized as "internal" recycling. "External" recycling also has been effectively employed on this level as well. The most common working of celebrity is at the level of the individual actor, but, clearly, celebrity can affect the audience view of relationships and thus of character interaction as well, as in the familiar example of actors appearing in some romantic context who are widely known (or widely assumed) to be carrying on a passionate affair in real life.

Celebrity, as we noted in speaking of its relationship to the work of the individual actor, while a powerful source of ghosting, is an ambiguous one, which may work either to reinforce or subvert the desired effect of the production, whether it involves the individual actor or the interrelationships of several actors. There is, however, a very different sort of external ghosting that in many periods of theatre history has been evoked by the bodies onstage and which is much more calculatedly created and for that reason much more consistently congruent with the planned effect of the production on its audiences. Here the external ghosting is not provided by previous acquaintance with the "real-life" existence of the actors but by previous acquaintance with the abstract positions their bodies assume onstage. Just as through its verbal component drama can be placed among and can be ghosted by literary parallels, through its visual component the theatre can be placed among and can be ghosted by parallel configurations drawn from the plastic arts. The *tableau vivant,* in which actors onstage are positioned so as to call up the image of a well-known painting or piece of sculpture, is particularly associated with the stage conventions of the nineteenth century, but examples of it can be found in most historical periods. The custom of posing living bodies in unmoving poses suggesting painting or statuary is well documented in medieval and Renaissance festivals and may well go back to classic times. In the late eighteenth century Beaumarchais incorporated copies of well-known paintings into his Figaro plays, and the practice of incorporating patriotic artwork, especially from the period's most popular artist, David, spread throughout the Paris theatre world in the Revolutionary years. Probably the David work most often reproduced was his powerful *The Death of Marat,* and, interestingly, this painting has continued to appear as a *tableau vivant* in theatrical productions in the late twentieth century. Peter Weiss calls for its reproduction at the climactic moment of his best-known play, *Marat/Sade,* and, indeed, many of the productions I have seen of this play, including Robert Wilson's at the Berliner Ensemble in 1999, have reproduced not only *The Death of Marat* but also a whole series of evocations of paintings of the era.

As I have remarked, the nineteenth-century stage was particularly fond of this device and provides some of its most familiar examples, such as the 1832 social drama, *The Rent Day,* created by Douglas Jerrold, one of the most popular dramatists of his time. *The Rent Day* opened with a tableau exactly recreating a then well-known genre painting of that same name, an effect, according to all reviews of the production, greeted with the enthusiastic applause of recognition. This reportedly moved the painter himself to tears when he attended the performance.[4] Even more striking was the use of painting in the second act, which both opened and closed with a tableau copied from a related painting, *Distaining for Rent.*

Although *Rent Day* utilizes the same technique as the live staging of *The Death of Marat* in Wilson's production, it represents a more extreme blending of painting and theatre, since Wilson is only quoting a well-known painting to make a dramatic point (a similar example would be the widespread use in the modern theatre of living quotes of Michelangelo's *Pietà,* recently seen, for example, in November 1999 in Marie Fornes's *Into the Dark,* which also employed the equally widespread quote of a Crucifixion pose). In *The Rent Day,* however, the painting is not simply a quotation for effect; it is the motivation for the play. The play tells the story of the painting. They are, or are assumed to be, the same narrative expressed in different media, theatre providing the dimensionality and movement through time forbidden to the painting. As the genre painting, with which the *tableau vivant* is particularly associated, has today fallen out of favor, one might assume that its theatrical use would have declined as well, but in fact both dramatists and directors continue to find it a powerful device for focusing reception. The American theatre in 1983 witnessed one of the most striking examples of a dramatic production based on a painting that has appeared in the history of this device, Stephen Sondheim's popular musical *Sunday in the Park with George.* The first act of this ingenious musical is built around the creation of the famous painting of Georges Seurat, *Un Dimanche à la Grande Jatte,* and the stunning climax of this act is the gradual building up of an exact duplicate of this panting on the stage, combining live figures and two-dimensional cut-outs.

Somewhat to my surprise, in the 1999–2000 New York season I witnessed within a two month period two major new productions that utilized the external ghosting of famous artworks in exactly the same way as such popular nineteenth-century painting/plays as *The Rent Day.* The first was one of three dance-theatre pieces by Susan

Stroman and John Weidman, presented at Lincoln Center under the collective title *Contact,* and was called *The Swing.* It was based on the familiar painting by Fragonard, reproduced in the theatre program and recreated onstage at the beginning and end of the piece, which concerned the relationships of the three people who appear in the painting. An even more self-conscious quotation of painting occurred in the new play by the British dramatist Shelagh Stephenson, *An Experiment with an Air Pump,* at the Manhattan Theatre Club. As the audience entered the theatre, they were greeted with a huge reproduction of this not very familiar painting that had been set up in front of the main curtain. When the play began, the painting was wheeled aside, to reveal behind it the cast of the play exactly reproducing the painting. As in *The Swing,* the play itself was concerned with an exploration of the relationships of these characters but also, as in *The Rent Day,* with an exploration of the social concerns suggested by the painting's subject matter, here the threats and promise of scientific experimentation.

Theatre's evocation of the external memories of familiar works of painting and sculpture suggests another frequently used type of external cultural memory, that of music. The theatre's tendency to incorporate elements of all other arts allows it to draw upon the audience's previous acquaintance with works in those other arts in a direct manner that is not possible in those other arts themselves. Greek critics were intrigued by the process they called *ekphrasis,* wherein a poet would attempt to capture the effect of painting in language and certain artistic movements, such as symbolism, have been fascinated by the possibilities of seeking the musical equivalents of colors or of poetic expression, but on the whole, at least since Lessing's famous eighteenth-century essay *Laocoon,* the main line of aesthetic theory and practice has, at least until the experimental movements of the twentieth century, kept the various arts distinct. Theatre has always worked to subvert these divisions, however, since it not only can imitate qualities of other arts but can in fact incorporate those arts themselves into its operations (causing no small confusion among those modernist theorists who insisted upon trying to determine what constituted the "essence" of each of the arts).[5] Just as theatre can incorporate actual paintings (as well as such visual "quotations" of paintings as the *tableaux vivants*), so it can incorporate actual musical passages, and in many periods and certain theatrical genres this has, of course, been a dominant element.

The most complex development of music within the Western theatrical tradition is, of course, the opera, which bears something of the same uneasy generic relationship to the world of music as the drama does to the world of literature. Most of the remarks that I have made in my comments on the "haunted text" apply equally strongly to the operatic tradition, and some of them even more strongly. Operatic works, like dramatic works, continually recycle certain basic stories and certain basic characters (some of them the same as in the dramatic tradition, such as Faust, others much more distinctly operatic, such as Orpheus). The continual restaging of certain standard works is, moreover, far more common in opera than in the theatre. A dedicated theatregoer will probably have many opportunities over a number of years to see certain plays by such major dramatists as Shakespeare, Ibsen, or Chekhov, but a dedicated opera-goer can hardly escape over a comparable period of time being offered many more stagings of a much smaller basic repertoire, grounded upon the standard works of Verdi, Mozart, Wagner, Bizet and Puccini. Thus, the ghosting of particular works is, if anything, even stronger in opera than it is in theatre.

Like other ghosting, musical ghosting in opera can draw upon either internal or external reference. External ghosting, utilizing familiar but nonoperatic musical material, such as the U.S. national anthem as a kind of leitmotif for Pinkerton in Puccini's *Madama Butterfly* is a frequently encountered device, but internal ghosting, drawing upon the audience's memories of previous operatic experience is even more common. The distinctiveness of musical styles and musical phrases encourages more use of aural "quotations" in operatic works, in addition to the visual ones that it shares with the spoken theatre. Buffa works with a parodic tone not surprisingly have made frequent use of this device. Offenbach's *Orphée aux enfers,* for example, quotes Orpheus' famous aria from Monteverdi, and Pepusch and Gay in *The Beggar's Opera,* in addition to the many popular airs that form the main musical body of the work, turn to grand opera for the work call of the gang of robbers, "let us take the road." The music actually used here is that of the Christian army liberating Jerusalem in Handel's then-popular *Rinaldo*. The device is, however, also to be found (although often with a comic edge) in much more serious works, most notably in the final act of Mozart's *Don Giovanni,* in which the onstage orchestra plays for the dining Don popular operatic selections; from Martín's *Una cosa rara;* Sarti's *I due litiganti;* and, finally, the familiar "Non più andrai" from Mozart's own *Le Nozze di Figaro.* Leporello's comment "this one I know only too well" inevitably draws a laugh from the audience, clear evidence that their musical memories, like his, have been stimulated by these quotes. For Mozart's original audiences, familiar with all three citations, the joke was surely even better.

The comparatively limited traditional repertoire of the opera provides its composers with a particularly attractive opportunity to play this sort of game with their audiences, an opportunity that postmodernist composers, already attracted to parody, pastiche, and quotation, have eagerly exploited. This can be clearly seen, for example, in *The Ghosts of Versailles* by William Hoffman and John Corigliano, presented at the Metropolitan Opera in 1991. As its title suggests, the work is full of ghostings, itself an opera within an opera developed as a sequel to two of the most popular and best-known works of the traditional repertoire, the Figaro operas of Mozart and Rossini. Not surprisingly, *The Ghosts* is filled with musical references to these and other composers, and the fact that Mozart also liked to include in his operas quotations of other familiar works adds to the fun and the complexity of this activity. Indeed, the first recognizable tune in the *Ghosts of Versailles,* emerging from the background of mysterious atonal glissandos and melodic fragments that suggest the world of the ghosts, is a faint and rather hollow but faithful rendition of the traditional French song "Marlbrough s'en va-t-en guerre," which Beaumarchais in his original play turned into a despairing love song for Cherubino and which Mozart converted again into the haunting "Voi che sapete." The elaborate ball scene at the Turkish Embassy that ends the first act, and which is itself an extended parody of late-eighteenth-century Orientalism in general and of Rossini's *Italiana in Algeri* in particular, is full of musical jokes and references. A single example may indicate the sort of games being played here. At one point the orchestra plays the opening of Figaro's aria "Se vuol ballare" from *The Marriage of Figaro,* a familiar theme instantly recognizable to a typical Metropolitan audience member. All sorts of associations flow out from this quotation. The context suggests Mozart's own occasional musical jokes of this sort and particularly the banquet scene in *Don Giovanni.* The familiar lines of the aria open up other and richer references, since this is the aria in which Figaro declares his independence from Almaviva in the metaphor of dance—no longer will he dance to Almaviva's tune but will cause Almaviva to dance to his. In *The Ghosts of Versailles* Figaro at this point is engaged in taking control of this dramatic action as well, by challenging Almaviva and soon after by declaring his independence also from playwright Beaumarchais. The struggle for control of the dramatic action, inaugurated in *The Marriage of Figaro* by this aria, with its close relationship to class struggle for control of the historical process, is here evoked as a part of new dramatic action in which both master and servant must confront a new claimant for that control, the artist, who dreams that by controlling the narrative he can lead the dance of history. Far from being a simple postmodernist playfulness with already familiar material, the evocation of musical memories encourages an audience to use ghosting to deepen their understanding of the implications of the dramatic action itself.

The forms of theatre that do not share opera's ambiguous position between the disciplines of music and drama have been no less interested in utilizing music for ghosting effects, both internal and external. Today we tend to associate a through line of musical accompaniment more with films or animated cartoons than with the spoken theatre, though in the nineteenth century the most familiar and popular theatrical form, the melodrama (the name originally referred to the mixture of drama and music), used music in a similar way, to announce characters and emphasize particular moods or shifts in the action. A complex system of musical reference grew up in the more than a century of this form's popularity, which combined internal and external references so that audiences watching a new melodrama were guided in their reception not only by the generic expectations of a form that regularly

recycled certain stock types—the aristocratic villain, the persecuted heroine, the honest hero, the comic friend—but also regularly recycled particular musical motifs that were associated with
these characters and with the emotional situations in which they
were placed in play after play. Some of these motifs were created
in the theatre, others borrowed from familiar classical or popular
music, but eventually all became part of a recognizable vocabulary
of the genre, recycled in the same way that the stock characters
were. Even today, when the nineteenth-century melodrama exists
largely in a rather caricatured social memory, certain repeated
tunes, the entry music of the villain, the "Hearts and Flowers" that
so often accompanied scenes of sentiment, still remain in that
memory as ghosts of the old melodrama tradition, along with the
top hat and curling mustaches of the villain.

Even theatres not so committed to a musical grounding have
often used musical quotation to underline the emotional impact
of a particular scene or situation or, in the case of the more familiar quotations, to encourage the audience to make some cultural
connection, often a parodic or ironic one, with the music. Familiar
anthems such as the *Marseillaise* or the *Internationale,* since they can
be relied upon to conjure up immediately a certain set of related
political, social, and cultural associations, are often used in this
manner, as Christoph Marthaler relied heavily upon familiar Swiss
patriotic and nationalist songs to sharpen the satiric barbs he was
directing toward this culture in *Hotel Angst.*

Pieces of music associated with certain moods or social practices, the *Wedding March* of Mendelssohn or Wagner or the *Funeral
March* of Chopin, provide another standard source, but almost any
piece of music, popular or classical, that can be reasonably relied
upon to recall to the audience certain useful associations may be
used by an imaginative director. Matthias Hartmann staged a
highly effective but unconventional production of Chekhov's *Three
Sisters* at the Berlin Volksbühne in the late 1990s. One of the most
distinguishing features was an experimentation with the passage of
time. Much of the performance was accompanied by an onstage
pianist (a practice much more common in contemporary Europe
than in the United States) whose musical "commentary" on the
action functioned somewhat in the manner of traditional melo-

drama. One of the most effective of his contributions was an extremely slow and deliberate playing of Chopin's *Minute Waltz,* lasting, of course, several minutes in this rendition. An amused ripple of laughter followed the opening notes of this piece, clearly indicating that the audience had recognized the ghosting of this familiar piece and had, moreover, seen how this distorted version related to the overall concept of the production.

A recognition of the role of musical ghosting in performance may serve as an indication of a more general matter. The reappearance of the physical body of an actor in a variety of different roles over a period of time is so familiar and important a part of the theatre experience that any regular theatregoer is to some extent aware of this aspect of theatrical recycling and quite possibly even of some of its implications for the process of reception. Much less obvious, and therefore much less remarked upon, however, is the fact that the body of the actor, if normally the most obvious, is by no means the only component on the stage that is regularly recycled. Any physical element (or for that matter any visual or aural element, not only music but also lighting or even sound effects), a setting, a costume, property, or item of scenery, can be and many have been used in more than one production and thus may carry with them certain memories of their previous usage even in a quite different play. In the remainder of this chapter I would like to consider, at least briefly, some of the operations of these other physical elements and some of the ways in which they, like the physical bodies of the actors that they adorn or surround, call upon the collective memory of the audience to affect the reception process.

In the classic theatres of China and Japan every type of visual element was regularly recycled, and often the same mask, the same costume, the same property, the same setting, will be utilized in a great number of different productions. Probably the most striking and familiar example of this is the classic Noh stage, with its invariable setting of four symbolic pillars, painted pine tree at the rear and roofed passageway, the *hashigakari,* with its three small pine trees and pebbled walk. Other parts of traditional performance are more variable, but all utilize at least some visual elements not unique to particular plays but common to many productions and providing a symbolic orientation for the audience whenever they appear. Certain Noh masks are confined to particular plays, but far more of them are general symbolic types that are used in a variety of similar plays and thus carry associations from play to play. The same is true of the costumes in the classic theatres of both Japan and China. Every type of character had a specific shape of costume, with particular decoration and particular colors. Faubion Bowers provides a notable example from the opening of a traditional cycle of Noh plays, a cycle that follows the same pattern, with the same figures, masks, properties, and costumes no matter which Noh plays are to be performed in the particular cycle. After the opening dance in this traditional opening section, the *Okina,* a character called Senzai appears. "He is invariably dressed in an elaborate costume of blue on which the white stork, a symbol of good fortune and eternity in Japan, has been embroidered or woven." After Senzai's dance, the comic figure Samba appears, wearing a specific traditional costume: "a conical hat of black and silver with a large red dot painted on it, and grand brocaded clothes," and carrying a traditional property: "the Buddhist *juzu,* or handbells, which he rings in somewhat sacrilegious mock piety."[6] Clearly, for audiences of the Noh theatre these familiar sights and sounds invoke memories of previous Noh productions and contribute importantly to establishing the proper mood.

The flamboyant Kabuki theatre is visually far more varied than the Noh, but it nevertheless inherited from the older Noh form a tradition of recycling. Many elements in the stage settings appear in production after production: the wooden gates that represent entrances to residences, the red-painted fences and sacred archways of the temples, the highway scenes with their inevitable pine trees, the sprays of cherry or plum blossoms above the stage, and so on. In costuming, certain styles, shapes, colors, and accessories are traditionally tied to certain characters and types of characters, a convention that has remained central to the operations and symbolism of this highly visual theatre. In the historical plays, the *jidai-mono,* the actor who plays the princess or young lady of high birth who is the hero of the play invariably appears in a special type of kimono called the *akahime,* of richly embroidered scarlet silk with a long hem. This special costume visually ties together such characters as the famous "Three Princesses" in the plays *Kinkakuji, Honcho Nijushi Ko,* and *Kamakura Sandai Ki,* considered the summit of the Kabuki actor's art. Similarly, the less central roles of the *samurai* warriors' wives in the same plays are always performed in a plainer kimono, the *kokumochi,* dark maroon, pale blue, or light green in color, with a black sash and collar and the white family crest on the back, breast, and sleeves.[7] In the case of particular important characters the traditional general costume would be further refined with specific details, but this merely constituted a refinement of recycling, not a breaking away from it, since different actors playing the same character in different productions were traditionally expected to appear in the same identical costume. A. C. Scott notes that "every traditional role had its costume strictly defined down to the last detail and woe betide any actor or costume man who ran counter to this."[8] The appearance of these costumes clearly called up associations in the audience's mind with similar characters in other plays, perhaps even played by the same actor, and provided orientation for each play's pattern of action and of character relationships.

I have already spoken of the *commedia dell'arte* as the most familiar example in the West of a form dependent to a very great degree upon recycling in textual elements, characters, and character relationships. Not surprisingly, the *commedia* also recycles costumes in a manner similar to although far less elaborated than that of the classic Japanese stage. Here, as in Japan, we find both specific types of costumes invariably worn by specific types of character as well as more individualistic variations worn by particularly popular variant characters, but both appearing in many different plays and productions over a period of many years and, in some cases, of generations of performance. Even today the costume of Harlequin, composed of the distinctive red, blue, and green triangles, conjures up at least faint memories of the rogue that delighted Europe for several centuries, and in the heyday of the *commedia* many of the most popular figures wore costumes that were as often repeated and as distinctive. The long red stockings, bright red jacket, trailing black coat, soft slippers, even the dagger and purse hanging from his belt, were as typical, for example, of Pantaloon, the eminent citizen of Venice, as the diamond motley was for Harlequin. So closely were traditional costumes tied to repeated characters that when the characters underwent significant changes over time the costumes were known to change with them. The costume of the cynical Brighella during the sixteenth and seventeenth centuries, reports Pierre Ducharte, "was composed of a jacket and full trousers, adorned with a braid of some sort of green material along the seams, which gave it the appearance of livery," but after the Renaissance, as Brighella "grew milder in temperament and habits. . . . His costume went through an evolution similar in spirit to that of his character, developing into a white frock coat with a turn-down collar; but his vest and trousers retained the trimmers of green braid."[9]

The kind of conscious and specific recycling of visual material, especially of costume, found in the *commedia* is far less common in subsequent European theatre than it has been in the Far East, though one might argue that certain traditional characters, such as Hamlet, have been generally, though by no means universally, associated with a costume of a particular shape, cut, and color. In Europe and the United States visual recycling in the theatre, until fairly recent times, operated in a different manner. The average European theatre from the Renaissance until the modern era tended to use a basic stock of costumes, settings, and properties for all plays, providing at least potentially a great variety of visual interconnections not necessarily anticipated in the dramatic text. Tate Wilkinson in his memoirs, published at the end of the eighteenth century, mentions one setting of wings and flat "of Spanish figures at full length, and two folding doors in the middle" that he first saw used at Covent Garden in 1747 and could still see in productions there as he was writing these memoirs forty years later. "I never see those wings slide on," he remarks tellingly, "but I feel as if seeing my very old acquaintance unexpectedly"—a striking expression of the potential effect of such recycling upon reception.[10] Small European theatres of this period might possess only a half-dozen or so complete settings, two or three interiors (most often a rustic cottage, a bourgeois salon, and a palace room), two or three exteriors (most likely a harbor, a woods, and a street scene), and perhaps one or two scenes of fancy (a hell, a glory, an oriental temple). Larger theatres might have three or four times that number, but this still did not provide much choice for any particular new production as we may see from the inventory of settings made in 1806 for the major French provincial theatre at Montpellier: a forest, a hamlet, an Asian forest, a desert, a public square, a grand salon, a "so-called Molière salon," a boudoir, a rustic chamber, the interior of a tent, a prison, a temple, a garden, a vestibule, a hell, and a glory.[11] The "so-called Molière salon" is an especially revealing item, showing how clearly a certain set was associated with a certain style of production. There is little doubt that the early-nineteenth-century patrons of the Montpellier theatre came to find the so-called Molière salon an "old acquaintance," just as Tate Wilkinson did the setting with Spanish figures. Already identified with the work of the country's most popular dramatist, it was very likely utilized in productions of the work of his many eighteenth-century imitators as well, ghosting their plays, as their texts, characters, and dramatic situations were already ghosted, by memories of the works of the comic master as experienced in the theatre.

The coming of romanticism, with its interest in local color and individualized scenic displays, by no means meant the end of this custom, which tradition and economics preserved in most European and American theatres all through the nineteenth century. The newspaper *Den Constitutionelle* in Christiania (Oslo) in 1841 complained that for the Norwegian premiere of Schiller's *Maria Stuart* in the same year "Queen Elizabeth's residence consisted of the Pompeian room which is familiar to us from every performance that we have been offered of the new French drama and which is now almost worn out." Similarly, when *Macbeth* was given for the first time in Norway (1844) the same periodical remarked that "the room in Macbeth's castle into which Duncan enters was the inevitable Pillared Hall, the backcloth of which is by now completely indistinguishable."[12]

An amusing testimony of the perseverance of this staging practice well into the twentieth century is provided by the opening of Luigi Pirandello's *Six Characters in Search of an Author*. The scene presumably shows the first rehearsal of another Pirandello play, *Each in His Own Role,* and the Prompter reads the written description of the setting: "Leo Gala's house. A curious room serving as dining-room and study." The Manager calls out to the Property Man: "Fix up the old red room," to which the Property Man, making a note, responds: "Red Set. All right."[13] This is the first statement in the play of the recurring theme of the disjuncture between the open-ended and unpredictable flow of life and its formalization and necessary falsification as it is converted into an artistic product. The highly individualistic "curious room" envisaged by the playwright and unique to this situation, is replaced by the generic "old red room," the setting, no doubt, for countless previous dramas whose ghosts will now visually haunt and thus compromise the uniqueness of the new narrative. This is, of course, precisely why romantic dramatists and designers revolted against the generic settings of the eighteenth century.

Although Pirandello sees scenic recycling as an object of amusement, it is nevertheless clearly still operative enough to be worthy of comment. The reform sought by the romantics was long in being generally accepted. The memoirs of Nemirovich-Danchenko, Stanislavsky's codirector at the Moscow Art Theatre, provide evidence that even in a fairly ambitious theatre at the end of the nineteenth century it was still the general theatrical custom to rely essentially upon a few generic settings: a garden, a wood, and a few basic rooms. As these rooms were used for production after production, they, and their normally minimal furnishings, began to develop associations with certain types of dramatic situations, so that the physical elements of the setting could and did bring to new plays associations with previous plays in the minds of the audience. The "tall lamp with a yellow shade" in the corner of one "small reception room" setting thus became associated, claims Nemirovich-Danchenko, with "comfortable love passages," while the curule chair in the "Gothic" or "Renaissance" setting was "stubbornly" referred to by at least one director as the "culture chair."[14] This sort of association by repeated reuse in similar circumstance is surely the most common sort of ghosting generated by standard stage scenery and properties. One might characterize it as the inanimate equivalent of the phenomenon of typecasting for actors, whereby a particular actor, by becoming associated with particular types of roles, arouses certain audience expectations by his very appearance. Indeed, the parallel could be carried further, by citing examples in which inanimate objects, like actors, have drawn upon the operations of celebrity, achieving certain effects in the theatre as a result of the audience's awareness of them in extratheatrical contexts. Just as the nineteenth-century theatre titillated audiences by offering William F. Cody playing himself in dramatic representations of his famous career, melodrama and spectacle houses of the same period would often seek to raise the emotional level (and commercial attractiveness) of productions by utilizing properties or costumes that were claimed to have significant real-life associations. One may find many theatre advertisements from Victorian England and the United States like that of London's Surrey Theatre for its production of *The Gamblers*, featuring a re-creation of a recent notorious poisoning case staged with the actual table, chairs, and even the fatal jug used in the real crime, all purchased for this purpose by the enterprising manager.[15] Similarly, Chicago's McVickers Theatre advertised for its 1889 production of *The Dark Secret* that "Captain William Andrews will appear in his twelve-foot dory in which he made his historic sea voyage,"[16] and New York's Windsor Theatre in 1883 for *Jesse James, the Bandit King* boasted of using "the original and only horses in the possession of Jesse James at the time of his death, Bay Raider and Roan Charger."[17]

A variety of forces have, as Nemirovich-Danchenko notes, much reduced this sort of recycling in the modern theatre. The romantic and later the realist authors and directors, insisting that each new play and indeed each new revival should be reconceived with totally new settings, costumes, and properties, provided a strong theoretical base for this change, and it was reinforced by economic and organizational changes in the theatre, most notably the replacement of the traditional rotating repertory organization with the long-running single production and the rise of the designers' unions, particularly in the United States, which specifically outlawed the recycling of design elements in order to provide more design opportunities for union members.

One may still, of course, find in any major ongoing nonprofessional theatre and in most ongoing professional theatres as well a stock of costumes, properties, and scenic elements that are regularly recycled, even though the expense of storage space and the pressure of the modern aesthetic for each production to have its own unique design statement both work against the simple pulling of items from stock and placing them repeatedly on the stage. I am sure that every university theatre has its equivalent of Cornell's old Dante chair, which, like Nemirovich-Danchenko's curule chair, has appeared regularly for years in Renaissance productions, but had the designers been able to manage a great variety in such furnishings they most likely would have done so, and, although university costume designers, unlike costume designers in America's professional theatre, can and do constantly recycle costumes, much ingenuity is used to prevent audiences from recognizing specific costumes from previous encounters with them.

Designer Robert Dahlstrom provided me with a telling anecdote demonstrating that actors also are aware of the possibilities and potential dangers of costume recognition by the audience. When Dahlstrom was designing a production of Aeschylus' *Oresteia* at the state theatre in Bergen, Norway, he decided to put the chorus of the *Agamemnon* in a variety of worn and battered military and functionary uniforms, drawn from a wide range of historical periods out of the theatre's costume stock. One actor, assigned a rather distinctive kepi to wear, flatly refused it. The problem, he insisted, was that he had worn that same distinctive hat when he had appeared a season before as the Good Soldier Schweik, and he argued, quite rightly in my opinion, that his appearance in it again would run the risk of giving the audience members the disturbing impression of recognizing "Schweik" as an alien and clearly disruptive presence among the chorus of Argive elders. Of course, in a production with a consciously postmodern orientation, more likely to be encountered today in Europe than in the United States, such a disruption might be consciously sought, and not only, as one might first expect, for some sort of Brechtian disruption of the dramatic illusion. One of the major reorientations of postmodernism has involved a shift from the romantic or new critical view of each work of art as essentially self-contained to a view of each work as existing in and best understood through a web of intertextual relationships. The conscious recycling of recognizable elements from other works can contribute significantly to dramatic productions reflecting this reorientation, as we have already noted in the work of Mesguich. One can therefore in the postmodern context readily imagine a production in which Schweik in his distinctive hat, or even the hat alone, might be used precisely to encourage an audience's awareness of an intertextual reference.

A clear example of that dynamic at work was provided by the intriguing modern metatheatrical play *La Répétition,* by Dominic Champagne, a Canadian play premiered onstage in 1990 and on television in 1992. Intertextuality is central to this work, which begins in the middle of a rehearsal of Chekhov's *The Seagull,* but, while Chekhov is echoed by actual lines, a more unusual visual intertextuality is provided by scenes in which two characters in the play sit wearing bowler hats beneath an isolated tree. No critic, and probably few audience members, missed this ghosting from Beckett's modern classic *Waiting for Godot,* even though not a line of that text was spoken.[18] Here, instead of Schweik, the familiar Didi and Gogo suddenly were seen in a quite alien play but consciously and calculatedly evoked by the production through visual quotation. A similar effect was achieved in Daniel Mesguich's 1989 production in Paris of Shakespeare's *Titus Andronicus,* when the ravaged and mutilated Lavinia drops to her knees facing the audience and emits a silent scream. The effect is chillingly appropriate to this dramatic action, but knowledgeable audience members also recognized that Mesguich was adding to the complexity of the moment by quoting one of the most famous visual images of the modern stage, Helene Wiegel's silent scream in the Berliner Ensemble production of Brecht's *Mother Courage,* when Courage has been informed of but does not dare vocally react to the death of her son.

In the traditional repertory theatres of Europe and the United States actors were often until fairly recent times required to provide some or all of their own costumes. Goethe's actors at Weimar were provided with fifty thaler annually to purchase their costumes, a bit more than was needed for a good middle-class suit or dress and not really enough for a court costume.[19] Thus, just as each theatre, except for a few large and well-financed houses, had only a limited number of available settings, each actor, except for a few well-connected and well-supported figures, had only a limited number of available costumes. Not uncommonly, then, the reappearance of an actor with a special "line of business" would echo not only earlier appearances of that particular actor but of his entire physical context. The father figure in a Molière comedy might thus appear in a subsequent Molière comedy not only in the same type of role but in the same "Molière salon" and wearing the same costume. Text, body, and visual setting all combined to encourage the ghosting of earlier productions.

Even when theatres of the seventeenth and eighteenth centuries provided on occasion more unusual or more expensive costumes, they were generally, like the settings of these theatres, limited in number, and so the reappearance of specific costumes in different productions was a far more common practice than it is today. Again, Goethe's theatre in Weimar provides a striking example, the coronation gown for the premiere of Schiller's *Mary Stuart*. Eduard Genast, the son of a leading Weimar actor, tells the story:

> The coronation procession presented a particularly difficult problem with our limited means; in order to present it in an even moderately suitable manner, the financial commission, of which I was a member, had to grit its teeth and make all sorts of purchases . . . The royal gown, however, was the real stumbling block. The enormous expense of it staggered Kirms, and since he was in charge of all the supplies of the court, he tried to pass off an old blue silk curtain for this purpose. Both Goethe and Schiller protested strongly. Finally the good Kirms gave in and gave his approval, though with glum looks, to the creation of a real coronation robe. It was, to be sure, of imitation velvet, and from now on had to be passed down from king to king like a grandmother's wedding gown in the old days.[20]

Clearly, the Weimar "coronation gown" became, like Nemirovich-Danchenko's culture chair or the Montpellier Theatre's Molière salon, a sign for a particular dramatic context, continually reinforced by the audience's memory of its previous appearances in other productions, though both Nemirovich-Danchenko and Genast obviously view this practice with an amused and rather ironical eye. In more modern times, in which theoretical, aesthetic, and even legal concerns are often allied against the practice of "passing down" a specific costume from production to production, such recycling is generally even more negatively considered, as the necessary but unfortunate recourse of production operations that unfortunately lack the resources to provide new and unique settings and costumes for every production.

Nevertheless, as already noted, certain modern directors and theatre companies in Europe and the United States, mostly experimental ones, have recognized the reception advantages in the calculated recycling of specific costumes and properties and have provided important exceptions to the widespread modern tendency to avoid or minimize this practice. During the 1970s England's Royal Shakespeare Company, in its cycle of Shakespearian histories collectively called *The Hollow Crown*, used in each successive play not only the same crown but also, much more strikingly and distinctly, a dazzling and historically quite inaccurate gold lamé coronation robe that, as the cycle continued, built up in the audience's mind associations with a series of kings who had worn it and thus brought to each new use a powerful accumulation of meaning and emotion.

A few companies have taken this process much further, consciously reusing physical material from one production in later productions in order to build a web of associations within their work. I have already mentioned one of the most familiar examples of this dynamic, the productions of Tadeusz Kantor, which especially in his last years, gained enormous power from the repeated appearances not only of the same actors but of the same costumes, properties, and the bizarre "machines" that were a kind of trademark of Kantor productions. This sort of production linkage through repeated use of the same elements is also the practice of one of Portugal's leading experimental companies, Cornucópia, founded in the 1970s by actor/director Luís Miguel Cintra. Cintra and his resident designer, Cristina Reis, arrange the flexible space in their Lisbon studio in a different manner for every production, but certain properties, costumes, and scenic elements are consciously repeated from production to production. Thus, connections are made among the ongoing new works of the company and also the wide range of European plays they present, such as Horváth's *Casimir and Caroline*, Jourdheuil's *Ah Q*, Büchner's *Woyzeck*.

The conscious recycling of a wide variety of elements from production to production forces repeating audiences (and the majority of audiences for such groups are repeating audiences) to recognize each new staging not only as one in a continuing series of works with important internal connections but also as works consciously constructed, with that constructedness foregrounded by the repeated elements. The primary motive that led romantic and realistic scenic designers to create totally new costumes, scenery, and properties for every production, was the motive of creating a stage world of perfect illusion, no element of which should remind the viewer that she was watching a theatrical construction and not a "slice of life." Today in the post-Brecht, postmodern theatre, a recognition of this constructedness, driven either by a Brechtian political desire to disrupt the dreamworld of naturalism or by a postmodern playfulness that delights in the artifice of art, has encouraged many such experimental companies to rely extensively upon recycling. A practice that was often in the past driven by primarily economic motives, the relative low expense of stock materials, today has been revived, driven much more by an artistic recognition of the relationship I have been tracing between recycling and reception.

One of the best known of the organizations involved in this process is the leading experimental theatre company in the United States, the Wooster Group. That group's involvement with cultural memory, quotation, and recycling is so complex, and so suggestive of what might be characterized as a central postmodern approach to these traditional theatrical concerns, that I will focus on them in more detail in a later, concluding section.

five

The Haunted House

I began my comments on the haunted body with Eric Bentley's useful "minimal" definition of the *theatrical situation:* "A impersonates B while C looks on." It may seem that this minimal definition consists only of two elements, A/B (the combined actor and character) and C, the audience, but the dynamic of "looking on" brings another element into this apparently simple equation, the necessity of a shared space, or, to be more accurate, two contiguous spaces, the one in which A/B appears and the one from which C is able to observe A/B. Here, then, is another fundamental part of the theatre, the contiguous spaces of A/B and C, most commonly configured as a stage and auditorium within a building devoted to theatrical performance. Our next concern, therefore, will be the various ways in which this elemental spatial dimension of theatre participates in or contributes to ghosting as it impacts upon reception.

Given the basic spatial relationship of all theatre, the contiguous spaces of performer and audience, the variety of forms this configuration has taken in various cultures and historical periods is enormous, as rich and varied as the forms of theatrical expression itself. As with dramatic texts and the varying traditions of acting, these different forms utilize recycling in quite different ways, but theatre spaces, like dramatic texts and acting bodies, are deeply involved with the preservation and configuration of cultural memory, and so they also are almost invariably haunted in one way or another, and this haunting of the space of performance makes its own important contribution to the overall reception of the dramatic event.

Normally, when we think of theatre, especially in terms of the space where it occurs, we think of a building erected specifically for that purpose. Indeed, in many European languages the words for the building and the art are the same, derived from the Greek word *theatron*, whose meaning, "a place for seeing," encapsulates the dynamic of the viewer/viewed confrontation. In most cultures and most historical periods, however, an important amount of theatrical activity does not take place in spaces specifically designated as "theatres." Before dealing with the ways in which recycling operates in more conventional and traditional venues, therefore, I would like to consider its important and complicated operations in some of the many other kinds of locations where theatre has been created.

It is clear that theatre existed long before theatres did. Peter Brook opens his book *The Empty Space* with the famous passage that gives its name to his study: "I can take any empty space and call it a bare stage. A man walks across this empty space whilst someone else is watching him, and this is all that is needed for an act of theatre to be engaged."[1] This simple formulation, like that of Bentley, reminds us that nothing is required for theatre except the space for the meeting of performer and audience and that, indeed, throughout history people have taken empty spaces of almost every conceivable kind and called them theatres. On the other hand, taken too literally, Brook's striking statement can also be misleading, on two levels. On the first level, as we all know, theatre is not yet present, as this example may seem to imply, when a man walks across an empty space with someone else watching. A certain perceptual contract is also necessary, an agreement that this action will be "framed" as theatre. In the quotation from Brook this contract is hidden in the opening phrase "and call it a bare stage." Neither the action of walking nor the observation of acting makes theatre but the placement of those two related acts within the "empty space" that the artist Brook has called into being as a theatre. On the second level Brook's use of the term *empty* suggests a phenomenological ground-zero that is also not accurate. Unlike that of Genesis, Brook's creative interpellation does not create a theatre out of a void but makes a theatre out of a space that previously was thought of as something else. The distinction is a critical one for this study because the "something else" that this space was before, like the body of the actor that exists before it interpellated into a character, has the potential, often realized, of "bleeding through" the process of reception, the process I have called ghosting.

Fundamental to modern semiotics is the insight that any part of our perceived world, even an "empty space," is inevitably layered with meanings. In his pioneering *Elements o\ ̅ ̅niology* Roland Barthes pointed out the virtual impossibility of discovering or creating a nonsignifying object in any society, since there is no reality except what is intelligible, and as social beings we structure our intelligible universe according to the semiotic systems of our culture.[2] Henri Lefebvre, in his seminal book on space, specifically rejects the concept of empty space, which is nothing more than "a form or container of a virtually neutral kind, designed simply to receive whatever is poured into it." It is, rather, "social morphology: it is to lived experience what form itself is to the living organism, and just as intimately bound up with function and structure."[3] The empty spaces that have been utilized for centuries for theatrical events are particularly susceptible to semiotization, since they are almost invariably public, social spaces already layered with associations before they are used for theatrical performance.[4] Through history, as publics have assembled for theatrical events, they have assembled in spaces already familiar to them in other contexts: around the Greek threshing floor, which brought to early performances ghosted memories of harvest and festival; in the squares in front of the great medieval cathedrals, where the imagination, like the vision, was dominated by religious imagery; in the fairground and marketplaces, ghosted by the images of commerce and trade; and in that most haunted of all sites, the village cemetery.

I have already noted that Michael Quinn's useful discussion of the effects of celebrity on the reception of individual actors has significant parallels in other production elements—in groupings of actors, even in inanimate stage objects. The same is true of these appropriated spaces, to which audiences also bring an extratheatrical acquaintance. Even when locations have been selected primarily because they were the most convenient or most available public space for a performance, they were necessarily to some degree ghosted in the minds of the public that came there by whatever psychic or semiotic role that the space played in the normal course of events, just as the local dentist in a community theatre production may continue to be ghosted by the audience's knowledge of his community life even if he were cast primarily for his handsome appearance or his resonant voice.

More often than not, however, those who have produced theatre have recognized and turned to their own ends the fact that public performance spaces often brought with them certain nontheatrical resonances, just as they have recognized and turned to their own ends the fact that the bodies of actors might be similarly haunted. This has been particularly the case with the type of performance that has become known as "site-specific performance" in the modern theatre. In such productions already written texts are placed in locations outside conventional theatres that are expected to provide appropriate ghostings in the minds of the audience, or, in more extreme cases, new works are created that are directly inspired by the extratheatrical associations of these locations. The French experimental director Armand Gatti, strongly committed to socially engaged theatre, has been particularly sensitive and successful in this sort of performance. His description of the role the theatre space played in one of his productions, dealing with a factory worker, demonstrates clearly how significant the effect of ghosting in such a space may be:

> With this kind of subject it's mostly the *place*, the architecture, that does the writing. The theatre was located not in some kind of Utopian place, but in a historic place, a place with a history. There was grease, and there were acid marks, because it was a chemical factory; you could still see traces of work; there were still work-clothes around; there were still lunch-pails in the corner, etc. In other words, all these left-over traces of hard work

had their own language, and you either used that language or you didn't say anything . . .That's why I wrote in an article "a play authored by a factory."[5]

The clearest and most straightforward type of theatrical recycling occurs when we recognize onstage an actor, a costume, or a property that we have seen before in another context, even a nontheatrical context, as in the personal "celebrity" of an acquaintance or a family member. Yet, as we noted in the case of the actor, a kind of haunting can be based on celebrity alone, when the audience has never before seen the person involved but brings to the theatre a strong image based upon reputation. Indeed, this is most commonly the case with the more macrocosmic celebrity of figures such as the well-known politician, the sports hero, or the rock star. Perhaps in such cases the term *fame* would be more exact. Either sort of celebrity, that based on direct personal experience and memory or that generated by cultural memory and the operations of the media, can provide powerful hauntings of the reception by material quite external to the performance at hand.

Theorists of tourism have often noted that physical locations, like individual human beings, can by the operations of fame be so deeply implanted in the consciousness of a culture that individuals in that culture, actually encountering them for the first time, inevitably find that experience already haunted by the cultural construction of these persons and places.[6] Mark Twain provides a typical example in his tourist classic *Innocents Abroad:*

> In a little while we were speeding through the streets of Paris and delightfully recognizing certain names and places with which books have long ago made us familiar. It was like meeting an old friend when we read "Rue de Rivoli" on the street corner; we knew the genuine vast palace of the Louvre as well as we knew its picture.[7]

Through the operations of the process of cultural memorialization that MacCannell calls "site sacralization," Twain can hail Paris locations he is actually seeing for the first time as "old friends," just as Tate Wilkinson can hail as "old acquaintances" the reused scenic pieces that occupy a place in the memory bank of his personal experience.

The most ancient records that we have of theatre activity are already closely associated with the process of site sacralization, of performance carried out in "haunted" locations. The narratives of cultural memory often have specific spatial associations, and many theorists, speculating about the origins of theatre, have suggested that it began with the reenactment of mythic, religious, or significant quasi-historical events in locations that were the actual or presumed site of these events and thus already haunted by memories of these events. Every faith has established holy places with real or legendary association to the great events in its founding or its development, places visited by pilgrims as an act of celebration or affirmation of that faith. Very commonly at the site of pilgrimage dramatic or quasi-dramatic observances are held, memorializing the religious events associated with that site and drawing much of their power from the cultural or historical memory of the site itself. The very first records that historians have associated with the theatre come from Abydos in Egypt, a pilgrimage site for nearly three thousand years, where mystery plays dealing with the story of Osiris were presented upon the very island that was honored as his place of burial.[8]

Quasi-theatrical performances were also held from a very early date at the Christian shrines in Jerusalem, as we may see from one of the earliest detailed reports of a pilgrimage to that city, that of Egeria in 381–84. The pilgrim reports that at such locations as the Upper Room, the Mount of Olives, and Golgotha, the faithful gathered on appropriate days to hear the Gospel account of events in those locations read. The recurring phrase *in the same day in the very place* suggests the importance of the setting to Egeria's experience. Nor were such observations restricted simply to the reading of appropriate texts. The events of Holy Week, from the triumphant entry into Jerusalem with pilgrims and townspeople greeting the bishop with palm branches and songs to the carrying of the Cross to Golgotha along the Via Dolorosa, were enacted in the appropriate locations in ceremonies whose power derived in large measure from the audience viewing the physical location as ghosted by the real events now being reenacted.[9]

Of course, the reenactment of religious scenes on the sites of their original occurrence is still found in many parts of the contemporary world, in traditional sites in the Holy Land and in new pilgrimage locations such as Hill Cumorah in upstate New York, where since 1937 the Mormon Church has presented annually a huge outdoor pageant on the site where Joseph Smith is said to have found the tablets establishing the Mormon faith. For many spectators attendance at such spectacles may still provide something of the religious experience felt by early pilgrims such as Egeria or the far more ancient participants in the rites at Abydos, but in our more secular world a significant portion of the spectators may be expected to bring a primarily historical rather than religious interest to such theatricalizations. Indeed, in many respects the modern tourist may be considered the direct descendant of the medieval pilgrim, and, for both, the desire to visit locations haunted by the cultural memory of past events has encouraged the development of dramatic or quasi-dramatic activities in these locations.

Although the earliest examples of this practice concern religious spaces and events, in the more secular modern world the reenactment of events in their actual or presumed locations has become more associated with historical than religious subjects. In a striking passage in his preface to *Cromwell* Victor Hugo articulated romanticism's new interest in exact historical settings:

> Exact locality is one of the first elements of reality. The speaking or acting characters alone do not engrave on the soul of the spectator the faithful impression of facts. The place where such a catastrophe occurred becomes a terrible and inseparable witness of it, and the absence of this sort of silent character makes the greatest scenes of history in the drama incomplete. Would the poet dare to assassinate Rizzo elsewhere than in Mary Stuart's chamber? Stab Henri IV elsewhere than in that rue de la Ferronier, obstructed with drays and carriages? Burn Joan of Arc elsewhere than in the old market-place?[10]

The point Hugo is making here is a theatrical one, arguing against the stock, constantly reused settings still common when he wrote and in favor of individualized stage settings that would serve as the proper and unique background for the unique romantic drama. But more recent performance practice has taken his advice in a much more literal manner and in fact restaged famous historical events in the rooms and public spaces where they actually occurred.

The postrevolutionary Russian theatre undertook such stagings on a scale never before attempted, the most famous example being Evreinov's famous *The Storming of the Winter Palace* in 1920, involving some eight thousand participants with arms and vehicles and set in the exact location where that event had taken place. The Civil War centennial in the United States between 1961 and 1965 and the bicentennial of the American Revolution a decade later provided a powerful stimulus for such activities in this country, so that countless battles and other historical events were reenacted in their historical locations. The attraction of such events for tourists was such that this practice has continued to expand since that time, with the result that every part of the country now offers examples of re-created historical events of all sorts, many of them on a regular and ongoing basis, a practice that has now also spread to many other countries around the world. Certain of these performances have repeating audiences, of course, who will bring to each new performance memories of previous ones. For most of the public, however, the spatial ghosting is primarily provided not by a personal familiarity with this place, as in the case of a medieval spectator who saw the locations of the events of Holy Week super-imposed upon familiar buildings around the Weinmarkt of his native Luzerne. Instead, the experience might be better compared to that of pilgrims who have visited Jerusalem during the centuries and seen reenactments of those same events staged in the actual streets of the ancient city, ghosted not by the pilgrims' personal memories of these streets but by cultural memories that made these streets, in Hugo's words, "silent witnesses" of the actual events being reenacted there.

So far I have been dealing with various ways in which "found" theatrical spaces may be haunted. The process is naturally different, but no less important, in more conventional theatre spaces, those created and maintained by their culture primarily for the presentation of this art. The distinction between the two is not always as clear as it might at first appear, a point powerfully argued by Richard Schechner in his important 1975 essay "Towards a Poetics of Performance," one of the founding documents of modern performance theory. Defining a theatre as "a place whose only or main use is to stage performances," Schechner argues that "this kind of space, a theatre place, did not arrive late in human cultures (say with the Greeks of the 5th century B.C.) but was there from the beginning . . . The first theatres were not merely 'natural spaces' . . . but were also, and fundamentally, cultural places."[11] The complex interweaving of space, memory, and cultural and geographical ghosting that is involved in the creation and ongoing use of "theatre spaces" is powerfully articulated in Schechner's evocation of the natural theatre spaces utilized by the Australian aborigines:

> Aborigine scenography creates a theatre out of a combination of natural and built elements. Each rock, waterhole, tree and stream is embedded in a matrix of legend and dramatic action. Thus a particular place is where a ceremony takes place, where a mythic event has happened in the past, where beings manifest themselves through songs and dances and where everyday and special actions converge—for example, a waterhole is a place where people come to drink and where ceremonies are enacted . . . a space may become a theatre by being "learned"— a novice is taught the legends, songs and dances associated with a space; geography itself is socialized; the uninitiated sees nothing but an out-cropping of rock or a waterhole, while the initiated experiences a dense theatrical setting.[12]

Even when permanent theatres began to be built, they continued to be haunted by the associations of the place where they were located. Long before the most famous of the ancient theatres, the Dionysian Theatre at Athens, was built, its location at the foot of the Acropolis was dedicated to the worship of that sponsoring god, an association reinforced by the central position of the altar to

Dionysos within the theatre itself. I have elsewhere dealt at length with the relationship between theatres from classic times to the present and their physical locations within the city.[13] Here I need only remark that the ghosts of a public's previous experience with a specific location—a town square, a threshing floor, a cemetery—are not completely exorcized when the improvised theatrical space imposed upon such locations is replaced by a permanent building, within which there are none of the visible traces of the area where theatre is located. Again, Richard Schechner pointed out the importance of and neglect by theorists of the audience's physical contextualization of the theatre experience: "In all cultures, people 'go to' the theatre: they make special times and places for it."[14] Often a theatre is located in a part of the city recognized as an "entertainment district," which has particular associations with leisure, pleasure, and, not infrequently, social marginality. In some cultures, as in classic Greece, the first theatres were located in sacred areas; in others, as in Elizabethan England, their surroundings were the most profane of the city.

An audience not only goes to the theatre; it goes to the particular part of the city where the theatre is located, and the memories and associations of that part of the city help to provide a reception context for any performance seen there. Clear evidence of this is provided by the fact that certain types of theatre have become known by the sections of the city with which they are most associated. Probably the most familiar examples are those productions that have been characterized by the name of the central entertainment district of the theatre capitals in which they were created: Broadway musicals in New York, West End dramas in London, Boulevard farces in Paris. Theatres in other, nonentertainment districts are nevertheless often as strongly colored by geographical associations as these highly visible commercial enterprises. Theatres in poorer neighborhoods have almost invariably also shared the associations of their surroundings. Enterprises such as London's Old Vic, claimed an observer in 1846, "have given a taint to the very districts they belong to." Such observers, naturally, attended such theatres, if at all, largely for the titillation of sampling a darker and more dangerous corner of society, willingly abandoning them to their local audiences, for whom they provided popular fare that became as associated with them as more respectable entertainment was with the more elegant ventures in the heart of the city. Thus, for example, in turn-of-the-century London the term *East End melodrama* united geographical, theatrical, generic, and class associations as clearly as did *West End drama,* and such associations unquestionably haunted the theatres of that district.

Gay McAuley, a performance studies scholar at the University of Sidney, has noted a striking contemporary Australian example of a theatre that both reflects this associative relationship with its geographical position and also manifests the ghosts of previous usage that we have noted in site-specific performances such as the factory utilized by Gatti:

> The Wharf Theatre in Sydney, home to the Sydney Theatre Company, is situated in a disused finger wharf on the harbor. There is a reminder of this past existence and the heavy manual labor that occurred there in the rough wooden floor of the pier that now constitutes the long indoor walkway patrons must negotiate before they reach the bar, restaurant, and the theatre itself. The connotations go further: the theatre seems to be located on the very edge of the continent, and the precariousness of its situation and the constant presence of water on all sides is a reminder of the importance of the sea for all the people who have worked on that wharf, the link with home for early settlers, their yearning for "over there," and their ambivalence toward the Australian landmass.[15]

The theatre building throughout the classic period and from the Renaissance onward has proven one of the few public buildings found in almost any normative list beginning with Vitruvius. Several such public buildings might be said to be repositories of cultural memory— libraries, for example, or public archives or museums as well as theatres. Theatres operate on the public imagination in a different way than these other repositories, however, since they are not concerned with the preservation or display of historical artifacts or documents but, rather, with the preservation and stimulation of historical memory itself. Not surprisingly, therefore, the theatre building has often been viewed as a domain of ghosts. Almost every one of the older theatres of Europe has accumulated its legends of haunting, and, as I have already noted, Japan's Noh theatre would not incorrectly be described as a place where ghosts appear to tell their stories, a trope found frequently in Western drama as well.

The close association of the theatre with the evocation of the past, the histories and legends of the culture uncannily restored to a mysterious half-life here, has made the theatre in the minds of many the art most closely related to memory and the theatre building itself a kind of memory machine. A striking and curious example of this is the renaissance "memory-theatres" of the Italian Giulio Camillo or the English Robert Fludd. Building upon the classic mnemonic device of remembering a series of items or concepts by mentally placing them in specific locations within a real or imagined architectural structure, these two most important memory theorists of the Renaissance each turned to the theatre as the ideal model for the storage of memory.[16] The dates of the development of these memory-theatres are striking. The most complete description existing of Camillo's memory-theatre comes from a correspondent of Erasmus, who notes in 1532 that the memory-theatre was the talk of Italy.[17] This is precisely the moment of the construction of the first renaissance theatres in that country; indeed, this same year, 1532, saw the opening and destruction by fire of what may have been the first such theatre, in Ferrara. When Robert Fludd's several-volume work was published (in two volumes, 1617 and 1619) permanent theatres were a familiar part of the London scene but still a fairly recent one, the first having appeared only forty years before, in 1576. The most famous of them all, the Globe, had opened in 1599 and been rebuilt in 1614, just as Fludd was creating his major work.[18]

Both Fludd and Giulio Camillo recognized a close cultural relationship between the concept of theatre and the dynamics of memory, but both postulated a theatre structure that was itself devoid of memory, serving merely as a mental repository for the materials of the mnemonic faculty, somewhat in the way a library provides a repository for the arrangement of and access to printed works. In order for these memory machines to operate, however, the mnemonically neutral space of the memory theatre became instantly bonded with memory material as soon as it began to be utilized. The actual physical theatres upon which these mental theatres were based also began their operations as largely neutral spaces within which cultural memory could be evoked, displayed, and, by theatre's inevitable interaction of performers and public, mutually created. As this process occurred, however, the neutral space of the theatre became itself haunted, both by the cultural memories it dealt with and the individual experiential memories of its public.

Strong, and inevitable, as the collective cultural associations and memory come to be in relationship to particular districts and neighborhoods of any city, the associations and memories that regular theatregoers develop over time in relationship to particular theatres naturally are on the whole even more specific and focused. Almost all of the ghosted elements of theatre that I have already discussed tend to be reinforced by their association with specific physical buildings. Certain dramatists, certain companies, certain actors, certain designers, often remain for years or even decades at a particular location, and so the audience memories of the previous work of those various theatre artists are reinforced by the fact that much or all of that previous work was experienced in the same physical surroundings. Although examples of this sort of memory and association may be found in all the performing arts, we find again in the case of the physical space that these associations, these memories, have been so much more strongly developed in theatre than elsewhere that they may be considered a particular feature of this art.

In many periods of theatre history, East and West, this sort of physical association has been reinforced by cultural establishment of specific buildings devoted not simply to the theatre but to a specific genre or subgenre of theatre, even, on occasion, to the work of a specific theatre artist. So we have, in the East, such theatrical and architectural institutions as the Grand Kabuki Theatres in Tokyo and Kyoto and the Kalakshetra Centre in Madras and, in the West, La Scala of Milan, Covent Garden in London, or the Comédie Française in Paris, whose very names evoke the spirits and images not only of particular types of drama but, particularly in the memories of their audiences, of specific great artists and productions associated with these spaces.

This dynamic is perhaps most clearly seen in the Western tradition in the opera, where the great opera houses, virtual synecdochic figures for a particular lifestyle and social class, are also powerful repositories of the cultural memory of that class. When opera developed as a distinct dramatic form in early-seventeenth-century Italy, an important part of that development was the establishment of theatres specifically devoted to this form, a necessary development considering that the opera demanded a distinctly different continuing group of artists than did the traditional spoken theatre. From 1637, when the first public opera house opened in Venice, until today, the opera theatre has remained a distinct subcategory of theatrical structures, building up its own complex web of reception associations involving particular great vocal artists, particular composers, particular musical and visual traditions, and, very significantly, a particular social ambiance, so that the very act of going to the opera has become, in the European tradition, ghosted not only by a host of artistic memories and associations but by social ones as well. This situation is notably reinforced not only by the prominent physical location of the great European opera houses but also by their opulent decoration. As I have already remarked, opera, with its comparatively small traditional repertoire, its small and normally highly traveled body of internationally famous stars, and its powerful sense of tradition, is surely the most consciously ghosted of the Western theatre forms, a fact emphasized by the only new opera commissioned by New York's Metropolitan Opera in the final quarter of the twentieth century, John Corigliano and William Hoffman's 1991 *The Ghosts of Versailles*.

The ghosting of a historical tradition was involved in this project from its beginning, when in 1980 the Metropolitan Opera Board decided to commission a work to mark the centennial of this theatre, in 1983, a work that would in some way consciously celebrate and continue this tradition. The result fulfilled this desire in a manner probably going beyond what the board originally expected or perhaps desired. I have already commented on Corigliano and Hoffman's ghostly recycling of operatic material from the tradition, a common enough operatic strategy given a fresh impetus by postmodernism's love of parody and pastiche, but rather more surprising and more directly relevant to my concerns in this chapter is that the opera also called specific attention to the opera house itself and its tradition-obsessed audience as a realm concerned with the dead past almost to the point of necrophilia.[19] Ghosts are everywhere in *The Ghosts of Versailles:* the ghosts of past operas, of famous operatic characters, of operatic visual and musical traditions, and of the historical and cultural surroundings in which these manifestations occurred. Appropriately, the onstage audience for which the central play-within-a-play is created is also composed of ghosts, seeking diversion in fanciful reworkings of traditional themes and material. The parallel to the traditionalist, ghost-ridden living audiences of the Metropolitan Opera itself was remarked upon by a number of the reviewers of the production, most notably by Edward Rothstein of the *New York Times*,[20] whose review was entitled "At the Met, Ghosts Come to Applaud." Rothstein argued that Corigliano and Hoffman had written a work that was not so much celebratory as engaged in cultural commentary and critique, a work about the difficulty, perhaps the impossibility, of creating something truly innovative in a form so haunted by its own past as the opera, especially in a cultural temple dedicated to the celebration of that past such as the Metropolitan. The ghostly aristocratic spectators onstage, suggested Rothstein, were clearly substitutes for the notoriously conservative Met audience: "apparently deadened and obsessed with the past."

The particular production demands of the opera, its emphasis upon the musical element of the performance and, to a significant if lesser extent, upon visual display, meant that from the very beginning the theatres devoted to it were quite distinct from those of the spoken drama, and so soon began to develop quite distinct repositories of cultural memory. This natural architectural/ generic division was soon supplemented in both in Europe and Asia by somewhat more arbitrary but for many generations equally powerful legislative divisions, which similarly operated to build strong mnemonic relationships between certain physical structures and certain genres, actors, authors, and modes of production. The main inspiration for this development in Europe was, not surprisingly, France, which in the seventeenth century became politically and culturally the center of the Continent and at the same time developed a love of system, order, and regularization that was admired and copied throughout Europe. During this period the theatre, like almost every aspect of French life and culture, was regularized and subjected to a systematic legislation conceived of and imposed from above, ultimately from the central temporal authority, the king. The spoken theatre was officially integrated into the royal and national system in 1680 with the establishment of the first national theatre, the Comédie Française, although the opera had already achieved a similar status a few years earlier. The popular *commedia dell'arte,* becoming increasingly a French genre, became, as the Comédie Italienne (later the Opéra-Comique), the third "official" French national theatre. For the next hundred years, until the upheaval of the Revolution, these remained the only three official theatres of France and served as an organizational model for other theatres throughout Europe.

These rigid and state-imposed divisions were, not surprisingly, overturned by the Revolution but reinstated by Napoléon in a much more complex system that restored the official association of particular genres with particular organizations and their physical theatres while recognizing the appearance of new and more popular genres at the turn of the century. An imperial decree of 1807 established the official number of theatres in Paris at eight, each with its own company and its own particular prescribed genre. There were four "major" theatres, two taking over the traditional spoken repertoire of the Comédie Française and the Comédie Italienne, and two presenting musical theatre, the Opéra and the Opéra-Comique. Four minor theatres were devoted to the new popular forms that had more recently emerged, two to the burgeoning genre of melodrama, one to peasant and dialect plays, and one to the vaudevilles, short plays with songs.[21]

For our concerns here, the most important aspect of such regularization was that a limited number of theatres were permanently established, with ongoing companies of actors and production staffs, clearly separated by type of theatre presented in each,

and, most important, each given a monopoly on this type of theatre. This meant that an audience going to a new French comedy
or tragedy or opera, through most of the eighteenth century,
would not only see it presented by essentially the same production
ensemble that had presented the last work of this type they had
seen but would experience it in exactly the same physical location.
Over a period of time these long-established national theatres
became increasingly conscious of and proud of their cultural
inheritance, so that the names and portraits of the composers and
dramatists whose works had been premiered on their stages were
worked into the interior decorations of their auditoriums, while
the portraits and busts of the great performers of the past decorated their foyers and stairways. So the public spaces of these great
national houses became (and still are today) visually haunted by
these evocations of their cultural tradition, and the audiences that
move (often on repeated occasions) through this field of cultural
memory into the performance space itself inescapably adds that
general cultural memory to its specific and individual memories of
theatrical experiences in these mnemonically highly charged surroundings.

The rise of nationalism in the early nineteenth century gave
new impetus to this tendency, when, in country after country
across Europe, new theatres were erected as a central part of the
encouragement of a new national and linguistic consciousness.
The long association in Europe of the theatre with the collection
and storage of cultural memory for a mass audience made it a
favored site for recalling and celebrating the myths, legends, and
history of the people to whose culture and traditions it was dedicated.[22] Although the specifically national orientation of most of
the great state theatres founded in the nineteenth century has
been modified by the growing internationalism of the modern
repertoire, the national theatre or theatres still remain among the
most prominent and familiar theatre structures in almost any
significant European city and for their publics are rich with memories and associations not only of that particular theatre and its history but of the local and national cultural heritage in general.

In Japan, as in Europe, there was a great flowering of theatre
beginning around 1600, when the already established traditional

Noh theatre was challenged by the appearance of two more popular forms, the Kabuki and the doll theatre, which developed into
the Bunraku. Although this flowering took place during the Tokugawa, or Edo, period (1603–1868), during which Japan pursued a
policy of strict isolation from the West, and although its three classic forms were far removed from Western dramatic models in subject matter, structures, and modes of production, this powerful
Eastern theatre tradition nevertheless displayed notable similarities to the West in the relationships between reception and recycling of elements of the theatre experience. I have already noted
similarities in the repetition of such elements as stock situations,
character types, and such physical elements as costumes, makeup,
and elements of the stage setting itself, and the congruence
between the two remote and distinct theatrical cultures when we
turn to the structures created to house theatrical performances. In
Japan, as in France, each theatre was dedicated to the performance of one of the three traditional types of theatre, though the
distinction was even more distinct, since, despite much borrowing
back and forth of narrative material between Kabuki and Bunraku
and by both from the older Noh, the performance traditions, even
the shape of the stage, were so distinct that an audience member
entering a theatre devoted to any of the three forms in the seventeenth century (and indeed still today) could instantly recognize
which sort of theatre was being offered there. This degree of architectural specificity was not at all to be found in the traditional divisions of the French and other European theatres, so that a spectator for any of the classic Japanese forms has always found, even in
an unfamiliar theatre, his receptions ghosted by much more
specific generic expectations than his European counterpart.

The national isolation of Japan during the Edo period was
repeated on every level of administrative organization, since the
policy of dividing every aspect of society into homogeneous groups
isolated from one another was as basic to Tokugawa culture as the
principle of centralization of power under the monarch was to sev-
enteenth-century France. The traditional gathering of artisans and
merchants into guilds, often hereditary and associated with a particular location, was strongly encouraged as a part of this social
structure by the Shogunate, and, as Earle Ernst notes in his study

of the Kabuki, this policy was applied during the seventeenth century to the theatres as well: "Troupes of actors, like the guilds, became hereditary units called *gekidan,* a system of organization which obtains today. In the larger cities theatres were permitted to be built only in specified areas."[23] Indeed, the Shogunate showed far more interest than any European government in regulating every aspect of the physical theatre: its size and shape, its seating arrangements, the size and composition of its roof and walls. Not surprisingly, as in Europe, the number of permanent theatres was strictly controlled by the granting of governmental permits and licences. From the mid-seventeenth century until 1714 the city of Edo (later Tokyo) was allowed only four Kabuki theatres—indeed, popularly known as the "Four Theatres," the Morita-za, the Naka-mura-za, the Ichimura-za, and the Yamamura-za. The Four Edo Theatres became three in 1714, when the Yamamura-za was the scene of a scandalous visit by a high court lady, causing the theatre to be closed forever (again there is a strange coincidental parallel with the governmental regulation of theatre in France, where the official public theatres were reduced from three to two in 1667 when the Comédie Italienne was closed for the next fifty years for alleged disrespect to the king's wife).

The three Edo theatres remained fixed, as did the similar numbers of theatres in Kyoto and Osaka, until the late nineteenth century.[24] Naturally, over a period of two centuries these three venerable structures underwent many remodelings and even total rebuildings (though an ever-watchful government strongly resisted any significant alterations), but for decades, indeed for generations, the Japanese theatregoing public attended not only a continually repeated repertoire but a repertoire played in a limited number of rigidly controlled structures, which inevitably built up the same rich web of performance traditions and associations as may be found in the long-standing state public theatres of the West such as the Comédie Française, the Vienna Burgtheater, and London's Drury Lane. One of the most powerful testimonies to the perceived importance of a theatre culture's previous associations with a particular building is offered by the many examples of theatres, East and West, destroyed by war or by fire (an all-too-frequent occurrence in the history of this art) that were rebuilt as precisely as possible in the manner of the old, familiar structure, even when more modern, more economical, or more convenient arrangements were possible.

The practice of exact recreation of destroyed theatrical venues, enforced by governmental legislation in Japan, was much less universally followed in the West, but there also the scrupulous reconstruction of well-known destroyed theatres has been an important architectural activity, even if driven by a somewhat whimsical mixture of patriotic, nostalgic, academic, or artistic motives rather than the more straightforward legislative ones of Japan. Theatre fires in the nineteenth century destroyed many of the handsome edifices built across Europe in the previous century, but not infrequently the replacement structures, as for example the locally beloved Celestines theatre in Lyon, France, were exact copies of the buildings they replaced, despite the considerably increased expense and in defiance of changing architectural taste. The extensive damage to European cities during World War II included many venerable theatre buildings, and, although many communities, especially in Germany, took the opportunity to rebuild with modern, state-of-the-art structures, a number of the most famous and beloved structures, such as the Semper Opera in Dresden, were lovingly restored down to the smallest decorative details in an attempt to defy, to the extent possible, the radical break in a cultural tradition represented by the destruction of the war. There have also been examples of theatres, threatened by bombing during the war or by peacetime destruction to make way for various urban developments, that have been carefully dismantled piece by piece and then reassembled in their original or an alternate location. London's famous and beloved Lyric Theatre, Hammersmith, is an example of the latter, now somewhat incongruously located on the upper floors of a much larger commercial building. The elegant rococo Cuvillies Theatre in the Munich Residenz is a striking example of the former, every bit of its ornate stucco interior dismantled (into some thirty thousand pieces) in 1943 and stored in the vaults of various castles about Munich, just six weeks before its former location was gutted by fire bombs, and then lovingly restored, like a giant jigsaw puzzle, in that location fifteen years later, where it still delights visitors today.

Whenever a famous theatre building today requires extensive remodeling or even rebuilding due to the ravages of fire or simple old age, there is now a quite predictable struggle among positions ranging from modernists, who would preserve nothing but the name, and traditionalists, who would restore the building in every detail. Generally speaking, the more famous the theatre is as a specific structure, the more likely it is that some variation of the latter position will triumph, in large part due to the knowledge of entrepreneurs and civic officials that the cultural and individual memories evoked by the reconstruction will make it more attractive to the potential public, even if those memories are evoked by a known simulation. The current rebuilding of La Fenice opera in Venice is perhaps the best-known recent example of this phenomenon.

Surely, the most striking and unusual example of the rebuilding of a destroyed theatre in modern times, however, has involved a theatre destroyed not within the memory of a single generation, many of whom can bring to the new structure their individual and specific memories of theatre experiences in the space of which it is a simulacrum, but of a theatre that has disappeared for several centuries, leaving only the most attenuated experiential memory in the scattered and thin records of diaries and other historical documents. I am speaking, of course, of the Shakespeare's Globe Theatre in London and of its rebuilding near its original location at the end of the twentieth century. Although the Globe, in the manner of other ongoing summer festival theatres, of which I will say more shortly, is gradually building an audience of repeating viewers, who bring to each new season the memories of previous experience at this theatre, surely the majority of those attending are still and will probably continue to be tourists and schoolchildren who are familiar with this famous theatre through reading and studying attempts at historical recreation. Although their physical experience of the theatre is a first-time one, ghosting nevertheless is centrally involved in that experience, though the ghosting is not the normal physical remembrance of a previously visited space but something closer to a "touristic" memory, or to that of the Jerusalem pilgrims mentioned earlier.

The traditional governmentally imposed limitations on the number of theatres, often coupled with a restriction of the production of certain dramatic genres to certain theatres, were frequently challenged during the eighteenth century and largely disappeared during the nineteenth century, or, more accurately, were incorporated into a more complex theatrical scene. The traditional national stages (often still divided into a theatre of the spoken word and two musical theatres, one for grand opera and one for lighter musical offerings) still provide in many cities the core of the theatre scene (in Paris these "national" stages still always appear first, in their own division, in any official listing of theatrical offerings), but the disappearance of the old monopolies and the rise of a bewildering variety of new genres and new production methods during the past two centuries have surrounded them with a great variety of alternative theatrical venues, today numbering in a major theatre center such as London, Paris, or New York into the scores, if not the hundreds.

This modern proliferation of venues has by no means diminished the ghosting of particular performance spaces for their audiences. Theatre audiences of the seventeenth and eighteenth centuries were offered far fewer venues in which to enjoy this art, but the total number of theatregoers was also much smaller, as was the variety of theatre offered. While none of the more recent ventures can compete with the accumulated historical memory of a Burgtheater or a Comédie Française, most of them have, for commercial, practical, political, or aesthetic reasons, or some combination of these, established some sort of image in the minds of their public.

This process was already clearly at work at the beginning of the nineteenth century. The Napoleonic legislation marking certain Parisian theatres as homes for particular popular genres such as vaudeville and melodrama was merely official recognition of an already existing fact, that these theatres, through their companies, their dramatists, their directors, and their audiences, were already firmly associated in the public mind with these genres. A Napoleonic spectator attending a theatre such as the Ambigu-Comique or the Vaudeville came with strong and clear expectations of what sort of offering was to be found there, expectations for the most part based upon previous visits to that same theatre. During the course of that century, as the romantics' vision of a theatre with ever-shifting generic boundaries was amply fulfilled, fresh approaches in playwriting, in acting, in direction or design, alone or in combination, often became associated with particular theatres, a phenomenon somewhat similar to the long-standing phenomenon of actors being associated with particular roles. Just as certain actors, sometimes to their frustration, would find new roles ghosted by a faithful public's memory of them in previous parts, certain theatres attracted a public that came expecting to find familiar types of material repeatedly given there, an expectation often encouraged by canny theatre managers.

When the new realistic drama, with its related interest in realistic detail in staging and acting, appeared at midcentury, for example, it became the specialty of particular theatres, so that the Prince of Wales Theatre in London and Montigny's Gymnase Theatre in Paris became locations almost synonymous in the mind of the theatregoing public with what came to be known in England as the "cup-and-saucer" drama, for its attention to such minutiae of everyday life. Occasionally, a particular genre would become so associated with a particular theatre that it would be designated by that name, such as London's Surrey melodramas, Savoy operas, or Aldwych farces. Attending a play is so much bound up with the rather complex physical experience of finding and experiencing a particular physical location that subsequent visits to this same location will almost inevitably evoke traces of previous ones, which theatre managers seeking to attract repeat audiences will often encourage just as actors will repeat a character or character type of proven popularity. Thus, it is not only venerable institutions such as the Comédie that particularly inspire ghosting of previous attendance in their audiences. Even a theatre that has been opened only a season or two, if it offers audiences sufficiently strong and distinct theatregoing experiences, can rely upon those experiences leaving impressions that will condition future visits to the same theatre.

The relation of this process to the passage of time and the experience of a single thoughtful theatregoer has been clearly described by Gay McAuley in a telling personal example of her associations with a particular famous London theatre, the Aldwych:

Due to the kinds of performance put on, a venue gains a certain reputation within a cultural community; it attracts a certain kind of spectator, repels others. Over a period of time the type of activity may change: for example, the Aldwych Theatre in London was so closely associated with farce in the 1920s that it gave its name to a genre—the "Aldwych farces"—but in the 1960s and 1970s, while it was the London base for the Royal Shakespeare Company, it became the primary venue for intelligent productions of the classics and of interesting new plays. Returning to London after an absence of several years in 1984 and knowing that the Royal Shakespeare Company had moved to the Barbican, I nevertheless found myself still checking the newspapers each week to see what was on at the Aldwych and being somewhat dismayed at the bland, commercial fare being offered. This personal anecdote illustrates both the way a given venue can come to seem causally connected to a particular kind of performance and the time lag involved before members of a cultural community recognize that change has occurred.[25]

Probably the most widespread association of particular theatres is with particular genres or subgenres, an association sometimes imposed (or legitimated) by state legislation, as with Napoléon's designation of certain theatres as homes of melodrama, but more often built up in regular theatregoers' minds by repeated offerings of similar fare, such as the Aldwych farces, the Savoy operas, or the cup-and-saucer comedies at the Prince of Wales. In either case the effect on repeating audiences is the same. They look to such theatres, and attend such theatres, as McAuley reports, with certain clear and not easily dislodged generic expectations that form an important part of the grounding of their reception of new work there.

For each theatregoing generation, such genre-based theatre associations may be supplemented by, or in some cases replaced by, associations with a particular artist. A certain actor, a certain director, a certain playwright, even a certain designer, if sufficiently distinctive, popular, and dominant and located over a reasonably long period of time at a single theatre, will almost certainly develop an audience that associates that theatre with that artist's work. Each new visit to such a theatre for such an audience is ghosted by the memories of previous exposure to that artist's work in that particular space. An audience member attending her first Richard Foreman production at the St. Mark's Theatre in the East Village (if today there is such a thing as a first-time Foreman audience member) may be puzzled by the normal Foreman interior, with its cabalistic signs, plexiglass screens, space traversed by lines, and so on, but for repeating audience members (the vast majority of any Foreman audience) these are all old friends, providing a familiar entry into the world of Foreman's dramatic imagination.

Molière, in the founding years of the Coméc Française, as leading actor, dramatist, and manager, so dominated the public experience of that theatre that it eventually acquired the popular label that it still bears today: "the house of Molière." Charles Ludlam, the innovative comic genius who created and guided New York's Theatre of the Ridiculous from the late 1960s until his untimely death in 1987, whom some critics called the modern Molière, attracted a similar devoted following to a theatrical space near Sheridan Square that became so identified with his work that attending it became for the faithful an important part of the Ridiculous experience. The symbolic parallel between these comic geniuses of two eras and their associated spaces extended even beyond death, since both Molière's and Ludlam's companies, not long after the death of their charismatic leaders, were evicted from the performance spaces that had become solidly associated with those leaders in the public mind.

Doubtless, the most famous theatre dedicated to the work of a single artist is the Festival Theatre created by Richard Wagner at Bayreuth solely for the performance of the Wagnerian canon, a function that it still fulfills today. Although Wagner designed the theatre to place full emphasis upon the stage visions and voices (hiding away the orchestra out of sight of the audience and requiring that the auditorium, contrary to normal practice of the time, be darkened during the performance), it would be foolish to suggest that the experience of attending a Wagnerian opera at Bayreuth is not affected by the physical experience of the theatre itself. There is a world of difference between seeing a production of such an opera at one of the world's great opera houses, Covent Garden or the Met, which present it in a space haunted by all of the social, cultural, and artistic associations and memories of grand opera as a genre, and seeing it at Bayreuth, specifically created as a living memorial to the work of a single composer.

Richard Schechner's insistence upon the importance of the geographical "framing" of theatrical performance is particularly significant in understanding the operations of an institution such as Wagner's Bayreuth. "Too little study has been made of the liminal approaches and leavings of performance," Schechner notes, "how the audiences get to, and into the performance place, and how they go from that space."[26] Schechner in this passage is thinking of the fairly familiar situation of audiences in a particular city, or village, who make their way to a district and a location within that general area and are conditioned in their response to the theatre by the memories and associations of that location. Bayreuth offers a much more extreme example of this dynamic, since it requires its audiences not merely to go to a different part of their city but to undertake a major journey to a location far from the areas they normally frequent and associated specifically with its theatrical offerings. Bayreuth has been called a place of artistic pilgrimage, and the term is quite appropriate, as its pilgrims, like their medieval religious counterparts, come from all over the known world to attend the ceremonies offered at a venerated shrine. Bayreuth is, moreover, a much clearer example of the dynamic of recycling that is the subject of this study than a medieval predecessor such as Santiago de Compostela, since for most of the pilgrims at the latter, their visit was a once-in-a-lifetime experience, ghosted not by previous acquaintance with the site but by the more abstract rumors and reports of it that inspired the journey in the first place. Modern Bayreuth is a very different matter. Only a limited number of pilgrims are admitted each year, the demand far exceeds the supply, and in general regular patrons are favored over newcomers for the few available seats. The result is that every season the audience is composed primarily of spectators who have made the pilgrimage before, many of them for many successive years. This is a particularly clear and concentrated example of a theatre in which the ghosting of memories of a particular venue are an essential, indeed inescapable, part of the total reception experience.

Bayreuth is thus a somewhat extreme example of what might be called a pilgrimage theatre, in which for the faithful (a significant majority of those attending) each new season is ghosted by memories not only of visiting this particular theatre in the past but indeed of the much more elaborate process of traveling across Europe or from some remote part of the world to come to Bayreuth. Here also the ghosting is reinforced by the fact that, although each season sees some new stagings, others remain in the repertoire to be repeated year after year, so that these faithful may also experience repeated viewings of the same spectacle in the same venue.

Although the Bayreuth experience is in certain ways unique, most of the features that mark it as a pilgrimage theatre can be found in varying degrees in theatres around the world. The success of Bayreuth has encouraged the establishment of regular summer theatre festivals in many countries. Some such theatres are, like Bayreuth, devoted entirely or primarily to the work of a single author (most commonly Shakespeare), but most are simply devoted to the bringing together of interesting recent work. None of these attract so complete a repeating audience as Bayreuth, but most of them attract a significant number of the same spectators year after year, just as long-established theatres in major cities generally come to rely upon a repeating "base" of faithful audience members who regularly subscribe and attend. I have many friends in Ithaca, in upstate New York, for whom a pilgrimage to the festival theatre in Stratford, Ontario, is an essential and invariable part of each summer, as I am sure it is for hundreds of others throughout the region.

Certain other theatres, not operating according to the summer festival model but more like traditional venues within the conventional season, nevertheless can take on many of the reception characteristics of a pilgrimage theatre. In recent times, when the international theatrical culture was dominated by the figures of famous directors, such theatres were often the home base of such a director. Thus, theatre pilgrims from around the world have for years made pilgrimage to two remote corners of Paris, to the Cartoucherie at Vincennes to attend the productions of Ariane Mnouchkine and to the Bouffes du Nord to see those of Peter Brook, just as music pilgrims from around the world have journeyed to Bayreuth. And the very different spaces of Mnouchkine's Théâtre du Soleil and Brook's Bouffes are now for repeating viewers (the vast majority of any audience) rich with ghostings of previous offerings by those directors in those spaces, just as Bayreuth is for devoted Wagnerians. Clearly, the directors of these two famous theatres are both well aware of the importance of the physical surroundings on their work and their audiences' reception of it, and each of their theatres provides a fascinating case study of the potentially powerful interactions between memory, theatrical space, and reception. When Peter Brook founded his International Center of Theatre Research in Paris in the early 1970s, he found a home for it in a comparatively remote and unfashionable abandoned theatre, the Bouffes du Nord.

Of course, Brook must have been aware, although doubtless few of his audience members have been, that this modest theatre is an important repository for the cultural memory of the modern theatre, since one of its most important pioneers, Lugné-Poë, introduced Parisian audiences to symbolism and to the later works of Ibsen here in the 1890s. For most of its almost century-long career of rather erratic production, however, the theatre was associated with less respectable offerings from the traditions of vaudeville and music hall, and for most spectators, when Brook reopened the theatre in 1971, it probably evoked few memories of any kind, since it had at that time been abandoned, closed, and deserted for twenty years. Instead of taking the obvious course of cleaning up and redecorating the space according to contemporary taste, however, Brook and his designer Chloé Obolensky made the bold decision to leave the peeling walls and broken plaster ornaments essentially as they found them, thus forcing even audience members totally unfamiliar with the theatre's extensive history to recognize that Brook's work was being carried out in a space long committed to theatrical work. The specific identities of the ghosts that haunted the Bouffes du Nord may have been unknown, but their spectral presence was very much felt. Today, of course, some thirty years of Brook productions in this distinctive space have layered their own memories upon it, and so the Bouffes has become haunted by the memories of Brook's own highly visible later career. In a review of Brook's 2001 production of *Hamlet* John Lahr pronounces the Bouffes du Nord, with "its eroding terra-cotta walls stained by weather and time," as "one of the most alluring theatres I've ever been in," and he astutely continues: "Its moody architecture forcibly encourages memory and the act of reimagination."[27] Here, linked with memory, is another one of those *re* words that seem so particularly well suited to the theatre experience.

Brook and Obolensky's emphasis on their space as a recycled one was unusual and striking on its own terms but became more so when, in 1987, Brook's epic production, the *Mahabharata,* was offered in New York by the Brooklyn Academy of Music. Brook found the traditional stages of the academy unsuited to his purposes, and so Harvey Lichtenstein, then president of the Brooklyn Academy, arranged for Brook to use a nearby theatre, the Majestic. Although it did not share the distinguished past of the Bouffes du Nord, it was a similarly elegant theatre that had been boarded up and abandoned for some twenty years. Obolensky, working with a New York architectural firm, not only repeated the decision taken in Paris to leave the theatre (at least in outward appearance) in its decayed state, but in fact to go much further than the company had gone in Paris to add artificial signs of distress, since the Majestic was in fact in somewhat better repair than the Bouffes had been. Obolensky and her colleagues dutifully painted holes and cracks in sound walls, exposed structural elements that had been carefully covered, and added broken plaster onto smooth surfaces. Michael Kimmerman, writing in the Architecture section of the *New York Times,* noted that "the guiding esthetic here is an appreciation of buildings that express their history. But in this case, the result is a contrived, self-conscious design."[28] "The challenge," commented Evan Carzis, one of the New York architects, "was to create the appearance of an old theatre in a state of decay. Our contractors laughed."[29]

Many reviewers noted that the Paris Bouffes had served as a model for this strange remodeling, but audience members who had actually visited Brook's Paris theatre noted that this was not simply a question of a repeated general style. The interior of the Majestic was turned into a kind of copy of the Bouffes, down to the types of decay and even the colors of the peeling paint on the auditorium walls. For them the theatre was ghosted not by memories of previous experiences in this space but of previous experience in another space of which this was a scrupulous imitation, somewhat akin to the careful reconstructions of famous theatres destroyed during the war. In the opening years of the Majestic, touring productions from the Bouffes du Nord dominated the repertoire there, and many critics wondered if a space so associated with Brook's aesthetic could successfully accommodate other productions. Now, some years and many productions later, the Majestic (now renamed the Harvey) has developed its own set of associations for its public, and its carefully distressed interior has become associated in the public mind much less with Brook and his Bouffes than with a certain type of international experimental production sponsored by the Brooklyn Academy.

The operations of ghosting at Mnouchkine's Théâtre du Soleil are equally elaborate but totally different. There a series of framing experiences, repeated with each visit, gradually lead spectators into Mnouchkine's world. These experiences begin with arrival at Vincennes, the final stop on one of the Paris subway lines (for a number of the Paris suburban theatres an audience member going by public transport must begin with going to the last stop on one of the subway lines, a most appropriate beginning for this excursion outside the normal bounds of the cultural community). At Vincennes the public is met by a shuttle bus operated by the theatre, the first transition from the everyday world to that of the theatre. One reviewer of Mnouchkine's famous production *L'Indiade* in 1987, quite perceptively began the review with an evocation of this journey:

> In the shuttle bus (*navette*) which leads from the Château de Vincennes subway stop to the Théâtre du Soleil, I feel the same flow of pleasure as on the seats in the bus to Orly airport: the sensation of finding myself in an intermediate space anticipating a flight away.[30]

Deposited by the bus at a gate leading into the domain of the theatre, the spectator enters a kind of magical kingdom, a cluster of buildings, outlined by lights, isolated in the Vincennes woods, converged upon, as at Bayreuth, by an international audience gathered in anticipation of a memorable theatre experience. The major theatre building is in fact three large adjoining halls, a reception hall in the center with a performance space on either side. In this center hall the final, and most distinctive, phase of the spectator's pilgrimage occurs, the "welcoming ceremony" (*cérémonie d'acceuil*), which has long been an essential part of Mnouchkine's aesthetic.

For each production this vast lobby is decorated with motifs related to the production and provided with an array of attractive stands and booths serving appropriate food, Indian dishes for *L'Indiade,* dishes from China for the 2000 production of *Tambours sur la digue,* set in a fairytale version of that country. Audience members are thus invited not only to enter the imaginary world of the production in the most tangible manner, by viewing its artifacts and ingesting its food and drink, but also to share the bridge between their own world and the one created by the apparatus of theatrical representation, since the area where the actors are making up and getting into costume is always visible from the central lobby area and accessible to the gaze of curious spectators, while the director herself serves consciously and visibly as the occasion's host, greeting spectators, serving food, and even cleaning tables and collecting used dishes for washing up. Not only does all of this repeated transitional ceremony, from *navette* to *acceuil,* call attention to the fact that the physical surroundings of a theatrical event are in fact an important part of the reception of that event, but in terms of the particular concern of this study they form a totality of repeated impressions that have now become a part of the Soleil experience. The Chinese food for *Tambours* may be different, but it is ghosted for most Soleil spectators by memories of other themed food eaten in this same space as part of the physical and emotional preparation for previous Soleil productions.

A kind of pilgrimage phenomenon, on a much more modest scale, can be found in most major theatre cities, where in addition to a clustering of theatrical venues in some kind of entertainment district (Times Square, the West End, the Boulevards) and normally in some kind of alternative "artistic" theatre district (Greenwich Village, the Latin Quarter) there are often individual theatres in unusual or remote locations, even for most theatregoing inhabitants of the city where they are situated, that specialize in unusual, experimental work, often that of a particularly interesting theatre artist, and so take on certain characteristics of pilgrimage theatres, in which the memory of previous experiences there includes that relative difficulty of access. The Mitterand project of decentralizing the French theatre institutionalized this phenomenon, so that in addition to its best-known pilgrimage theatres, those of Brook and Mnouchkine, Paris is surrounded by a ring of equally remote suburban theatres, at Nanterre, Sartrouville, Créteil, Saint-Denis, Gennevilliers, and so on, originally designed to attract a local audience but which popular young experimental directors from Patrice Chereau in the 1960s to Stanislas Nordey today have in fact made into pilgrimage theatres for a visiting public. The Riverside Studios or Donmar Warehouse in London or the Brooklyn Academy of Music in New York, all associated not with particular artists but with a certain range of modern experimental work, are other well-known examples of this same dynamic.

For most of the history of the theatre, and in most theatrical cultures, the usefulness of a permanent physical structure answerable to the needs of theatre in general or of a particular type of theatre has meant that the most common of all theatre experiences has involved audiences returning repeatedly to the same physical place or places to see there performances of much the same type created and performed by a continuing group of artists, all of which encourages the operations of ghosting upon reception. Ghosting generated by the repeated use of a certain physical space has much diminished in the modern commercial theatre. Certainly, the major theatres of Broadway or London's West End have very clear associations with particular types of plays and style of production, but as individual theatres, with a very few exceptions, they are almost totally interchangeable in the public imagination and memory. This is, of course, a direct result of the fact that such theatres have no ongoing association with any particular artist or organization. They are purely commercial properties, rented serially by a sequence of productions that almost certainly will have no relationship one to another except that they are all commercial enterprises. I am sure that most regular New York theatregoers share my vagueness about most Broadway theatres and cannot generally remember in which of a number of similar theatres in almost identical locations they saw any particular commercial play unless they consult the program.

Nevertheless, even in these conditions most inimical to the associations of a particular venue, the desire to place new theatrical experiences within an ongoing physical context is not totally extinguished. In the New York theatre programs, themselves highly commercial operations that provide almost none of the supplementary material about the play being seen that make many European theatre programs so much more informative and interesting, one can still regularly find, in addition to the obligatory cast list and the advertisements, two special sections that provide powerful encouragements of ghosting in the reception process. The first is the almost inevitable artistic biographies of the performers, emphasizing past roles that the audience may have seen. And, although it might be argued that this feature, quite aside from ghosting, provides audience members with a kind of list of artistic credentials, the other feature can hardly serve any such secondary purpose. It is a short essay entitled "At This Theatre," giving a one-page history of the theatre's productions, growing more detailed in recent years. Since audiences can hardly be interested in a theatre's "credentials" as they might be in an actor's, such a feature can surely serve no other purpose than to recall previous experiences in this venue, otherwise difficult to distinguish from its Broadway rivals. Most regular theatregoers that I know read this little essay with great pleasure, recalling previous evenings in this theatre and thus building a memory context that in other periods other theatres have possessed without this artificial stimulus.

The pleasure of such ghosting was emphasized to me when a colleague told me of a recent New York theatre experience. Attending Andrew Lloyd Webber's *Aspects of Love* at New York's Royale Theatre, he found that the sight of "the intimacy of the auditorium and the slight curve of the standing-room area at the back of the stalls" suddenly evoked in him the ghost of that same area more than forty-five years earlier, when, "as a college boy hungry for theatre," he had stood there to watch Julie Andrews making her New York debut in the musical *The Boy Friend*. So struck was he by this theatrical ghosting that he remarked upon it to the woman ushering him to his seat. "I was here then, too," she replied. Her first job had been as an usherette for that production, at which time she, Julie Andrews, and my colleague must all have been about the same age, nineteen. "This was a great moment," my colleague concluded in reporting the incident to me,[31] probably in fact a greater moment for him than anything offered onstage that evening. His pleasure in this experience demonstrated for me once again how important for us, and yet how underrated, are the ghosts of our previous theatregoing.

Ghostly Tapestries: Postmodern Recycling

*A*s the previous chapters have argued, any theatrical production weaves a ghostly tapestry for its audience, playing in various degrees and combinations with that audience's collective and individual memories of previous experience with this play, this director, these actors, this story, this theatrical space, even, on occasion, with this scenery, these costumes, these properties. In certain theatrical cultures, especially those with a strong commitment to continuity of the production apparatus, this recycling is particularly noticeable; in others, especially those with a strong commitment to artistic originality and innovation, it may be less so but has always been central to the functioning of theatre as a repository and living museum of cultural memory. All of the characteristics of theatre as a cultural activity contribute to its effectiveness in this project: the variety of physical and abstract material it utilizes, the large amount of this material that has been directly taken over from other, nontheatrical contexts, and its special production conditions, which involve the assembling in a particular place a public, performers, and a preexisting text, along with a substantial collection of other memory-haunted material products.

The particular use to which theatrical recycling is put naturally varies from culture to culture, indeed from production to produc-

165

tion, and often has operated in ways unanticipated by the producing organization itself, but, to the extent that it has been consciously employed, it has normally been utilized in one of three ways. By far the most common is as a kind of reception shortcut. Theatre being a highly concentrated form (occupying only, as Shakespeare notably observed, "the two hours' traffic of our stage"), it has always sought to provide orientation aides in the form of such devices as already known plots, already familiar characters, already experienced situations. A second utilization, somewhat less common but also deeply embedded in the operations of theatre, is of recycling for ironic purposes, when the audience's previous knowledge of or experience with some element of the dramatic production reveals to them an incongruity between the apparent situation onstage and what they know or assume to be the real situation. This is most familiar in the dramatic script, in which, for example, previous familiarity with the structure of tragedy or with known tragic narratives have allowed dramatists ever since Sophocles to utilize this technique. Thus, recycling can be and has been used with equal success either to reinforce or to undermine the drama being presented.

A third, and by no means insignificant, encouragement of recycling in theatre arises from the fact that this art, in order to survive, must attract an ongoing public, a concern particularly important in those eras and cultures in which the theatre has functioned primarily as a commercial enterprise. Here the importance of an audience's previous familiarity with and interest in a particular story or a particular dramatic version of it, a particular character, a particular theatre and its type of offerings, a particular actor, dramatist, director, even on occasion a designer (such as Julie Taymor today), has encouraged the foregrounding of that recycling as a means of attracting that audience. Both the public and often the commercial nature of the theatre, and the fact that it is composed of so many different elements and artists, any of which can potentially appeal to a public's previous positive experience, gives this dynamic a richness and variety that again is not found in any other art form.

Beyond such practical considerations, however, lies the deeper connection of theatre as a human activity with the dynamics of cultural memory itself. The simultaneous attraction to and fear of the dead, the need continually to rehearse and renegotiate the relationship with memory and the past, is nowhere more specifically expressed in human culture than in theatrical performance.

The rise of the romantic theatre, with its emphasis on the organic unity of each work of art, its worship of originality, and its suspicion of the kind of repeated experience offered by the traditional genres, and then of the realistic theatre, with its attempt to create the illusion of a nontheatrical slice of life, discouraged, during most of the nineteenth and twentieth centuries, certain traditional forms of recycling, such as the stock characters, plots, costumes, and scenery of earlier periods. Most of these forms in fact continued but in much more subtle incarnations. Such basic theatrical practices as the recycling of traditional scripts through revivals and the recycling of the bodies of familiar actors in different parts of course continued, but both practices were profoundly influenced by the romantic/realistic aesthetic. Revivals, which had often in the pre-romantic era been quite satisfied with repeating the composition, even the gestures of past interpretations (generations of Hamlets, for example, from Betterton onward, knocked over a chair in the Queen's bedchamber in their surprise at seeing the ghost), now stressed their difference from their absent originals (and by emphasizing difference, as postmodern theorists have noted, have indirectly reinscribed these absent originals). Actors were highly praised for being able to assume apparently totally different characters play to play, and *typecasting* or *always playing the same character* became terms and phrases of critical opprobrium. The modernist movement, although it took many forms, still continued in general to follow the direction encouraged in the theatre by both romanticism and realism, to remove from any work as much extraneous material as possible, in search of some essential quality or expression. Such an orientation is not necessarily theoretically opposed to the process of recycling, but it places strict limits upon it, rejecting all material not involved with what is seen as the essential qualities of the art.

In the late twentieth century the shift in artistic practice and theory that has become known as postmodernism opened the theatre, at least in the hands of more experimental companies and directors, to a new interest in the artistic and reception possibilities of recycling, although, in most cases, with distinctly different goals than those of pre-romantic production and with a much freer reuse of material drawn from a much wider range of sources. In direct opposition to the concept of organic unity that in various ways dominated aesthetic theory and practice from romanticism to modernism, postmodernism delights in the eclectic, in unexpected and innovative juxtapositions of material, creating new relationships, effects, and tensions. The recycling of material in a postmodern theatrical production will therefore be much more varied and surprising than in a more traditional work. The production of a play by Chekhov, Ibsen, or Shakespeare by a postmodern director such as America's Robert Wilson, France's Daniel Mesguich, or Germany's Frank Castorf may well include the most astonishing variety of recycled material: bits and pieces of other plays or literary works, newsreels or other documentary film from a wide range of historical periods, songs and dances from a variety of popular culture sources, quotations from or projected pieces of familiar films and videos, current and past political references, and so on. A German critic, writing recently of the work of Castorf, for example, characterized his theatre as "pulp fiction," manifested most clearly in its "continual play with citations and clichés."[1]

The range of recycled material that can be utilized even (or sometimes especially) in a familiar classic text by such directors is almost unlimited and certainly not limited by the original setting or performance tradition of the text. A great deal of this recycling is of extratheatrical material, but it normally relies almost as heavily as does more traditional theatrical recycling upon an audience's previous acquaintance with the recycled material.

This complex recycling of extratheatrical material has not replaced the traditional varieties of recycling within the genre in these productions; indeed, as a rule, they summon up traditional theatrical ghosts as well, to an extent and with a degree of self-consciousness rarely, if ever, found in the mainstream theatre of conventional realism. Some idea of the complexity and centrality of recycling in the postmodern theatre may be suggested by a brief survey of the importance and variety of its operations in the work of what is probably the best-known contemporary experimental theatre group in the United States, New York's Wooster Group.

We may begin with noting the name of the group, a reference to the physical location on Wooster Street, remote from the midtown world of the commercial New York theatre but in the heart of Soho, a center of the New York experimental art world. The Performing Garage on Wooster Street, where the group creates and displays its productions, most often in the form of ongoing experimentation, has been its home from the beginning and is now in the minds of its audiences inextricably bound up with memories of Wooster Group productions. For older patrons with an interest in experimental theatre, the space is doubly haunted, since it was the home before the Wooster Group of Richard Schechner's Performance Group, which attracted much attention in the late 1960s and early 1970s and whose history forms part of the genealogy of the Wooster Group itself.

The bodies of the actors are the most obvious and the most traditional type of recycling in the Wooster Group, since the company, in the manner of many theatre groups around the world and over the centuries, has remained relatively stable over a period of years. Indeed, one might argue that in this sense the group was ghosted from its very beginning, since several of its key members had also been associated with Schechner's Performance Group. Even members who have left the group to go on to work in other venues, such as Willem Dafoe, return from time to time to perform with their former colleagues, bringing with them ghosts of their non–Wooster Group activities.

One particularly striking and contemporary sort of body ghosting is made possible by a combination of the group's general recycling of material and its duplication of bodies within a single production by the use of video. Very often an actor whose physical body is visible to the audience can also simultaneously be seen by them on a video screen, sometimes synchronically with the visible body and other times, and more directly germane to this study, presented as a recording taped at some other time. A particularly memorable example occurred in *Brace Up!* when the actor Ron Vawter was both seen apparently weeping onstage while a simultaneous video showed him applying the glycerine tears and commenting on their appearance. This is a clear example of the ongoing interest of the group in providing continual illusion-destroying devices that emphasize the constructedness of its performances.[2] After Vawter's death, however, the video of his preparation continued to be shown in productions, functioning now like the ghosts of legend, in the absence of his physical body.

Around and involving these recycled bodies, the company weaves for each production a network of other material, much of it also recycled. David Savran, in the first extended study of the Wooster Group aesthetic, suggested that the group worked with five types of raw material, most of them recycled from previous work of the group or out of the general culture: recordings, previously written dramatic material (most notoriously from Arthur Miller's *The Crucible*, prompting a highly publicized lawsuit against the company by that author), prerecorded film and video, the performance space left over from the last production, and the dance and movement work of the group itself.[3] To this already rich collection of recycled material one should add costumes and properties, since these elements also are often drawn either from previous productions or from recognizable sources elsewhere in the national or global culture. Kate Valk, as the narrator in *Brace Up!* appeared in a man's gray suit drawn from the visual memory of the company itself, because it had previously been worn by Willem Dafoe in one of the group's best-known productions, *Routes 1 & 9*. The kimono-like costume worn by Joan Jonas, on the other hand, evoked external references, as assistant director Marianne Weems has explained: "that's definitely from Noh. But it also is a reference to Yamamoto, the famous fashion store around the corner."[4] The character Masha's kimono, in turn, appeared again in more distinctly Japanese surroundings in the subsequent (1993) production *Fish Story*, a reworking of O'Neill's *Emperor Jones* refracted through influences from traditional and contemporary Japanese performance quotations. In turn, certain physical elements from *Fish Story*, in its various forms, such as a set of highly distinctive portable stools and a blood-red plastic flyswatter, resurfaced in a later revised version of *Brace Up!* that was presented in 1994.

This flow of elements from one production to another is

encouraged by the fluidity of the productions themselves. Most Wooster Group productions are offered as work "in progress." Few of the company's productions are ever considered totally finished (indeed, a 1999 revival of a work from the early days of the group, *North Atlantic* [1984], was advertised as a "rework in progress"), and one production may gradually evolve into another (as happened with the various versions of *Fish Story*), with the natural accompanying flow from one to the other of costumes, properties, effects, and the bodies of the actors. The Wooster Group may in a certain sense be said to have returned to a traditional practice of many theatres, East and West, before the advent of the particularized stages of romanticism and realism, in relying upon a stock of settings, properties, and costumes that are regularly reused in different production contexts.

The practice, however, is now utilized with a very different effect in mind, one much more theatrically self-conscious, in the manner of most postmodernist work. The recycled settings, costumes, and properties of the traditional theatre, to the extent that they consciously registered as recycled in the imaginations of their audiences, served primarily as symbolic references to certain conventionalized and frequently repeated theatrical manifestations: traditional character types, traditional locations of dramatic action, traditional situations and relationships. The recycled physical material in Wooster Group productions evokes not echoes of such generalized theatrical tropes but, rather, echoes of the ongoing operations and experiments of the group itself. The Moscow Art Theatre's reappearing tall lamp with the yellow shade may have become a kind of sign for romantic scenes, but the Wooster Group's blood-red flyswatter conjures up no such conventionalized associations, only memories of its previous appearance in the complex texture of images in an ongoing performance project.

The same thing is true of the physical setting. A single basic setting has appeared in almost every Wooster Group production since *Nyatt School* in 1970. This is a rectangular platform raised twenty inches off the floor and nearly as wide as the theatre interior, with ramps along its right and left sides for entrances and another entrance provided by a stair downstage center. Along the entire length of the upstage edge there is a twenty-four-foot gray institutional reading table placed on the floor, its top even with the stage. When actors are seated there, their backs are against the rear wall of the theatre and their lower bodies hidden, and a row of actors seated and reading in this position has been a recurring image, production to production. Metal tubing frames the stage horizontally and vertically on all sides. In its geometrical, nonrealistic abstraction and its use for many different plays, this repeating space has something in common with the traditional Japanese Noh stage, possibly a conscious echo, since the Noh theatre has provided inspiration for a number of costumes, properties, and movements in various Wooster Group productions.

Unlike the classic Noh stage, however, the Wooster Group setting has been moved to different locations in relationship to the audience over the years. It has most often been used in its original position, after *Nyatt School*, for *North Atlantic* (1984 and 1999), *L.S.D.* (1984), *Frank Dell's The Temptation of St. Anthony* (1987) and *Brace Up!* (1992), but it was also turned back to front for *Point Judith* (1979) and moved against the left wall of the theatre for *Routes 1 & 9* (1981). The Wooster Group designer Jim Clayburgh, in speaking of the set for *Brace Up!* credited this reworking of the same basic setting to the methodology of director Elizabeth LeCompte:

> Since Liz likes to start thinking about something with a set in mind, it's easier for her to start with the set or an idea of the set in place, and the easiest way to get that is to sort of look at what you have in the closet and pull it out, and maybe turn it inside out, which is in fact what we did.[5]

Using "what you have in the closet" has become an important part of the Wooster Group aesthetic, which consciously and regularly practices every sort of recycling so far discussed: the theatre itself, its stage, its texts, the bodies of the actors, their costumes and properties, as well as the modern technological recycling offered by film, sound tape, and, most important, video.

This ubiquitous recycling is one of the most striking features of the productions by the Wooster Group, but it is a practice by no means unique to the group. It is probably the best-known and most visible group in the United States that consciously recycles a wide variety of elements from production to production, though other examples could be cited today from around the world. To the traditional theatrical reasons for recycling, the Wooster Group adds others that are more distinctively characteristic of performance concerns of our own time. As I have observed earlier, the primary motive that led romantic and realistic scenic designers to create totally new costumes, scenery, and properties for every production and encouraged actors in this tradition to seek characters so original that audiences, ideally, were unaware while watching them of previous performances by themselves or anyone else was the motive of creating a stage world of perfect illusion, no element of which should remind the viewer that she was watching a theatrical construction and not a "slice of life."

Among the other effects of recycling today is one in particular that is now much more important than it has been in most other periods. It is that, in conscious opposition to the aesthetic of realism, recycling today often serves to call the attention of the audience to the constructedness of the theatrical performance, to its status as a product not spontaneously appearing but consciously assembled out of preexisting elements, many of them already known to the observers from other, somewhat different contexts. Such a recognition of constructedness is actively pursued both by the engaged theatre descended from Brecht, which has found recycling a useful tool in its project of disrupting the dreamworld of naturalism, and by the playful postmodern theatre, taking joy in the artifice of art. A practice that in the past was sometimes driven by artistic convention, sometimes by audience desire, sometimes by the demands of publicity, sometimes by economic concerns, but always springing from the deeper entanglement of theatre itself with the operations of individual and social memory, has appeared with new power, new prominence, and new motivations today. Once again, both for traditional and for quite contemporary reasons, the recycling of every theatrical element—from the script, through the bodies of the actors, to the whole visual and aural context in which they are received—is being recognized as central to the theatrical experience by some of the most respected and influential of today's companies and their publics.

Notes

Chapter 1

1. Herbert Blau, *The Eye of Prey* (Bloomington: Indiana University Press, 1987), 173.

2. Richard Schechner, *Between Theatre and Anthropology* (Philadelphia: University of Pennsylvania Press, 1985), 36–37.

3. Joseph Roach, *Cities of the Dead* (New York: Columbia University Press, 1996), 3.

4. Elin Diamond, intro., *Writing Performances* (London: Routledge, 1995), 2.

5. Bert O. States, *Dreaming and Storytelling* (Ithaca: Cornell University Press, 1993), 119.

6. Jacques Derrida, "Signature Event Context," *Limited Inc.*, trans. Elisabeth Weber (Evanston: Northwestern University, 1988), 18. The implications of this insight for performance are discussed in my book *Performance: A Critical Introduction* (London: Routledge, 1996), 65–66, 171.

7. Roland Barthes, *Image, Music, Text,* trans. Stephen Heath (New York: Hill and Wang, 1977), 146; italics mine.

8. Hans Robert Jauss, *Toward an Aesthetic of Reception,* trans. Timothy Bahti (Minneapolis: University of Minnesota Press, 1982), 22–23.

9. Stanley Fish, *Is There a Text in This Class?* (Cambridge: Cambridge University Press, 1980), 349.

10. Michael Goldman, *On Drama: Boundaries of Drama, Borders of Self* (Ann Arbor: University of Michigan Press, 2000), 8.

11. Freddie Rokem, *Performing History* (Iowa City: University of Iowa Press, 2000), 6.

12. Ben Brantley, "Verily, He Talks the Talk," *New York Times,* June 16, 2000, E1.

13. Victor Hugo, "Préface à *Cromwell,*" *Oeuvres complètes,* 18 vols. (Paris: Le Club Français du Livre, 1967), 3:63.

14. Hugo, "Note" to *Ruy Blas,* ed. Gerard Sablayrolles (Paris: Larousse, 1965), 299; italics mine.

15. Peter J. Rabinowitz, "'What's Hecuba to Us?' The Audience's Experience of Literary Borrowing," in *The Reader in the Text,* ed. Susan R. Suleiman and Inge Crosman (Princeton: Princeton University Press, 1980), 241.

16. Jonathan Kalb, *The Theater of Heiner Müller* (Cambridge: Cambridge University Press, 1998), 118.

17. Ibid., 159.

18. Ibid., 108.

19. Robert Simonson, "Making Yourself Heard on Broadway," *Playbill* 19:1 (October 31, 2000): 74.

Chapter 2

1. Bharata, *Natyasastra,* trans. and ed. G. K. Bhat (Poona, India: Bhandarkar Oriental Research Institute, 1975), 115.

2. Zeami, *Kadensho, or The Flower Book,* trans. Nobori Asaji (Osaka, Japan: Union Services Co., 1975), 71–72.

3. Zeami, *Sando,* 154, qtd. in Thomas Blenman Hare, *Zeami's Style* (Stanford: Stanford University Press, 1986), 54.

4. Samuel Leiter, *New Kabuki Encyclopedia* (Westport, Conn.: Greenwood Press, 1997), 343.

5. Aristotle, *Poetics,* trans. S. H. Butcher (London: Macmillan, 1932), 37.

6. Ibid., 47.

7. Romain Rolland, *Le Théâtre du peuple* (Paris: Hachette, 1913), 124.

8. Jacques Peletier du Mans, *Art poétique,* bk. 2, chap. 7, cited by Elliott Forsyth, *La Tragédie française de Jodelle à Corneille* (Paris: Nizet, 1962), 98.

9. Christian Biet, *Oedipe en monarchie: tragédie et théorie juridique à l'âge classique* (Paris: Klincksieck, 1994), 12.

10. Ibid., 116.

11. This teleological orientation is found everywhere in Aristotle, but one familiar example is in his comments on the evolution of tragedy, which, he says, "advanced by slow degrees; each new element that showed itself was in turn developed. Having passed through many changes, it found its natural form, and there it stopped" (*Poetics,* 19).

12. Netta Zagagi, *The Comedy of Menander: Convention, Variation and Originality* (Bloomington: Indiana University Press, 1995), 15–16.

13. Comments Valéry, "The character of Faust and of his fearful companion have the right to all reincarnations" (Paul Valéry, *Mon Faust* [Paris: Gallimard, 1946], 7).

14. J. I. Crump, *Chinese Theatre in the Days of Kublai Khan* (Tucson: University of Arizona Press, 1980), 181.

15. Kenneth Burke, *A Grammer of Motives* (New York: Prentice-Hall, 1945), 503–17.

16. D. C. Muecke, *The Compass of Irony* (London: Methuen, 1969), 71.

17. Bert O. States, *Irony and Drama: A Poetics* (Ithaca: Cornell University Press, 1971), xv–xvi.

18. G. G. Sedgewick, *Of Irony: Especially in Drama* (Toronto: University of Toronto Press, 1948), 32–33.

19. Bertrand Evans, *Shakespeare's Comedies* (Oxford: Clarendon Press, 1960). Evans calls this discrepant awareness "Shakespeare's favourite dramatic condition" and uses it as a key to understanding all of the comedies (337).

20. Sophocles, *Oedipus the King,* trans. David Grene, in *The Complete Greek Tragedies,* ed. David Grene and Richmond Lattimore (Chicago: University of Chicago Press, 1991), 1:21.

21. Zeami, *Atsumori,* in *Masterworks of the No Theatre,* ed. and trans. Kenneth Yasuda (Bloomington: Indiana University Press, 1989), 236.

22. Jean Cocteau, *The Infernal Machine,* trans. Albert Bermel, *The Infernal Machine and Other Plays* (Norfolk, Conn.: New Directions, 1963), 17.

23. Edward Fitzball, *Jonathan Bradford; or, The Murder at the Road-Side Inn* (London: Thomas Hailes Lacy, 1833), 12.

24. John J. Winkler and Froma I. Zeitlin, eds. *Nothing to Do with Dionysos?* (Princeton: Princeton University Press, 1990), 2.

25. Marvin Carlson, *The Theatre of the French Revolution* (Ithaca: Cornell University Press, 1966), 132, 199.

26. February 12, 1806, qtd. in Emmy Allard, *Friedrich der Grosse in der Literature Frankreichs* (Halle: Max Niemeyer, 1913), 125.

27. See Marvin Carlson, "Nationalism and the Romantic Drama in Europe," in *Romantic Drama,* vol. 2 in the Romanticism Subseries of the *Comparative History of Literatures in European Languages,* International Comparative Literature Association (Philadelphia: J. Benjamins, 1994), 139–52.

28. Pierre Lanéry, *Bibliographie raisonnée et analytique des ouvrages relatifs à Jeanne d'Arc* (Paris: Librairie Techener, 1894). Jan Joseph Soons adds 142 more titles in his study, *Jeanne d'Arc au Théâtre, 1890–1926* (Purmerend, Neth.: J. Muusses, 1929).

29. Yoshinobu Inoura and Toshio Kawatake, *The Traditional Theatre of Japan* (New York and Tokyo: John Weatherhill, 1981), 158.

30. The various versions are discussed in Lawrence Marsden Price, *Inkle and Yarico Album* (Berkeley: University of California Press, 1937).

31. Aristotle, *Poetics*, 37.

32. Ibid., 11.

33. See Fred W. Householder Jr. "ΠΑΡΩΙΔΙΑ" *Classical Philology* 39:1 (January 1944): 3.

34. An extensive discussion of this aspect of the play may be found in Peter Rau, *Paratragödia, Untersuchungen einer komischen Form des Aristophanes* (Munich: Beck, 1967). See also Margaret A. Rose, *Parody: Ancient, Modern and Post-modern* (Cambridge: Cambridge University Press, 1993), esp. 18–19.

35. Robert F. Willson, *"Their Form Confounded": Studies in the Burlesque Play from Udall to Sheridan* (The Hague: Mouton, 1975), x.

36. Virginia Scott, *The Commedia dell'Arte in Paris, 1644–1697* (Charlottesville: University Press of Virginia, 1990), 288–92.

37. Fritz Brukner, *"Die Alt-Wiener Parodie": Jahrbuch deutscher Bibliophilen und Literaturfreunde* 21–22 (1937): 83–103.

38. Margaret A. Rose, *Parody/Meta-Fiction: An Analysis of Parody as a Critical Mirror to the Writing and Reception of Fiction* (London: Croom Helm, 1979), 28.

39. Linda Hutcheon, *A Theory of Parody* (New York: Methuen, 1985), 101.

40. E. Droz, *Compte-rendu* of Gustave Cohen, *Receuil de farces inédites du XVe siècle, Bibliothèque d'Humanisme et Renaissance* 11 (1949): 301–2.

41. At least this is the commonly accepted current theory, most convincingly argued by Jean Rychner in *Contribution à l'étude des fabliaux*, 2 vols. (Geneva: E. Droz, 1960).

42. Grace Frank, *Medieval French Drama* (London: Oxford University Press, 1960), 246.

43. A survey of what is known of ancient Greek folk and fairy tales may be found in the article *"Märchen"* by Friedrich Aly, in *Paulys Realencyclopädie der Klassischen Altertumswissenschaft*, ed. Georg Wissowa (Stuttgart: Alfred Druckenmuller, 1928) 14:254–81. Theodor Zielinski's *Die Märchenkomödie in Athen* (St. Petersburg: Kranz,1885) argued for a direct connection between Aristophanic plays and this material, a view widely discredited but recently at least partially rehabilitated by Kenneth J. Reckford in *Aristophanes' Old-and-New Comedy* (Chapel Hill: University of North Carolina Press, 1987), esp. 89–92.

44. Katia Canton, *The Fairy Tale Revisited* (New York: Peter Lang, 1994), 20–21.

45. Thelma Niklaus, *Harlequin Phoenix* (London: Bodley Head, 1956), 169.

46. One of the earliest and still one of the most complete collections of information on these figures is V. De Amicis, *La Commedia popolare latine e la commedia dell'arte* (Naples, 1882).

47. Elaine Fantham, "The Earliest Comic Theatre at Rome: Atellan Farce, Comedy and Mime as Antecedents of the *commedia dell'arte*," in

Domenico Pietropaolo, *The Science of Buffoonery: Theory and History of the Commedia dell'Arte* (Toronto: Dovehouse Editions, 1989), 25.

48. Most notably, Pierre Louis Duchartre, in *La Commedia dell'Arte*, trans. T. Weaver (New York: Dover Books, 1966), 24–29.

49. Ibid., 114.

50. Sidney G. Ashmore, ed., *The Comedies of Terence* (New York: Oxford University Press, 1908), 5.

51. Fantham, "Earliest Comic Theatre," 26.

52. Niklaus, *Harlequin,* 54.

53. Traditionally, the type of dramatic action such stock characters appear in has been as predictable as the characters themselves, but in the modern era, with its love of novelty, its playfulness with generic expectations, and its self-consciousness about narrative techniques, this tie between stock characters and stock narrative structures is not nearly so certain. The popular television series "Xena: Warrior Princess" features a stock heroic trio of Xena, her companion Gabrielle, and their comic sidekick Joxer and even certain opponents that reappear in a number of episodes, such as Ares and Callisto, but, although many episodes follow the fairly predictable narrative pattern of the old-fashioned western (the savior figure rides into town, confronts and defeats the forces of evil, then rides on to other adventures), other episodes quite consciously and obviously place the familiar cast of characters in totally alien narratives—in musical comedies, in film noir settings, in classic locked-room detective fictions, and so on.

54. Philip Auslander, *Liveness* (London: Routledge, 1999), 33.

55. Nicholas Rowe, *The Works of Mr. William Shakespeare,* 6 vols. (London: Jacob Tonson, 1709), 1:xiii–ix. Although earlier documentation of this specific command is lacking, William Green, in his study of the play, feels that circumstantial evidence argues in its favor. *Shakespeare's Merry Wives of Windsor* (Princeton: Princeton University Press, 1962), 54.

56. David Grimsted, *Melodrama Unveiled* (Chicago: University of Chicago Press, 1968), 186.

57. Walter J. Meserve, *Heralds of Promise: The Drama of the American People during the Age of Jackson, 1829–1849* (New York: Greenwood Press, 1986), 122–27.

Chapter 3

1. Eric Bentley, *The Life of the Drama* (New York: Atheneum, 1964), 150.

2. Pierre Rémond de Sainte-Albine, *Le Comédien* (Paris, 1749), 228.

3. Earle Ernst, *The Kabuki Theatre* (New York: Oxford University Press, 1956), 200.

4. Arthur Pougin, *Dictionnaire Historique et Pittoresque du Théâtre* (Paris: Firmin-Didot, 1885), 327–28.

5. Ibid., 407.

6. L.-Henry Lecomte, *Napoléon et le monde dramatique* (Paris: H. Daragon, 1912), 148.

7. *Quarterly Review* 17 (1812): 449.

8. Dion Boucicault, qtd. in Dutton Cook, *Hours with the Players,* 2 vols. (London: Chatto and Windus, 1881), 2:89–90.

9. Ibid., 2:90.

10. Joseph Roach, *Cities of the Dead* (New York: Columbia University Press, 1996), 93.

11. Thelma Niklaus, *Harlequin Phoenix* (London: Bodley Head, 1956), 72.

12. Ibid., 76.

13. Roach, *Cities,* 16.

14. Thomas Whitfield Baldwin, *The Organization and Personnel of the Shakespearean Company* (Princeton: Princeton University Press, 1927), 177.

15. Bente A. Videbaek, *The Stage Clown in Shakespeare's Theatre* (Westport, Conn.: Greenwood Press, 1996), 4.

16. Walter J. Meserve, *Heralds of Promise: The Drama of the American People during the Age of Jackson, 1829–1849* (New York: Greenwood Press, 1986), 104–6.

17. See Francis Hodge, *Yankee Theatre* (Austin: University of Texas Press, 1964), esp. 225–36.

18. William Winter, *Life and Art of Edwin Booth* (New York: Macmillan, 1894), 161.

19. Francis Wilson, *Joseph Jefferson* (New York: Charles Scribner's Sons, 1906), 37.

20. Anthony Sher, *The Year of the King* (London: Methuen, 1985), 28–29.

21. H. L. Mencken, *Prejudices: Second Series* (New York: Alfred A. Knopf, 1920), 208–9.

22. Bert O. States, *Great Reckonings in Little Rooms* (Berkeley: University of California Press, 1985), 200.

23. Richard Moody, *Edwin Forrest: First Star of the American Stage* (New York: Alfred A. Knopf, 1960), 104.

24. Alan Schneider, *Entrances* (New York: Viking, 1986), 232–33.

25. Harry Haun, "Good Company," *Playbill* 19:1 (October 31, 2000): 16.

26. Gherardi, *Théâtre Italien,* 6 vols. (Amsterdam: Adrian Braakna, 1701), 1:67.

27. *New York Newsday,* October 11, 1991, 52.

28. Rosette Lamont, "France's National Theatres: Belt-Tightening Time," *Western European Stages* 5:2 (Fall 1993): 14.

29. "The Secret Garden," *New Yorker* 67 (December 9, 1991): 88.

30. *New York Times,* January 23, 2000, "Arts and Leisure," 9.

31. This sort of complicated layering of ghosted acting references, or ghosting within ghosting, is more common than one might suppose. The

already cited *Bon Appetit!* provides another, quite different working out of this process. Joseph Roach offered me yet another from his theatrical memories. Roach recalls that when Olivier played James Tyrone in *Long Day's Journey into Night* (an interpretation I will discuss at the conclusion of this chapter in a different context) he rose at one point to what seemed like seven feet tall (after having shambled around the stage previously, making the audience wonder how he ever could have been a commanding stage personality) to imitate Edwin Booth summoning him (James Tyrone) to compliment him on his acting—Olivier ghosting his younger self, in the role of James Tyrone ghosting his young self, ghosting the memory of Edwin Booth.

32. Roach, *Cities*, 2.

33. Ibid., 78.

34. Lawrence Barrett, *Edwin Forrest* (New York: Benjamin Blom, 1969), 98.

35. Samuel Leiter, *New Kabuki Encyclopedia* (Westport, Conn.: Greenwood Press, 1997), 290–91.

36. John Downes, *Roscius Anglicanus* (1706), ed. Judith Milhous and Robert D. Hume (London: Society for Theatre Research, 1987), 55.

37. See Gerald Eades Bentley, *The Jacobean and Caroline Stage,* 7 vols. (Oxford: Clarendon Press, 1941–68), 2:597.

38. Downes, *Roscius,* 52n.

39. Thomas Davies, *Dramatic Miscellanies,* 3 vols. (London: Thomas Davies, 1784), 3:171–72, qtd. in Roach, *Cities,* 80.

40. Toby Lelyveld, *Shylock on the Stage* (Cleveland: Case Western Reserve University Press, 1960), 23.

41. William W. Appleton, *Charles Macklin: An Actor's Life* (Cambridge: Harvard University Press, 1960), 49–50.

42. Michael Quinn, "Celebrity and the Semiotics of Acting," *New Theatre Quarterly* 4 (1990): 154–61.

43. Jiří Veltrusky, "Contribution to the Semiotics of Acting," in *Sign, System and Meaning: A Quinaquagenary of the Prague Linguistic Circle,* ed. Ladislav Marejka (Ann Arbor: Michigan Slavic Studies, 1976).

44. Quinn, "Celebrity," 155.

45. All Langtry's biographies connect the scandals of her private life to her popularity in the theatre. See, for example, James Brough, *The Prince and the Lily* (London: Hodder and Stoughton, 1975), 278–79.

46. Freddie Rokem, *Performing History* (Iowa City: University of Iowa Press, 2000), 212; italics mine.

47. Qtd. in Robert Baldick, *The Life and Times of Frédérick Lemaître* (London: Hamish Hamilton, 1945), 156.

48. States, *Great Reckonings,* 199–200.

49. Ibid., 190.

50. "Day by Day," *New York Times,* July 18, 1986, B4:6.

51. The complexity of the moment is increased by the fact that Olivier is playing one of the great popular actors of the last century and the father of the playwright. The celebrity/biography of both James O'Neill and Eugene O'Neill adds a further level of ghosting to this powerful moment under the light.

52. Although, as with literary criticism, performative intertextuality may invite audiences to think of parallels they had never noticed before, as here, for example, the themes of female sexuality/chastity, buried guilt, maternity, legitimacy, and the ruthless pursuit of truth at all costs.

Chapter 4

1. Samuel Leiter, *New Kabuki Encyclopedia* (Westport, Conn.: Greenwood Press, 1997), 291.

2. Michal Kobialka, "Spatial Representation: Tadeusz Kantor's Theatre of Found Reality," *Theatre Journal* 44:3 (October 1992): 338–39.

3. Jean Alter, *A Socio-Semiotic Theory of Theatre* (Philadelphia: University of Pennsylvania Press, 1990), 137.

4. Louis James, *Fiction for the Working Man, 1830–1850* (London: Oxford University Press, 1963), 150.

5. Most notably, Clement Greenberg, "After Abstract Expressionism," *Art International,* 6 (1962); and Michael Fried, "Art and Objecthood," in *Minimal Art,* ed. Gregory Battcock (New York: Dutton, 1968).

6. Faubion Bowers, *Japanese Theatre* (New York: Hill and Wang, 1952), 16.

7. A. C. Scott, *The Kabuki Theatre of Japan* (New York: Collier Books, 1966), 139–40.

8. Ibid., 136.

9. Pierre Louis Duchartre, *The Italian Comedy,* trans. Randolph Weaver (New York: Dover, 1966), 164.

10. Tate Wilkinson, *Memoirs* (York: Wilson, Spence and Mawman, 1790), 4:92.

11. Marvin Carlson, "A Theatre Inventory of the First Empire," *Theatre Survey* 9:1 (May 1970): 36–49.

12. From Roderick Rudler, "Scenebilledkunsten i Norge for 100 år siden," in *Kunst og kultur,* 1961, qtd. in Michael Meyer, *Ibsen* (Garden City, N.Y.: Doubleday, 1971), 106n.

13. Luigi Pirandello, *Six Characters in Search of an Author,* trans. Edward Storer, in *Naked Masks,* ed. Eric Bentley (New York: Dutton, 1952), 212–13.

14. Vladimir Nemirovich-Danchenko, *My Life in the Russian Theatre,* trans. John Cournos (New York: Little, Brown, 1936), 90.

15. H. Chance Newton, *Crime and the Drama* (London: St. Paul, 1927), 96.

16. *Chicago Sunday Tribune,* January 13, 1889.

17. *New York Herald,* February 6, 1883.

18. Louise Vigeant, "Clin d'oeil et coup de chapeau: *La Répétition* de Dominic Champagne," *Jeu* 64 (1992): 97.

19. Eduard Genast, *Aus dem Tagebuche eines alten Schauspielers* (Leipzig: Voight and Günther, 1862), 141.

20. Ibid., 140.

Chapter 5

1. Peter Brook, *The Empty Space* (New York: Avon, 1969), 9.

2. Roland Barthes, *Elements of Semiology,* trans. A. Lavers and C. Smith (London: Cape, 1967), 41–42. I have considered this matter with particular reference to theatre in the essay "Semiotics and Non-Semiotics in Performance," *Modern Drama* 28:4 (December 1985), 670–75.

3. Henri Lefebvre, *The Production of Space,* trans. Donald Nicholson-Smith (Oxford: Blackwell, 1991), 93–94.

4. Lefebvre puts it succinctly: "(Social) space is a (social) product." Ibid., 26.

5. Armand Gatti, "Armand Gatti on Time, Place, and the Theatrical Event," trans. Nancy Oakes, *Modern Drama* 25:1 (March 1982): 71–72.

6. See, for example, Dean MacCannell's discussion of the process he calls "site sacralization," in *The Tourist* (New York: Schocken Books, 1976), 44–47; or John Urry on the tourist gaze in his book of the same name (London: Sage, 1990), 3–4.

7. Mark Twain, *Innocents Abroad* (New York: New American Library, 1966), 83.

8. R. T. R. Clark, *Myth and Symbol in Ancient Egypt* (London: Thames and Hudson, 1959), 65.

9. E. D. Hunt, *Holy Land Pilgrimage in the Later Roman Empire, A.D. 312–460* (Oxford: Clarendon Press, 1982), 112–16, 123.

10. Victor Hugo, *Oeuvres complètes,* 18 vols. (Paris: Le Club Français du Livre, 1967), 3:63.

11. Richard Schechner, *Essays on Performance Theory, 1970–1976* (New York: Drama Book Specialists, 1977), 110.

12. Ibid., 119.

13. Marvin Carlson, *Places of Performance: The Semiotics of Theatre Architecture* (Ithaca: Cornell University Press, 1989), esp. 61–97.

14. Schechner, *Essays,* 122.

15. Fay McAuley, *Space in Performance* (Ann Arbor: University of Michigan Press, 1999), 47

16. The most complete study of this intellectual tradition is Frances A. Yates, *The Art of Memory* (New York: Penguin, 1966).

17. Qtd. in ibid., 135.

18. Indeed, Yates has argued (a view not widely accepted by other writers on the Globe) that Fludd's work should be considered a major source in hypothetical reconstructions of that famous building. See Yates, *Theatre of the World* (Chicago: University of Chicago Press, 1969).

19. It is tempting to omit the *almost*. Joseph Roach has suggested the close ties between memory, performance, and the attraction of the dead in "History, Memory, Necrophilia," in *The Ends of Performance,* ed. Peggy Phelan and Jill Lane (New York: New York University Press, 1998), 23–30. Indeed, *The Ghosts of Versailles* might be read in part as a dramatic meditation upon the shift in relationship to the dead during the Age of Enlightenment (the period in which the ghosts of the play actually lived) cited by Roach and theorized by the French historian Pierre Nora. The older system was based upon "environments of memory," sites of active participation through behavioral memory of ghosts and ancestral spirits, a system replaced in the modern era by "places of memory," the artificial sites of the modern production of national and ethnic memories. In these terms the Met's *Ghosts* can be seen as the evocation of an "environment of memory" within a "site of memory," drawing an important part of its power from the tensions between competing memorial systems.

20. June 5, 1992.

21. Marvin Carlson, *The Theatre of the French Revolution* (Ithaca: Cornell University Press, 1966), 285–86.

22. See my essay "Nationalism and the Romantic Drama in Europe," in *Romantic Drama,* ed. Gerald Gillespie (Philadelphia: John Benjamins, 1994), 139–52.

23. Earle Ernst, *The Kabuki Theatre* (New York: Oxford University Press, 1956), 5.

24. Ibid., 40, 44.

25. McAuley, *Space,* 41–42.

26. Schechner, *Essays,* 122.

27. John Lahr, "Hamlet Minceur," *New Yorker,* December 18, 2000, 100.

28. Michael Kimmelman, "Putting Old Wrinkles into a Theater's New Face," *New York Times,* October 25, 1987, 41.

29. "Restoring a Theater to Its Decrepit State," *New York Times,* October 12, 1987, B1.

30. Sophie Cherer, "*L'Indiade,*" *Sept à Paris,* December 21, 1987.

31. The colleague was Scott McMillin, professor of English at Cornell University, who first told me of this experience soon after it happened and provided more details in an email message to me on June 12, 2000.

Chapter 6

1. Ralph Hammerthaler, "Das Kino und sein Double," *Suddeutsche Zeitung,* December 1, 1998.

2. Euridice Arratia, "Island Hopping: The Wooster Group's *Brace Up!*" *TDR* 36:4 (Winter 1992): 130.

3. David Savran, *Breaking the Rules: The Wooster Group* (New York: TCG, 1988), 51.

4. Arratia, "Island Hopping," 125.

5. Quoted in ibid., 124.

References

Allard, Emmy. *Friedrich der Grosse in der Literatur Frankreichs.* Halle: Max Niemeyer, 1913.

Alter, Jean. *A Socio-Semiotic Theory of Theatre.* Philadelphia: University of Pennsylvania Press, 1990.

Aly, Friedrich. "*Märchen.*" In *Paulys Realencyclopädie der Klassischen Altertumswissenschaft,* ed. Georg Wissowa, 14:254–81. Stuttgart: Alfred Druckenmuller, 1928.

Appleton, William W. *Charles Macklin: An Actor's Life.* Cambridge: Harvard University Press, 1960.

Aristotle. *Poetics.* Trans. S. H. Butcher. London: Macmillan, 1932.

Arratia, Euridice. "Island Hopping: The Wooster Group's *Brace Up!*" *TDR* 36:4 (Winter 1992): 121–42.

Ashmore, Sidney G., ed. *The Comedies of Terence.* New York: Oxford University Press, 1908.

Auslander, Philip. *Liveness.* London: Routledge, 1999.

Baldick, Robert. *The Life and Times of Frédérick Lemaître.* London: Hamish Hamilton, 1945.

Baldwin, Thomas Whitfield. *The Organization and Personnel of the Shakespearean Company.* Princeton: Princeton University Press, 1927.

Barrett, Lawrence. *Edwin Forrest.* New York: Benjamin Blom, 1969.

Barthes, Roland. *Elements of Semiology.* Trans. A. Lavers and C. Smith. London: Cape, 1967.

———. *Image, Music, Text.* Trans. Stephen Heath. New York: Hill and Wang, 1977.

Bentley, Eric. *The Life of the Drama*. New York: Atheneum, 1964.

Bentley, Gerald Eades. *The Jacobean and Caroline Stage*, 7 vols. Oxford: Clarendon Press, 1941–68.

Bharata. *Natyasastra*. Ed. and trans. G. K. Bhat. Poona, India: Bhandarkar Oriental Research Institute, 1975.

Biet, Christian. *Oedipe en monarchie: tragédie et théorie juridique à l'âge classique*. Paris: Klincksieck, 1994.

Blau, Herbert. *The Eye of Prey*. Bloomington: Indiana University Press, 1987.

Bowers, Faubion. *Japanese Theatre*. New York: Hill and Wang, 1952.

Brantley, Ben. "Verily, He Talks the Talk." *New York Times,* June 16, 2000.

Brook, Peter. *The Empty Space*. New York: Avon, 1969.

Brukner, Fritz. *"Die Alt-Wiener Parodie." Jahrbuch deutscher Bibliophilen und Literaturfreunde* 21–22 (1937): 83–103.

Burke, Kenneth. *A Grammer of Motives*. New York: Prentice-Hall, 1945.

Canton, Katia. *The Fairy Tale Revisited*. New York: Peter Lang, 1994.

Carlson, Marvin. *Goethe and the Weimar Theatre*. Ithaca: Cornell University Press, 1978.

———. "Nationalism and the Romantic Drama in Europe." In *Romantic Drama*, vol. 2 in the Romanticism Subseries of the *Comparative History of Literatures in European Languages*. International Comparative Literature Association. Philadelphia: J. Benjamins, 1994.

———. *Performance: A Critical Introduction*. London: Routledge, 1996.

———. *Places of Performance: The Semiotics of Theatre Architecture*. Ithaca: Cornell University Press, 1989.

———. "Semiotics and Non-Semiotics in Performance." *Modern Drama* 28:4 (December 1985): 670–75.

———. "A Theatre Inventory of the First Empire." *Theatre Survey* 9:1 (May 1970): 36–49.

———. *The Theatre of the French Revolution*. Ithaca: Cornell University Press, 1966.

Cherer, Sophie. "*L'Indiade.*" *Sept à Paris,* December 21, 1987.

Clark, R. T. R. *Myth and Symbol in Ancient Egypt*. London: Thames and Hudson, 1959.

Cocteau, Jean. *The Infernal Machine*. Trans. Albert Bermel. In *The Infernal Machine and Other Plays*. Norfolk, Conn.: New Directions, 1963.

Cook, Dutton. *Hours with the Players*, 2 vols. London: Chatto and Windus, 1881.

Crump, J. I. *Chinese Theatre in the Days of Kublai Khan*. Tucson: University of Arizona Press, 1980.

De Amicis, V. *La commedia popolare latine e la commedia dell'arte*. Naples, 1882.

Derrida, Jacques. *Limited Inc*. Evanston: Northwestern University Press, 1988.

Diamond, Elin. Introduction. *Writing Performances*. London: Routledge, 1995.

Downes, John. *Roscius Anglicanus* (1706). Ed. Judith Milhous and Robert D. Hume. London: Society for Theatre Research, 1987.

Droz, E. *Compte-rendu* of Gustave Cohen, *Receuil de farces inédites du XVe siècle. Bibliothèque d'Humanisme et Renaissance* 11 (1949): 301–2.

Duchartre, Pierre Louis. *La Commedia dell'Arte*. Trans. T. Weaver. New York: Dover Books, 1966.

Ernst, Earle. *The Kabuki Theatre*. New York: Oxford University Press, 1956.

Evans, Bertrand. *Shakespeare's Comedies*. Oxford: Clarendon Press, 1960.

Fantham, Elaine. "The Earliest Comic Theatre at Rome: Atellan Farce, Comedy and Mime as Antecedents of the *commedia dell'arte*." In Domenico Pietropaolo, *The Science of Buffoonery: Theory and History of the Commedia dell'Arte*. Toronto: Dovehouse Editions, 1989.

Fish, Stanley. *Is There a Text in This Class?* Cambridge: Cambridge University, 1980.

Fitzball, Edward. *Jonathan Bradford; or, The Murder at the Road-Side Inn*. London: Thomas Hailes Lacy, 1833.

Forsyth, Elliott. *La Tragédie française de Jodelle à Corneille*. Paris: Nizet, 1962.

Frank, Grace. *Medieval French Drama*. London: Oxford University Press, 1960.

Fried, Michael. "Art and Objecthood." In *Minimal Art*, ed. Gregory Battcock. New York: Dutton, 1968.

Gatti, Armand. "Armand Gatti on Time, Place, and the Theatrical Event." Trans. Nancy Oakes. *Modern Drama* 25:1 (March 1982): 69–81.

Genast, Eduard. *Aus dem Tagebuche eines alten Schauspielers*. Leipzig: Voight and Günther, 1862.

Gherardi. *Théâtre Italien*, 6 vols. Amsterdam: Adrian Braakna, 1701.

Goldman, Michael. *On Drama: Boundaries of Drama, Borders of Self*. Ann Arbor: University of Michigan Press, 2000.

Green, William. *Shakespeare's Merry Wives of Windsor*. Princeton: Princeton University Press, 1962.

Greenberg, Clement. "After Abstract Expressionism," *Art International* 6 (1962): 30–35.

Grimsted, David. *Melodrama Unveiled*. Chicago: University of Chicago Press, 1968.

Hammerthaler, Ralph. "Das Kino und sein Double." *Suddeutsche Zeitung*, December 1, 1998.

Hare, Thomas Blenman. *Zeami's Style*. Stanford: Stanford University Press, 1986.

Haun, Harry. "Good Company." *Playbill* 19:1 (October 31, 2000): 16.

Hodge, Francis. *Yankee Theatre*. Austin: University of Texas Press, 1964.

Householder, Fred W., Jr. "ΠΑΡΩΙΔΙΑ." *Classical Philology* 39:1 (January 1944): 1–9.

Hugo, Victor. "Note" to *Ruy Blas*. Ed. Gerard Sablayrolles. Paris: Larousse, 1965.

————. "Préface à *Cromwell*," *Oeuvres complètes*. 18 vols. Paris: Le Club Français du Livre, 1967.

Hunt, E. D. *Holy Land Pilgrimage in the Later Roman Empire, A.D. 312–460.* Oxford: Clarendon Press, 1982.

Hutcheon, Linda. *A Theory of Parody.* New York: Methuen, 1985.

Inoura, Yoshinobu, and Toshio Kawatake, *The Traditional Theatre of Japan.* New York and Tokyo: John Weatherhill, 1981.

James, Louis. *Fiction for the Working Man, 1830–1850.* London: Oxford University Press, 1963.

Jauss, Hans Robert. *Toward an Aesthetic of Reception.* Trans. Timothy Bahti. Minneapolis: University of Minnesota Press, 1982.

Kalb, Jonathan. *The Theater of Heiner Müller.* Cambridge: Cambridge University Press, 1998.

Kimmelman, Michael. "Putting Old Wrinkles into a Theater's New Face." *New York Times,* October 25, 1987, 41.

Kobialka, Michal. "Spatial Representation: Tadeusz Kantor's Theatre of Found Reality." *Theatre Journal* 44:3 (October 1992): 329–56.

Lahr, John. "Hamlet Minceur." *New Yorker,* December 18, 2000, 100–101.

Lamont, Rosette. "France's National Theatres: Belt-Tightening Time," *Western European Stages* 5:2 (Fall 1993): 13–20.

Lanéry, Pierre. *Bibliographie raisonnée et analytique des ouvrages relatifs à Jeanne d'Arc.* Paris: Librairie Techener, 1894.

Lecomte, L.-Henry. *Napoléon et le monde dramatique.* Paris: H. Daragon, 1912.

Lefebvre, Henri. *The Production of Space.* Trans. Donald Nicholson-Smith. Oxford: Blackwell, 1991.

Leiter, Samuel. *New Kabuki Encyclopedia.* Westport, Conn.: Greenwood Press, 1997.

Lelyveld, Toby. *Shylock on the Stage.* Cleveland: Case Western Reserve University Press, 1960.

MacCannell, Dean. *The Tourist.* New York: Schocken Books, 1976.

McAuley, Fay. *Space in Performance.* Ann Arbor: University of Michigan Press, 1999.

Mencken, H. L. *Prejudices: Second Series.* New York: Alfred A. Knopf, 1920.

Meserve, Walter J. *Heralds of Promise: The Drama of the American People during the Age of Jackson, 1829–1849.* Westport, Conn.: Greenwood Press, 1986.

Meyer, Michael. *Ibsen.* Garden City, N.Y.: Doubleday, 1971.

Muecke, D. C. *The Compass of Irony.* London: Methuen, 1969.

Nemirovich-Danchenko, Vladimir. *My Life in the Russian Theatre.* Trans. John Cournos. New York: Little, Brown, 1936.

Newton, Chance. *Crime and the Drama.* London: St. Paul, 1927.

Niklaus, Thelma. *Harlequin Phoenix.* London: Bodley Head, 1956.

Pirandello, Luigi. *Six Characters in Search of an Author.* Trans. Edward Storer. In *Naked Masks,* ed. Eric Bentley. New York: Dutton, 1952.

Pougin, Arthur. *Dictionnaire historique et pittoresque du théâtre.* Paris: Firmin-Didot, 1885.

Price, Lawrence Marsden. *Inkle and Yarico Album.* Berkeley: University of California Press, 1937.

Quinn, Michael. "Celebrity and the Semiotics of Acting," *New Theatre Quarterly* 4 (1990): 154–61.

Rabinowitz, Peter J. "'What's Hecuba to Us?' The Audience's Experience of Literary Borrowing." In *The Reader in the Text,* ed. Susan R. Suleiman and Inge Crosman. Princeton: Princeton University Press, 1980.

Rau, Peter. *Paratragödia, Untersuchungen einer komischen Form des Aristophanes.* Munich: Beck, 1967.

Reckford, Kenneth J. *Aristophanes' Old-and-New Comedy.* Chapel Hill: University of North Carolina Press, 1987.

Rémond de Sainte-Albine, Pierre. *Le Comédien.* Paris, 1749.

Roach, Joseph. *Cities of the Dead.* New York: Columbia University Press, 1996.

———. "History, Memory, Necrophilia." In *The Ends of Performance,* ed. Peggy Phelan and Jill Lane. New York: New York University Press, 1998.

Rokem, Freddie. *Performing History.* Iowa City: University of Iowa Press, 2000.

Rolland, Romain. *Le Théâtre du peuple.* Paris: Hachette, 1913.

Rose, Margaret A. *Parody, Ancient, Modern and Post-modern.* Cambridge: Cambridge University Press, 1993.

———. *Parody/Meta-Fiction: An Analysis of Parody as a Critical Mirror to the Writing and Reception of Fiction.* London: Croom Helm, 1979.

Rowe, Nicholas. *The Works of Mr. William Shakespeare.* 6 vols. London: Jacob Tonson, 1709.

Rychner, Jean. *Contribution à l'étude des fabliaux.* 2 vols. Geneva, E. Droz, 1960.

Savran, David. *Breaking the Rules: The Wooster Group.* New York: TCG, 1988.

Schechner, Richard. *Between Theatre and Anthropology.* Philadelphia: University of Pennsylvania Press, 1985.

———. *Essays on Performance Theory, 1970–1976.* New York: Drama Book Specialists, 1977.

Schneider, Alan. *Entrances.* New York: Viking, 1986.

Scott, A. C. *The Kabuki Theatre of Japan.* New York: Collier Books, 1966.

Scott, Virginia. *The Commedia dell'Arte in Paris, 1644–1697.* Charlottesville: University Press of Virginia, 1990.

Sedgewick, G. G. *Of Irony: Especially in Drama.* Toronto: University of Toronto Press, 1948.

Simonson, Robert. "Making Yourself Heard on Broadway." *Playbill* 19:1 (October 31, 2000).

Soons, Jan Joseph. *Jeanne d'Arc au Théâtre, 1890–1926.* Purmerend, Neth.: J. Muusses, 1929.

Sophocles. *Oedipus the King.* Trans. David Grene. In *The Complete Greek Tragedies,* ed. David Grene and Richmond Lattimore. 2 vol. Chicago: University of Chicago Press, 1991.

States, Bert O. *Dreaming and Storytelling.* Ithaca: Cornell University Press, 1993.

———. *Great Reckonings in Little Rooms.* Berkeley: University of California Press, 1985.

———. *Irony and Drama: A Poetics.* Ithaca: Cornell University Press, 1971.

Twain, Mark. *Innocents Abroad.* New York: New American Library, 1966.

Urry, John. *The Tourist Gaze.* London: Sage, 1990.

Valéry, Paul. *Mon Faust.* Paris: Gallimard, 1946.

Veltrusky, Jiří. "Contribution to the Semiotics of Acting." In *Sign, System and Meaning: A Quinaquagenary of the Prague Linguistic Circle,* ed. Ladislav Marejka. Ann Arbor: Michigan Slavic Studies, 1976.

Videbaek, Bente A. *The Stage Clown in Shakespeare's Theatre.* Westport, Conn.: Greenwood Press, 1996.

Vigeant, Louise. "Clin d'oeil et coup de chapeau: *La Répétition* de Dominic Champagne." *Jeu* 64 (1992): 95–100.

Wilkinson, Tate. *Memoires.* York: Wilson, Spence and Mawman, 1790.

Willson, Robert F. *"Their Form Confounded": Studies in the Burlesque Play from Udall to Sheridan.* The Hague: Mouton, 1975.

Wilson, Francis. *Joseph Jefferson.* New York: Charles Scribner's Sons, 1906.

Winkler, John J., and Froma I. Zeitlin, eds. *Nothing to Do with Dionysos?* Princeton: Princeton University Press, 1990.

Winter, William. *Life and Art of Edwin Booth.* New York: Macmillan, 1894.

Yates, Frances A. *The Art of Memory.* New York: Penguin, 1966.

———. *Theatre of the World.* Chicago: University of Chicago Press, 1969.

Zagagi, Netta. *The Comedy of Menander: Convention, Variation and Originality.* Bloomington: Indiana University Press, 1995.

Zeami. *Atsumori,* in *Masterworks of the No Theatre.* Ed. and trans. Kenneth Yasuda. Bloomington: Indiana University Press, 1989.

———. *Kadensho, or The Flower Book.* Trans. Nobori Asaji. Osaka, Japan: Union Services Co., 1975.

Zielinski, Theodor. *Die Märchenkomödie in Athen.* St. Petersburg: Kranz, 1885.

Index

Abbot, Bud, 93
acting, 8–10, 13–15, 50, 52–95
Adam, John-Louis, 38
Ah Q (Jourdheuil), 130
"All in the Family," 72
Alter, Jean, 106
Amphitryon 38 (Giraudoux), 36
Andreini, Francesco, 60
Andrews, Julie, 164
Antigone (Anouilh), 25
Arabian Nights, 21, 43
Arden of Feversham, 34
Aristophanes, 36, 41, 71
Aristotle, 18–19, 21–23, 25, 35–36, 176
Arlequin Anée, 48
Arlequin Deucalion, 48
Arlequin Mercure Galant, 48
Arlequin Phaéton, 48
Armin, Robert, 61–62
Arsenic and Old Lace (Kesselring), 91
Artaud, Antonin, 14
Aspects of Love (Webber), 163
As You Like It (Shakespeare), 87
Atellan farce, 45–46
Atrides, Les (Mnouchkine), 106

Atsumori (Zeami), 30
Auber, Daniel, 38
Aude, Joseph, 50
Auslander, Philip, 47
Austin, J. L., 4

Baldwin, Thomas, 61
Bancroft, Squire, 153
Barrett, Lawrence, 81–82
Barry, Spranger, 101
Barrymore, John, 80
Barthes, Roland, 4–5, 133
Beaumarchais, Pierre-Augustin
    Caron de, 49–50, 109, 112, 116–17
Beauty and the Beast (Ashman), 44
Beggar's Opera, The (Gay), 115
Beier, Karen, 107
Benjamin, Walter, 14
Bentley, Eric, 52–53, 131–32
Bérénice (Racine), 38
Bergson, Henri, 90
Bernhardt, Sarah, 65, 68, 80, 92, 101
Best Man, The (Vidal), 15
Betterton, Thomas, 58, 83, 167
Biancolelli, 60
Biet, Christian, 24

Bizet, Georges, 115
Blau, Herbert, 1, 78
Blumenfeld, Alan, 77
Bois, Curt, 87–88
Bon Appetit! (Stapleton), 71–72
Bondy, Luc, 101
Booth, Edwin, 65, 80, 181
Boucicault, Dion, 56
Bowers, Faubion, 120
Boy Friend, The (Wilson), 164
Brace Up! (Wooster Group), 169–70, 172
Brando, Marlon, 67, 77
Brantley, Ben, 9–10
Brecht, Bertolt, 80, 86, 107, 173
Breth, Andrea, 102–3
Breuer, Lee, 104
Britannicus (Racine), 108–9
Brook, Peter, 103, 106–7, 132–33, 158–60
Bunraku, 20, 35, 106, 148
Burke, Kenneth, 28
burlesque drama, 37

Cabaret (Kander and Ebb), 67
Caesar, Sid, 77
Camille (Dumas), 65
Camillo, Giulio, 142
Carzis, Evan, 159
Casimir and Caroline (Horváth), 130
Castorf, Frank, 101, 168
Cats (Webber), 44
Cesares, Maria, 73
Champmesle, Mlle., 72
Chanfrau, Francis S., 64
Chantecler (Rostand), 68
Chekhov, Anton, 102–3, 168
Chereau, Patrice, 103, 162
Cherry Orchard, The (Chekhov), 102, 107
Chikamatsu, 34–35
Child, Julia, 71–72
Chinese classical drama, 28
Cid, Le (Corneille), 38, 72
Cintra, Luís Miguel, 129
Clayburgh, Jim, 172

Cobb, Lee J., 67
Cody, William F., 88, 125
Cohen, Gustav, 40
comedy, 39–41
commedia dell'arte, 45–48, 53–54, 60–61, 63, 93, 109–10, 121–22
Contact (Stroman and Weidman), 114
Contes du temps passé de ma mère Oie (Perrault), 41, 43
Cook, Dutton, 56
Coquelin, Constant, 65, 68
Coriolanus (Shakespeare), 65
Cosa rara, Una (Martín), 116
Costello, Lou, 93
costume, 120–22, 126–29
Crébillon, Claude-Prosper Jolyot de, 27
Critic, The (Sheridan), 37
Cromwell (Hugo), 137
Cronyn, Hume, 93–94
Crowbar (Wellman), 2
Crucible, The (Miller), 170
Crump, D. J., 28
cummings, e. e., 14
curtain calls, 90–92
Cyrano de Bergerac (Rostand), 65, 68, 109–10

Dafoe, Willem, 169–70
Dahlstrom, Robert, 126
Danjuro IX, Ichikawa, 82
D'Annunzio, Gabriele, 68
Dark Secret, The, 125
Davies, Thomas, 83
Dead Class, The (Kantor), 105
Death of a Salesman (Miller), 67
Death of Marat, The (David), 112–13
Debureau, 89
Derrida, Jacques, 4, 14, 17
Diamond, Elin, 2
Dimanche à la Grande Jatte, Un (Seurat), 113
Dinner Party, The (Simon), 71
Doggett, Thomas, 84
Doll House, A (Ibsen), 100

Don Giovanni (Mozart), 116–17
Don Juan, 34
Don Quixote (Cervantes), 37
Dorval, Marie, 13
Downes, John, 83
Doyle, Arthur Conan, 64
Droz, Eugènie, 40
Ducharte, Pierre, 122
Due litiganti, I (Sarti), 116
Duse, Eleanora, 68, 92, 101

Each in His Own Role (Pirandello),
   123
Egeria, 136
Eliot, T. S., 14
Elizabeth, Queen of England, 49
Emperor Jones, The (O'Neill), 170
Ernst, Earl, 148
Euripides, 15, 82
Evans, Bertrand, 29
Experiment with an Air Pump, An
   (Stephenson), 114

Falstaff, 49, 61
Fantasticks, The (Schmidt and Jones),
   98
Fantham, Elaine, 45
Faust, 34, 78, 115
Faust (Goethe), 108
F@ust, Version 3.0, 34
féeries, 41, 43
Figaro, 49–50
Fish Story (Wooster Group), 170–71
Fludd, Robert, 142, 184
folk and fairy plays, 42–43, 48, 178
Fontanne, Lynne, 93–94
Forbidden Broadway (Alessandri), 38
Foreman, Richard, 104, 155
Forrest, Edwin, 65, 68, 101
Foscari, 33
Fourposter, The (deHartog), 94
Frank, Grace, 40
Frank Dell's The Temptation of St.
   Anthony (Wooster Group), 172
Frederick the Great, 33
Freud, Sigmund, 25

Frogs, The (Aristophanes), 36–37
Funeral March (Chopin), 118
Fura dels Baus, 34
Fushikaden (Zeami), 19

Gamblers, The, 125
Garrick, David, 13, 65, 101
Gatti, Armand, 134
Genast, Eduard, 128
"General Hospital," 75–76
Gherardi, 71–72
ghosting, 7–8, 58–63, 66, 71, 75,
   79–81, 85, 91, 94–105, 109–19,
   133–36, 138–39, 142–45, 148, 152,
   159–64, 181
Ghosts (Ibsen), 1
Ghosts of Versailles, The (Hoffman and
   Corigliano), 116–17, 144–45, 184
Gielgud, John, 91–92, 94
Gillette, William, 64
"Gilligan's Island," 47
Gin Game, The (Coburn), 94
Gladiator, The (Bird), 68
Gluck, Christoph Willibald, 38
Goethe, Johann Wolfgang von, 38,
   61, 127–28
Goldman, Michael, 6
Goldoni, Carlo, 109
Goldsmith, Oliver, 43
Good Soldier Schweik, The (Hašek),
   126
Grammer, Kelsey, 9–10
Granville-Barker, Harley, 101
Gray, Spaulding, 14–15, 47, 73
Grease (Jacobs and Casey), 70
Greek New Comedy, 25, 35, 45–47
Greek tragedy, 22–23
Grigolli, Olivia, 110
Grillparzer, Franz, 38
Grotowski, Jerzy, 107
Guys and Dolls (Loesser, Swerling,
   Burrows), 77

Hamlet (Shakespeare), 4, 7, 65, 67,
   78–81, 83, 90, 95, 99, 101, 108–9,
   167

Hamletmachine (Müller), 14
Hardy, Oliver, 93
Harlani, 38
Harlequin, 48–50
Harlequin and Cinderella, 48
Harlequin and Guy Fawkes, 48
Harlequin and Jack the Giant Killer, 48
Harlequin and William Tell, 48
Harlequin Dr. Faustus, The, 48
*Harlequin Jack Horner and the
  Enchanted Pie,* 48
Harlequin Neptune, 48
Hart, Charles, 83
Hartmann, Matthias, 118–19
Harvey (Chase), 91
Hebbel, Friedrich, 38
Hegemon the Phasian, 36
Henry IV (Shakespeare), 49
Henry V (Shakespeare), 105
Henry VIII (Shakespeare), 83
Hermann, 33
Hernani (Hugo), 38
Hill, George, 63–64
Hoffmann, Philip Seymour, 71
Hölderlein, Friedrich, 14
Hollow Crown, The (Shakespeare),
  129
Homer, 36
Horace, 22, 41
horizon of expectations, 5–6
Hotel Angst (Marthaler), 110, 118
Hotel "Zur schönen Aussicht"
  (Horváth), 110
Hugo, Victor, 12–13, 137–38
Hume, Robert, 83
Hutcheon, Linda, 39

Ibsen, Henrik, 1, 61, 168
Indiade, L' (Cixous), 106, 161
Infernal Machine, The (Cocteau), 31
Inoura, Yoshinobu, 34
intertextuality, 4–5, 8, 17, 19, 72, 74,
  77, 95
Into the Dark (Fornes), 113
Into the Woods (Sondheim), 43–44
Iphigenia in Aulis (Euripides), 105

irony, 28–29
Irving, Henry, 65
I Shall Never Return (Kantor), 105
Italiana in Algeri (Rossini), 116

Jauss, Hans Robert, 5
Jefferson, Joseph, 65
Jekyll and Hyde (Bricusse and Wild-
  horn), 44, 75–76
Jesse James, the Bandit King, 125
Jeu de la feuillée (Adam de la Halle),
  41, 88
jidaimono, 20
Joan of Arc, 34, 101
John Gabriel Borkman (Ibsen), 101
Jonas, Joan, 170
Jonathan Bradford (Fitzball), 32
joruri, 20
Julius Caesar (Shakespeare), 77, 101

Kabuki, 20–21, 35, 54, 59, 82–83,
  98–99, 105–6, 120–21, 148–50
Kalb, Jonathan, 14
Kantor, Tadeusz, 104–5, 107–8, 129
Kathakali, 106
Kawatake, Toshio, 34
Kean, Edmund, 13, 65
Kemble, John Philip, 65
Kemp, Will, 61–62
Kimmerman, Michael, 159
Kinder- und Hausmärchen (Grimm),
  42
King Lear (Shakespeare), 62, 65, 108
Kirms, Franz, 128
Kiss Me, Kate (Porter), 44
Kleist, Heinrich von, 38
Kobialka, Michal, 104
Koshiro V, Matsumoto, 99
Kyogen, 35

La Brie, Mlle., 111
La Grange, Charles Varlet, 111
Lahr, Bert, 69
Lahr, John, 159
Lamont, Rosette, 73
Lane, Nathan, 77

Langtry, Lillie, 87
Laocoon (Lessing), 114
Laughter on the 23rd Floor (Simon), 76–77
Laurel, Stan, 93
Lavelli, Jorge, 73
Lawless, Lucy, 70, 75
LeCompte, Elizabeth, 172
Lefebvre, Henri, 133
Leiter, Samuel, 20–21, 82
Lekain, 13
Lelyveld, Toby, 84
Lemaître, Frédérick, 13, 64
Let the Artists Die (Kantor), 105
Libussa, 33
Lichtenstein, Harvey, 159
Life of the Taiko, 20
Lindsay, John, 92
Lion King, The (John), 44
Locatelli, 60
London Merchant, The (Lillo), 35
Long Day's Journey into Night (O'Neill), 92–93, 181
Ludlam, Charles, 155
Lugné-Poë, Aurélien-Marie, 158
Lunt, Alfred, 93–94

Macbeth (Shakespeare), 9–10, 65, 123
MacCannell, Dean, 135
Macklin, Charles, 83–85, 87
Macready, William, 65, 101
Madame Butterfly (Puccini), 115
Madonna, 89
Magic Flute, The (Mozart), 38
Mahabharata, 21
Mahabharata, The (Carriere), 107
Malkovich, John, 69
Mamet, David, 69
Mantegna, Joe, 69
Marat/Sade (Weiss), 112
Marble, Dan, 63–64
Maria Martin or The Red Barn, 35
Maria Stuart (Schiller), 123, 128
Marie Tudor (Hugo), 108
Marivaux, Pierre, 108–9

Marriage of Figaro, The (Beaumarchais), 117
Mars, Mlle., 57
Marshall, Herbert, 73
Martin, Mary, 67
Marx brothers, 93
Marx, Karl, 14
McAuley, Gay, 141, 153–54
McGillin, Howard, 74–75
Medeamaterial (Müller), 25
medieval drama, 33, 40–41
Mein Kampf (Tabori), 73
Meisl, Karl, 38
melodrama, 42
"Melrose Place," 75–76
Menander, 25, 27, 46
Mencken, H. L., 67
Merchant of Venice, The (Shakespeare), 83–85
Mère coupable, La (Beaumarchais), 50
Merry Wives of Windsor, The (Shakespeare), 49
Mesguich, Daniel, 2, 80, 95, 108–10, 127, 168
Meyerhold, Vsevelod, 80, 102–3, 107
Midsummer Night's Dream, A (Shakespeare), 107
Milhous, Judith, 83
Minute Waltz (Chopin), 119
Miser, The (Molière), 111
Misérables, Les (Boubil and Schonberg), 44
Mitterand, François, 162
Mnouchkine, Ariane, 105–6, 158, 160–62
Molière, 47, 61, 78, 109, 111, 123, 128, 155
Mon Faust (Valéry), 27, 78
Monteverdi, Claudio, 115
Montigny, Adolphe, 153
Moody, Richard, 68
Mose the fireman, 50, 64–65
Mosher, Greg, 73
Mother Courage (Brecht), 127
Mourning Becomes Electra (O'Neill), 25

Mousetrap, The (Christie), 98
Mozart, Wolfgang Amadeus, 115–16
Muecke, D. C., 28
Müller, Heiner, 14
musical comedy, 44
Musset, Alfred de, 40

Napoleon, 55, 146, 153–54
Nataka, 19
Natyasastra (Bharata), 18–19, 21–22, 35, 54
Nemirovich-Danchenko, Vladimir, 124–26, 128
Niklaus, Thelma, 43, 60
N.I.Ni, 38
Noh drama, 3, 18–21, 23, 30, 35, 57, 59, 98, 119–20, 142, 148, 172
Nordey, Stanislas, 162
Northanger Abbey (Austin), 37
North Atlantic (Wooster Group), 171–72
Nozze di Figaro, Le (Mozart), 116
Nyatt School (Wooster Group), 171–72

Oblensky, Chloé, 158–60
Oedipe (Voltaire), 26
Oedipus (Sophocles), 20–22, 24–26, 29–31
Old Wives Tale, The (Peele), 41
Olivier, Laurence, 66–67, 92–93, 181
O'Neill, Eugene, 182
O'Neill, James, 65, 182
opera, 115–17, 144–46
Orbach, Jerry, 98
Oreste (Voltaire), 26
Oresteia (Aeschylus), 106, 126
Orphée (Cocteau), 73
Orphée aux enfers (Offenbach), 115
Orpheus, 115
Osiris, 136
Othello (Shakespeare), 65, 67
Our Town (Wilder), 15, 73

pantomime, British, 42–43
parody, 36–40, 71–72

Patinkin, Mandy, 74–75
Peletier du Mans, Jacques, 24
Perinet, Joachim, 38
Perrault, Charles, 42
Phantom of the Opera (Webber), 44
Philip Glass Buys a Loaf of Bread (Ives), 107
Pietà (Michelangelo), 113
Pirandello, Luigi, 124
Pixérécourt, Guilbert Charles de, 38
Plautus, 46
Poetics (Aristotle), 18–19, 22
Point Judith (Wooster Group), 172
Post, C. R., 25–26
postmodernism, 11, 13–15
Pougin, Arthur, 55
Psyche (Corneille), 41
Puccini, Giacomo, 115

Quarrel of the Ancients and the Moderns, 24
Quinn, Michael, 85–89, 133

Rabinowitz, Peter, 14
Ragtime (McNally, Flaherty, Arens), 44
Ramayana, 21
Real Inspector Hound, The (Stoppard), 37
realism, 12–13, 18
Redgrave, Michael, 91
Rehearsal, The (Villers), 37
Reilly, John C., 71
Reis, Cristina, 129
Rent (Larson), 44, 98
Rent Day, The (Jerrold), 112–13
Répétition, La (Champagne), 127
Richard II (Shakespeare), 106
Richard III (Shakespeare), 66, 108
Richardson, Ralph, 91–92
Rinaldo (Handel), 115
Rival Queens, The (Lee), 83
Roach, Joseph, 2, 58, 79, 81, 83, 181
Rokem, Freddie, 7, 87
Rolland, Romain, 23
Roman comedy, 46

romanticism, 11–13, 18, 24, 42
Romeo and Juliet (Shakespeare), 95, 108–9
Rome sauvée (Voltaire), 26
Ronconi, Luca, 103
Rose, Margaret, 39
Rothstein, Edward, 145
Routes 1 & 9 (Wooster Group), 73, 170, 172
Rowe, Nicholas, 49
Rühmann, Heinz, 87–88

Sainte-Albine, Pierre Rémond de, 53
Salvini, Tommaso, 65
Sando (Zeami), 19–20
Sanokama I, Ichinatsu, 54
Sartre, Jean-Paul, 14
Savran, David, 170
Saxe-Meiningen, George II, Duke of, 101, 103–4
Scarlet Pimpernel, The (Knighton and Wildhorn), 44
scenery, 12–13, 122–27
Schechner, Richard, 1, 139–40, 156, 169
Schikaneder, Emanuel, 38
Schiller, Friedrich, 38, 61, 78, 128
Schneider, Alan, 69
Schreiber, Liev, 80
Scott, A. C., 121
Seagull, The (Chekhov), 102–3, 108–9, 127
Searle, John R., 4
Secret Garden, The (Simon and Norman), 74–75
Sedgewick, G. G., 29
"Seinfeld, " 47
semiotics, 133
Semiramis (Voltaire), 26
Seneca, 24
Serban, Andrei, 80, 99
sewamono, 20
Shakespeare, William, 14, 38, 61–62, 66, 77, 151, 157, 168
Shepard, Sam, 69
Sher, Anthony, 66

Sihanouk (Cixous), 106
Simonson, Robert, 14
site-specific theatre, 134–38
Six Characters in Search of an Author (Pirandello), 123–24
Smith, Joseph, 137
Sophocles, 24, 166
South Pacific (Rodgers and Hammerstein), 67
Speed-the-Plow (Mamet), 89
stand-ins, 76–77
Stanislavsky, Konstantin, 80, 102–3, 107
Stapleton, Jean, 71–72, 75
States, Bert, 3, 28, 67, 78, 90–91
Steele, Richard, 35
Stein, Peter, 102–3
Sting, 89
Storming of the Winter Palace, The (Evreinov), 138
Streetcar Named Desire, A (Williams), 67, 77
Strehler, Giogio, 103, 108
Sunday in the Park with George (Sondheim), 113
surrogation, 79–80
Swan, The (Egloff), 43
Sweeney Todd (Sondheim), 44
Swimming to Cambodia (Gray), 73
Swing, The (Fragonard), 114

tableau vivant, 112–13
Tales of Heike, 14, 20
Tales of Ise, 20
Talma, François Joseph, 13
Tambours sur la digue (Cixous), 106, 161
Tandy, Jessica, 93–94
Tartuffe (Molière), 55
television sitcoms, 47
Tempest, The (Shakespeare), 92, 107–8
Terence, 46
Threepenny Opera, The (Brecht), 89
Three Sisters, The (Chekhov), 103, 118–19

Titus Andronicus (Shakespeare), 108, 127
Today is My Birthday (Kantor), 104–5
Toledo, P., 40
tourism, 135–36
True West (Shepard), 70
Twain, Mark, 135
Twelfth Night (Shakespeare), 101, 105
typecasting, 8–9

Valk, Kate, 170
Vawter, Ron, 169–70
Veltrusky, Jiří, 85
Verdi, Giuseppe, 115
Voltaire, 26, 38, 61

Wagner, Jack, 75
Wagner, Richard, 115, 155–57
Waiting for Godot (Beckett), 69, 127
Warhol, Andy, 14
Water-Hen, The (Witkiewicz), 105

Wedding March (Mendelssohn), 118
Wedding March (Wagner), 118
Wellman, Mac, 2
Wiegel, Helene, 127
Wielopole, Wielopole (Kantor), 44
Wild Duck, The (Ibsen), 94–95
Wild Party, The (La Chiusa), 44
Wild Party, The (Lippa), 44
Wilkinson, Tate, 122–23, 136
Willson, Robert F., 37
Wilson, Robert, 107, 112–13, 168
Winge, Stein, 95
Wings of Desire (Wenders), 87–88
Wooster Group, 15, 169–73
Woyzeck (Büchner), 130

Xena, Warrior Princess, 70

Yankee, Stage, 63–64

Zagagi, Netta, 27
Zeami, 18–23